Lecture Notes in Computer Science   10969

Commenced Publication in 1973
Founding and Former Series Editors:
Gerhard Goos, Juris Hartmanis, and Jan van Leeuwen

More information about this series at http://www.springer.com/series/7408

João Eduardo Ferreira · George Spanoudakis
Yutao Ma · Liang-Jie Zhang (Eds.)

Services Computing – SCC 2018

15th International Conference
Held as Part of the Services Conference Federation, SCF 2018
Seattle, WA, USA, June 25–30, 2018
Proceedings

 Springer

Editors
João Eduardo Ferreira
University of São Paulo
São Paulo
Brazil

George Spanoudakis
City, University of London
London
UK

Yutao Ma
Wuhan University
Wuhan
China

Liang-Jie Zhang
Kingdee International Software Group Co.
Shenzhen
China

ISSN 0302-9743   ISSN 1611-3349   (electronic)
Lecture Notes in Computer Science
ISBN 978-3-319-94375-6   ISBN 978-3-319-94376-3   (eBook)
https://doi.org/10.1007/978-3-319-94376-3

Library of Congress Control Number: 2018947328

LNCS Sublibrary: SL2 – Programming and Software Engineering

Printed on acid-free paper

This Springer imprint is published by the registered company Springer International Publishing AG
part of Springer Nature
The registered company address is: Gewerbestrasse 11, 6330 Cham, Switzerland

Preface

Services account for a major part of the IT industry today. Companies increasingly like to focus on their core expertise area and use IT services to address all their peripheral needs. Services computing is a new science that aims to study and better understand the foundations of this highly popular industry. It covers the science and technology of leveraging computing and information technology to model, create, operate, and manage business services. The 2018 International Conference on Services Computing (SCC 2018) contributes to building the pillars of this important science and shaping the future of services computing.

SCC has been a prime international forum for both researchers and industry practitioners to exchange the latest fundamental advances in the state of the art and practice of business modeling, business consulting, solution creation, service delivery, and software architecture design, development, and deployment.

This volume presents the accepted papers for SCC 2018, held in Seattle, USA, during June 25–30, 2018. For SCC 2018, we accepted 12 full papers, including ten research track papers and two application and industry track papers. Each was reviewed and selected by at least three independent members of the SCC 2018 international Program Committee. We are pleased to thank the authors whose submissions and participation made this conference possible. We also want to express our thanks to the Organizing Committee and Program Committee members, for their dedication in helping to organize the conference and reviewing the submissions. We owe special thanks to the keynote speakers for their impressive speeches.

May 2018

João Eduardo Ferreira
George Spanoudakis
Yutao Ma
Liang-Jie Zhang

Organization

General Chairs

J. Leon Zhao   City University of Hong Kong, SAR China
Keqing He   Wuhan University, China

Program Chairs

João Eduardo Ferreira   University of São Paulo USP, São Paulo, Brazil
George Spanoudakis   City, University London, UK

Program Co-chair

Yutao Ma   Wuhan University, China

Application and Industry Track Chairs

Andreas Wombacher   Aurelius Enterprise, The Netherlands
Walid Gaaloul   Institut Mines Telecom, France

Short Paper Track Chair

Georgia M. Kapitsaki   University of Cyprus, Cyprus

Publicity Chair

Shuiguang Deng   Zhejiang University, China

Services Conference Federation (SCF 2018)

General Chairs
Calton Pu   Georgia Tech, USA
Wu Chou   Essenlix Corporation, USA

Program Chair
Liang-Jie Zhang   Kingdee International Software Group Co., Ltd, China

Finance Chair
Min Luo   Huawei, USA

Panel Chair

Stephan Reiff-Marganiec   University of Leicester, UK

Tutorial Chair

Carlos A Fonseca   IBM T.J. Watson Research Center, USA

Industry Exhibit and International Affairs Chair

Zhixiong Chen   Mercy College, USA

Organizing Committee

Huan Chen (Chair)   Kingdee Inc., China
Jing Zeng (Co-chair)   Tsinghua University, China
Cheng Li (Co-chair)   Tsinghua University, China
Yishuang Ning (Co-chair)   Tsinghua University, China
Sheng He (Co-chair)   Tsinghua University, China

Steering Committee

Calton Pu   Georgia Tech, USA
Liang-Jie Zhang (Chair)   Kingdee International Software Group Co., Ltd, China

SCC Program Committee

Nuno Antunes   University of Coimbra, Portugal
Katt Basel   Norwegian University of Science and Technology,
    Norway
Ladjel Bellatreche   LIAS/ISAE-ENSMA, France
Bruno   University of Coimbra, Portugal
Allen Wei-Lun Chang   Tamkang University, Taiwan, China
Pietro Colombo   University of Insubria, Italy
Luciano Vieira de Araujo   University of São Paulo, Brazil
YiXin Diao   IBM T.J. Watson Research Center, USA
Pedro Furtado   University of Coimbra, Portugal
Kurt Geihs   University of Kassel, Germany
Alfredo Goldman   University of São Paulo, Brazil
Jun Han   Swinburne University of Technology, Australia
Shigeru Hosono   NEC Co. Ltd., USA
Yen-Hao Hsieh   Tamkang University, Taiwan, China
Christian Huemer   Vienna University of Technology, Austria
Fuyuki Ishikawa   National Institute of Informatics, Japan
Rushikesh Joshi   IIT Bombay, India
Eleanna Kafeza   Athens University of Economics and Business, Greece
Natalia Kryvinska   University of Vienna, Austria

Samantha Kumara	University of Aizu, Japan
Shruti Kunde	Tata Consultancy Services Limited, Hong Kong, SAR China
Gibson Lam	Hong Kong University of Science and Technology, Hong Kong, SAR China
Rodrigo Alves Lima	Georgia Tech, USA
Zakaria Maamar	Zayed University, UAE
Paci Federica Maria	University of Southampton, UK
Massimo Mecella	University of Rome, Italy
Suoratik Mukhopadhyay	Louisiana State University, USA
Seog Chan Oh	GM Research, USA
Marcio Katsumi Oikawa	Federal University of ABC, Brazil
Bruno Padilha	University of São Paulo, Brazil
Bhanu Prasad	Florida A&M University, USA
Norbert Ritter	University of Hamburg, Germany
Rafael Liberato Roberto	Federal University of Technology – Parana, Brazil
Andre Luis Schwerz	Federal University of Technology – Parana, Brazil
Jun Shen	University of Wollongong, Australia
Richard Mark Soley	Object Management Group, USA
Liang Tang	Florida International University, USA
Chao Wang	University of Science and Technology of China, China
Chong Wang	Wuhan University, China
Jie Xu	University of Leeds, UK
I-Ling Yen	University of Texas at Dallas, USA
Muhammed Younas	Oxford Brookes University, UK
Xiaofeng Yu	Nanjing University of Finance and Economics, China
Daphne Soe-Tsy Yuan	National Chengchi University, Taiwan, China

Contents

Research Track: Services Algorithm

Program Recommendation Algorithm Based on Tag Association Model

Fulian Yin, Xiaowei Liu[✉], Congcong Zhang, and Rongge Xu

Communication University of China, Chaoyang District, Dingfuzhuang,
East Street No. 1, Beijing, China
yinfulian@cuc.edu.cn, cuclxw@163.com,
1007358526@qq.com, 399329885@qq.com

Abstract. The existing content-based recommendation techniques can't provide personalized recommendation for each user while mining the potential interest of them. In order to solve this problem, we analyze the viewing behavior of users, the attribute of programs and the association of tags to establish the user-tag model, program-tag model and tag-tag model. To realize the improved algorithm 1, the relationship among user, program and tag is reasonably used. In consideration of related interest, the original interest is also taken into account to realize the improved algorithm 2. After the optimization, accuracy and recall rate increase by 0.41% and 0.49% respectively.

Keywords: Tag association · Combination model
Content-based recommendation · Personalized TV program recommendation

1 Introduction

Nowadays, the integration of TV media and Internet media is becoming an inevitable trend as the era of media convergence coming at a rapid pace. Following this trend, new business targets at the audiences of television and gives them with user attribute. As one way of watching TV programs, video-on-demand service makes it easy for users to find programs they're interested in among a large amount of video resources. In this way, users could find the programs they want to watch quickly without the restriction on time. After choosing programs, users may also hope to get more information about other programs, this kind of information is very important for TV operators to retain the audience. Therefore, the personalized recommendation is necessary. In 1998, Das and his partners presented a system that was applied to the system named TV Advisor [1]. Consumers could enter like or dislike by rating a set of 10 TV program subject categories on a 7 point Likert scale, and then the system will make adjustments on the basis of their choices to recommend relative TV programs to them. In recent years, the multi-angle analysis and novelty became main stream in researches on TV program recommendation system, and new ideas such as the concept of

Supported by "the Fundamental Research Funds for the Central Universities" (3132018XNG18 46) and "The National Social Science Fund of China" (GD1739).

© Springer International Publishing AG, part of Springer Nature 2018
J. E. Ferreira et al. (Eds.): SCC 2018, LNCS 10969, pp. 3–18, 2018.
https://doi.org/10.1007/978-3-319-94376-3_1

confidence user and the theory of demographic stereotyping are brought into discussion [2, 3]. The development of TV program recommendation will last for a long period of time. In this period, the improvement of the traditional algorithm and the new innovation are both worth of research.

The concept of recommendation system was proposed by two scholars Resnick and Varian in the literature [4] in 1997. In the past over 20 years, personalized recommendation system has been widely used in e-commerce, video sites, music radio, social networks, personalized reading and other fields. In the meantime, relative algorithms are widely studied by the relevant personnel, and also have a good commercial value. In the development of personalized recommendation, some classical methods come to light, such as collaborative filtering recommendation method, content-based recommendation method, graph-based recommendation method and so on. Because of the Internet sites have lots of content resources, content-based recommendations are increasingly applied in practice, and using tags to realize recommendations is one of the most typical methods. Xia and his partners established a product system of user interest model and improved the accuracy of recommendation effectively by the interest model of social tag clustering optimization [5]. Douglas Eck and his partners used a set of enhanced classifications, and mapped the audio function to the social tags collected from the network, to avoid the common problem "cold start" in the system [6]. Content-based recommendation also involves a lot of research points, which has made good recommendation effects [7, 8]. In addition, there are some relevant researches based on content-based recommendation and other methods. For example, literature [9] put forward a new tag-based recommendation, which was combined with the content filtering and collaborative filtering technology to improve the coverage rate and diversity. In the literature [10], a well-working hybrid recommendation method was proposed based on network structure and tags, in which the user preference model was constructed by using TF-IDF and users' support degree. Literature [11] also proposed a hybrid filtering method to get the benefit of both collaborative filtering and content-based filtering. As for the relationship between the user, project and tag, literature [12] proposed a method for extracting the correlation information between the user, item and tag from the social tagging system. In addition, the tag itself also has relevant research, such as the study of the tag system [13].

In this paper, the relationship between the user and tag, the program and tag, the tag and tag are respectively extracted based on the user viewing data and program lists. On the basis of these relationships, we establish the user-tag model, program-tag model and tag-tag model then use the association between the tags to tap the potential interest of users and achieve two kinds of improved algorithms. Finally, we use several indicators to evaluate the algorithms compared with the collaborative filtering algorithm we have realized [14].

2 Traditional Collaborative Filtering Algorithm Based on Combination Model

2.1 User-Tag Model and Program-Tag Model

The user-tag model and the program-tag model are designed to reflect the relationship between user and tag as well as the relationship between program and tag by the numerical value. In the models, the tags are from the video sites, mainly including director tags, actor tags, region tags, and type tags. Users spend time on different tags by watching different programs in their viewing behavior. In those tags, some are which users always spend their time on, like plot, love, some are tags with users' obvious preference, such as war, romantic and so on. If the latter tags can be highlighted in value, it will further highlight the characteristics of the user's viewing preference. In order to describe the user's preference for the tags better, it is necessary to use the TF-IDF formula. The classical TF-IDF formula has a wide range of applications in many fields of information science, especially in the field of information retrieval. This field often extracts keywords in the text to apply in the TF-IDF formula, and the key words used here are the tags of the programs.

The establishment of the user-tag model is intended to describe the relationship between user and tag, and to lay the data base for the implementation of the recommendation algorithm. The user's choice of the programs is independent, so the user's viewing behavior reflects the user's viewing characteristics, which can be demonstrated by the data corresponding to the tags. We set the number of users as n, the number of tags as M, then the user-tag model is a $n \times M$ matrix as Fig. 1 shows.

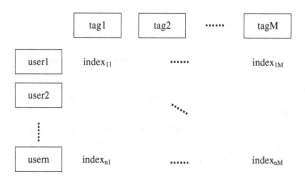

Fig. 1. Schematic diagram of user - tag model

By using the statistics of the length of time that the user spends on each tag, we can get the length of time that the current user spends on the current tag, which is represented by T_i, the length of time that the current user spends on all tags is represented by T. Then we use n_i to represent the number of users who spend time on the current tag. According to the TF-IDF formula, the method of numerical calculation in the matrix is as following:

$$Index_{user-tag} = \frac{T_i}{T} \times \log\left(\frac{n}{n_i}\right) \tag{1}$$

in this formula T_i/T corresponds to the first half part of TF-IDF formula. The greater the user's interest in the current tag is, the greater the value will be. And $\log\left(\frac{n}{n_i}\right)$ corresponds to the second half part of TF-IDF formula. For the public tags that many users spend time on, this value will be relatively small, on the contrary, this value will be relatively large.

The establishment method of the program-tag model is similar to the user-tag model, and it aims to describe the relationship between the program and tag by using the tags of each program in the program list. In on-demand programs which have matched the tag, each program has 1 to 19 tags. According to the idea of flat tag, the tags are classified into the same dimension to describe the program [13].

We set the number of programs as N, the number of tags as M, and the program-tag model is an $N \times M$ matrix. The schematic diagram is shown below (Fig. 2).

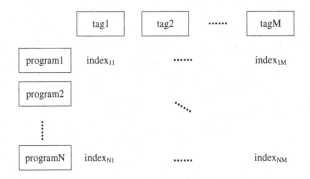

Fig. 2. Schematic diagram of program - tag model

The tags for each program in the on-demand program list are the data base of the program-tag model. We use x to represent the number of times that the current tag appears in the list of programs, X to represent the total number of tags in the current list of programs, and use N_i to represent the number of programs marked by the current tag. In the program-tag model, the numerical calculation method based on the TF-IDF formula is as following:

$$Index_{program-tag} = \frac{x}{X} \times \log\left(\frac{N}{N_i}\right) \tag{2}$$

in this formula, $\frac{x}{X}$ corresponds to the first half part of TF-IDF formula, and $\log\left(\frac{N}{N_i}\right)$ corresponds to the second half part of TF-IDF formula. If some programs are labeled as the public tag, latter value will be relatively small. For those tags only marking a few programs, when the current program has been marked, the latter value will be relatively large.

2.2 Traditional Collaborative Filtering Algorithm Based on the Two Models

Collaborative filtering algorithm is a classic algorithm in the recommendation field. In this paper, it is implemented by the use-tag model and program-tag model for comparison with improved algorithms.

The collaborative filtering algorithm we used here is a collaborative filtering algorithm based on the user. First of all, we need to calculate the similarity between users to obtain the similar users by the user-tag model. In this model, each user has a user-tag vector. By calculating the cosine similarity between the user-tag vectors, the similarity value between one user and others can be obtained. Then, we can find some users with larger value after ranking, to be served as reference users of the current user. The calculation method of cosine similarity is shown in the following formula:

$$cos_{l,k} = \frac{\overrightarrow{user_l} \cdot \overrightarrow{user_k}}{\left|\overrightarrow{user_l}\right| \cdot \left|\overrightarrow{user_k}\right|} \tag{3}$$

in this formula, $\overrightarrow{user_l} \cdot \overrightarrow{user_k}$ is the dot product of two user-tag vectors. They do the modular arithmetic, then multiply, and get $\left|\overrightarrow{user_l}\right| \cdot \left|\overrightarrow{user_k}\right|$.

These similar users' favorite programs can be used as recommendation reference for the current user. Combining programs that similar users have seen in the test set, and removing the duplicates, we can get the current user's proposed recommendation list. In this list, the number of programs is uncertain, so we need to filter out the most worthy recommendation programs as the user's recommendation list. This should be observed from the dual perspective of the user and the program. Each user-tag vector in the user-tag model represents the user's viewing feature, which reflects the user's property. In the program-tag model, each program also has a corresponding program-tag vector that represents the properties of the programs. Do dot product of user-tag vector and program-tag vector, we can obtain dot product value we need. The more tags whose overlap value of two vectors is not 0, and the bigger value of the coincidence part is, the bigger value of dot product will be, and the users are more likely to enjoy the programs. By this method, a list of recommended programs of customized length can be obtained.

3 Improved Algorithms Based on Combination Model

3.1 New Tag - Tag Model

In this paper, one of the core elements of the improved algorithms is the construction of the tag-tag model.

Just as the user-tag model is a description of the relationship between user and tag, the program-tag model is a description of the relationship between program and tag, tag-tag model is designed to describe the relationship between tags. The association between tags is established on the tags which mark the same program. This relationship reflects the similarity or correlation between tags. For example, comedy and funny appear together could reflect their similarity, spy and military appear together reflect the relevance. In on-demand programs, each program will be labeled by 1 to 19 tags. They occur together in the same program's tag sequence, so there is a potential association. If the number of the tags contained in the tag sequence for each program is m, according to the principle of permutation and combination, the number of tags is $m(m-1)/2$. In addition, the number of a program's tags must be more than 1. As defined in the above section, the number of all tags is M, and the tag-tag matrix is a $M \times M$ matrix. The schematic diagram is shown below (Fig. 3).

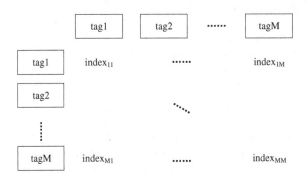

Fig. 3. Schematic diagram of tag - tag model

In the figure, we take numerical value $index_{M1}$ as an example. It represents the co-occurrence count of tags with $tagM$ and $tag1$ appearing in the on-demand program list. In order to make the normalized total count for facilitating the subsequent calculation, we convert the co-occurrence count to the co-occurrence rate in the matrix. Taking the tag rate of the corresponding position of $index_{M1}$ as an example, the formula is as following:

$$ratioindex_{M1} = \frac{index_{M1}}{\sum_{i=1}^{M} index_{Mi}} \tag{4}$$

in this formula, the value of co-occurrence rate reflects the relative relationship between $tag1$ and $tagM$ in the all tags' environment. The larger the similarity or correlation between the tags is, the larger the co-occurrence rate will be.

In the on-demand program viewing data, the user's viewing time is very important reference data. Therefore, we use the length of time again in the tag-tag model to make the tag-tag model carry user's preference. Each user can create a table about time of total tags, in which the minimum value is 0 for meaning of the user hasn't spent any time on the current tag.

In order to adjust the co-occurrence rate by the length of time, we need to obtain the normalized numerical value of the following three kinds of conditions: if we want to increase the data, the value should be greater than 1; if the we want to decrease the data, the value should be bounded between 0 and 1; if nor increase or decrease, which means the time user spends on the current tag is 0, the value should be 1. The initial data can be obtained through the processing of the corresponding time of the tags. Take numerical calculation of *tagM* as an example. The formula is as following:

$$factor = \begin{cases} \frac{timelong_M - \overline{timelong}}{timelong_M} + 1, timelong_M \neq 0 \\ 1, timelong_M = 0 \end{cases} \tag{5}$$

in this formula, $\overline{timelong}$ is the average value of the corresponding time for each tag, the formula is as following:

$$\overline{timelong} = \frac{\sum_{i=1}^{M} timelong_i}{M} \tag{6}$$

The factor calculated by the formula is mostly larger than 0. However, for some tags with extremely small time value, the factor value is less than 0. In addition, if user spends a lot of time on some tags, the factor value will be much greater than 1. These special cases are not conducive to the retention of original tag-tag association. Therefore, the numerical value of factor needs to be further processed. The formula of factor's normalization is shown as following:

$$realfactor = \begin{cases} factor, factor \in [0.01, 1.99] \\ 0.01, factor \in (-\infty, 0.01) \\ 1.99, factor \in (1.99, \infty) \end{cases} \tag{7}$$

By the above method, each user can get factors of tags corresponding to their viewing preference whose values are bounded between 0.01 and 1.99. By multiplying these values and the value of the corresponding tag lines in the tag-tag model, we can get a tag-tag model with user's personalized preference, which will make the results more consistent with the user's interest in the following recommendations.

3.2 Improved Algorithm 1 Based on Combination Model

The improved algorithm 1 is based on the relationship among user, tag and program, the hierarchical relationships between them is shown in the Fig. 4. The first link indicates the relationship between the user and tag, and each user's favorite tags can reflect his viewing behavior. The second link indicates the relationship between the tags, and the related tags are mined by user's favorite tags. The third link indicates the relationship between the program and tag. From the related tags, we can get corresponding programs, and obtain the recommendation program list.

The detailed steps of the algorithm are as follows:

(1) Extract the corresponding lines of the current user from the user-tag model, which is the current user's user-tag vector. Each tag in the vector corresponds to the values: $count1, count2, \ldots, countn$. Sort and get the top m tags, they are $label1, label2, \ldots, labelm$, respectively.

(2) Extract the corresponding lines of $label1, label2, \ldots, labelm$ from the tag-tag model, and sum up each column to get the corresponding values of each tag:

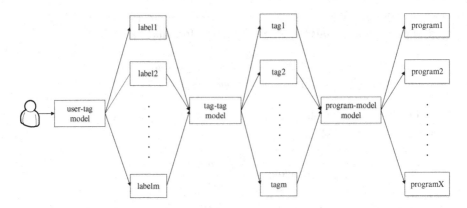

Fig. 4. Diagram of the hierarchical relationships between the user, tag and program

$sum1, sum2, \ldots, sumn$. Sort these values and get the top m tags corresponding to their values, they are $tag1, tag2, \ldots, tagm$, respectively.

(3) Extract the corresponding columns of $tag1, tag2, \ldots, tagm$, from the program-tag model, and sum up each rows to get the corresponding values of each program: $add1, add2, \ldots, addn$. Sort these values and get the top X programs which have not been watched by the user to form a list of recommendation programs.

Among them, step (1) finds the tags with large values from the current user's user-tag vector. These tags show the user's viewing records and reflect the user's viewing preferences. Step (2) finds the well-associated tags by the user's favorite tags in the tag-tag model, which could find out the potential interest preference by the original interest preference, and the potential interest preference is similarly reflected by tags. Finally, step (3) gets the well-associated programs in the program-tag model, and then recommends them to the users.

Compared to the collaborative filtering algorithm, this algorithm not only considers the relationship between the user and program, but also integrates the relationship between the tags. Using the associated tags to recommend, we can tap user's potential interest, which is associated with the original interest. In addition, the method assures the recommendation program list is not repeated with programs they have seen.

However, this algorithm is also one-sided, after getting the user's associated tags, it will only use the associated tags to recommend, and completely ignore the user's original interest. Therefore, the improved algorithm 2 is proposed in the next section on the basis of algorithm 1, in which the original interest and associated interest are both integrated into the recommendation.

3.3   Improved Algorithm 2 Based on Combination Model

The improved algorithm 2 also begins from the user-tag model, but its idea is some of different from the improved algorithm 1. The improved algorithm 1 only uses the associated tags to provide recommendations, although this has the effect of mining the potential interest of users, the effect of integrating the user's original interest is also worth trying.

A brief flow diagram of the improved algorithm 2 is shown in the Fig. 5.

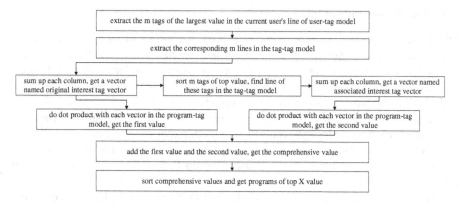

Fig. 5. Flow diagram of the improved algorithm 2

The detailed steps of the algorithm are as follows:

(1) Extract the corresponding lines of the current user from the user-tag model, which is the current user's user-tag vector. Each tag in the vector corresponds to the values: $count1, count2, \ldots, countn$. Sort and get the top m tags, they are $label1, label2, \ldots, labelm$, respectively.

(2) Extract the corresponding lines of $label1, label2, \ldots, labelm$ from the tag-tag model, and sum up each column to get the corresponding values of each tag: $sum1, sum2, \ldots, sumn$. Sort these values and get the top m tags corresponding to their values, they are $tag1, tag2, \ldots, tagm$, respectively.

(3) Find the corresponding vectors of $label1, label2, \ldots, labelm$ in the tag-tag model, and sum up each column of each vector to get a new vector, which is the original interest tag vector **V1**. In the same way, find the corresponding vectors of $tag1, tag2, \ldots, tagm$. By the above method, we can get the associated interest tag vector **V2**.

(4) **V1** and each program-tag vector in the program-tag model do dot product, to get the values of each program: $num11, num12, \ldots, num1N$. **V2** and each program-tag vector in the program-tag model do dot product, to get the values of each program: $num21, num22, \ldots, num2N$. By summing up the values, the new values of each program are obtained: $(num11 + num21), (num12 + num22), \ldots, (num1N + num2N)$. Sort these values and get the top X programs which have not been watched by the user to form a list of recommendation programs.

In the above steps, original interest tag vector and associated interest tag vector reflect the interest preferences and related interest preference of the users according to the viewing behavior and tag correspondence, respectively. Then they do dot product with each line in the program-tag model respectively and get their corresponding values, add the two values together, and we can get the comprehensive numerical value to select the programs with comprehensive consideration of user's interest, thus providing a comprehensive recommendation list.

4 Experiment and Analysis of the Result

4.1 Evaluation Indicators

Off-line test is used in the experiment to evaluate the results of the recommendation. The algorithms are realized by training set and tested by test set. Because of the differences between the algorithms, their evaluation results also have some differences. By analyzing the differences, we can get the advantages and disadvantages of them, and provide the basis for the subsequent optimization. In order to evaluate the recommendation in the experiment comprehensively, the accuracy, recall rate, coverage rate and average popularity level (novelty) are used. Accuracy and recall rate belong to the same category of the evaluation indicators, which are consistent in most cases. And coverage rate and novelty are also consistent in most cases. These combinations can make the evaluation more balanced.

Accuracy and recall rate are commonly used to measure the effect of Top-N recommendation. The user set is represented as U, and $R(u)$ is the recommendation list based on the historical behavior of the training set, $T(u)$ is a list of user viewing behaviors on the test set. The definition of the accuracy rate is as following:

$$Precision = \frac{\sum_{u \in U} |R(u) \cap T(u)|}{\sum_{u \in U} |R(u)|} \tag{8}$$

The definition of the recall rate is as following:

$$Recall = \frac{\sum_{u \in U} |R(u) \cap T(u)|}{\sum_{u \in U} |T(u)|} \tag{9}$$

In the experiment, $|R(u) \cap T(u)|$ represents the number of programs, which are overlapping parts between the programs which are recommended for the users in the training set and the programs watched by users in the test set. The accuracy indicates the proportion of the overlapping programs in the recommended programs. Recall rate indicates the proportion of the overlapping programs in the programs that are watched by users in the test set.

Coverage rate can be used to describe the capacity about the long tail mining of the recommendation system. The coverage rate is defined as the ratio of the collection of items which can be recommended for the user set U in the total collection of items. If the recommendation system only recommends popular items, the proportion of these items in all items is small, and then the coverage rate will be relatively low. If the recommendation system can make most items appear in the recommendation list, the capacity about the long tail mining is strong, the coverage rate will be correspondingly high.

Using I to represent the collection of all the items, the coverage rate can be expressed as following:

$$Coverage = \frac{\left| \sum_{u \in U} R(u) \right|}{|I|} \tag{10}$$

In the experiment, $\left|\sum_{u \in U} R(u)\right|$ represents the program list, which is obtained after merging and removing duplicate of all users' recommended programs in the user set. I represents a list of all on-demand programs.

Novelty is usually measured by the average popularity level of the recommended results. Unpopular items often make users feel novel, therefore, smaller the value of average popularity level is, larger the degree of novelty will be. In the recommendation system based on the tag, we define the popularity $popular(i)$ as the number of tags that are marked by the users. The definition of the average popularity level is as following:

$$AveragePopularity = \frac{\sum_u \sum_{i \in R(u)} log(1 + popular(i))}{\sum_u \sum_{i \in R(u)} 1} \tag{11}$$

On the whole, in the experiments of this paper, recommendations by collaborative filtering involve a range of programs that are based on similar users, and two kinds of improved algorithms are to find the programs that the users may be interested in. The improved algorithm 1 only considers the potential interest of the user, so it has disadvantages in the accuracy and recall rate, the improved algorithm 2 make up for this deficiency. Then we use the specific experimental data to show the result.

4.2 Evaluation and Comparative Analysis

Experiments 1–4 introduce the comparative analysis of the experiment result according to the accuracy, recall rate, coverage rate and average popularity level. The improved algorithm 1 and the improved algorithm 2 both have 5 groups of experiment, in which the number of tags is 5, 10, 15, 20 and 25. The improved algorithms are compared with the collaborative filtering algorithm. In order to see the contrast between them clearly, we draw the line charts with various indicators of the collaborative filtering algorithm, the improved algorithm 1 and the improved algorithm 2. Particularly, collaborative filtering algorithm does not involve different number of tags, so only the vertical coordinate values are significant.

Experiment 1: Comparative Analysis of Accuracy
Figure 6 is the comparison line chart of the accuracy. (a) is a comparison chart of three algorithms. (b) is a comparison chart of the improved algorithm 1 and the improved algorithm 2.

As can be seen from the graph (a), the accuracy of collaborative filtering algorithm is higher than the improved algorithm 1 and the improved algorithm 2. In the graph (b), with the integration of the user's original interest, the accuracy of the improved algorithm 2 is higher than the improved algorithm 1. The result also shows that when the number of tags is selected in a certain range, if it increases, the accuracy of two improved algorithms rises too.

Experiment 2: Comparative Analysis of Recall Rate
Figure 7 is the comparison line chart of the recall rate. (a) is a comparison chart of the three algorithms. (b) is a comparison chart of the improved algorithm 1 and the improved algorithm 2.

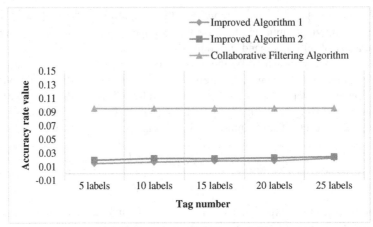

(a) Comparison of three algorithms

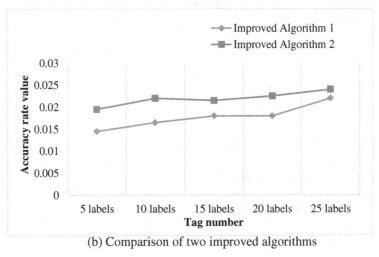

(b) Comparison of two improved algorithms

Fig. 6. Comparison chart of the accuracy rate of the three algorithms

As can be seen from the graph (a), the recall rate of collaborative filtering algorithm is higher than the other two algorithms. In the graph (b), after the integration of the user's original interest, the recall rate of the improved algorithm 2 is higher than the improved algorithm 1 on the whole. But when we select 25 tags, the recall rate of the improved algorithm 2 is slightly lower than the improved algorithm 1. In a way, within a certain range, the number of tags increases, the recall rate of the improved algorithm 1 rises too.

Experiment 3: Comparative Analysis of Coverage Rate
Figure 8 is the comparison line chart of the coverage rate.

As the chart shows, for the coverage rate, the improved algorithm 1 is better than the collaborative filtering algorithm. It shows that more programs can be covered, and

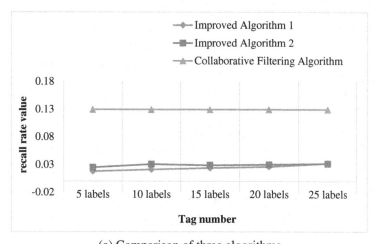

(a) Comparison of three algorithms

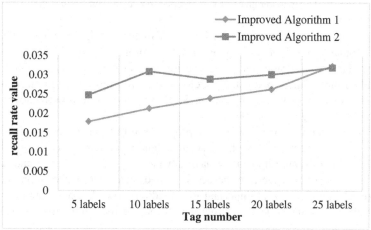

(b) Comparison of two improved algorithms

Fig. 7. Comparison chart of the recall rate of the three algorithms

also indirectly shows that recommended popular programs of the improved algorithm 1 are fewer than that of collaborative filtering algorithm. When we select 5 and 10 tags, the coverage rate of improved algorithm 2 is lower than the improved algorithm 1, but higher than the collaborative filtering algorithm. When the number of tags is increasing, the coverage rate reduces a lot. Therefore, although the accuracy and recall rate are more advantageous in the large number of tags, the coverage rate is more advantageous when the number of tags is small.

Experiment 4: Comparative Analysis of Average Popularity Level (Novelty)
Figure 9 is the comparison line chart of the average popularity level.

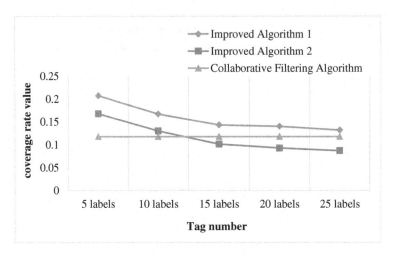

Fig. 8. Comparison chart of the coverage rate of the three algorithms

As can be seen in the comparison line chart of the average popularity level, the average popularity level of the two improved algorithms is similar. The two lines almost overlap in the graph, and both are lower than the line of the collaborative filtering algorithm. That's to say, the novelty of the two improved algorithms is better than the collaborative filtering algorithm. So they can provide a more novel list of recommendation programs for users.

In summary, the improved algorithms proposed in this paper are trying to tap the potential interest of users. Although the accuracy and recall rate are not as good as the collaborative filtering algorithm, they have advantages in coverage rate and novelty, especially in the novelty. Despite the accuracy and recall rate of the improved algorithms are relatively low, it is important to provide users with a novel and surprising recommendation list in on-demand programs. It may be more attractive to users.

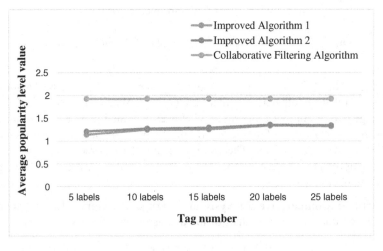

Fig. 9. Comparison of the average popularity level of the three algorithms

5 Conclusion

In this paper, we make full use of the relationship between the user, program and tag, and form an association between them. In this way, we establish the user-tag model, tag-tag model and program-tag model to reflect the relationship between user and tag, tag and tag, program and tag. On the basis of the three models, the improved algorithm 1 not only provides users with personalized recommendation, but also taps the potential interest of users. The improved algorithm 2 integrates user's original interest on the basis of the improved algorithm 1. The experimental results show that the improved algorithms are not as good as the collaborative filtering algorithm in terms of accuracy and recall rate, but the coverage rate and novelty are better than it. In addition, after optimizing the improved algorithm 1, accuracy and recall rate increase by 0.41% and 0.49% in the result of improved algorithm 2. However, coverage rate and novelty degree decrease. The improved algorithms still have room for improvement of accuracy and recall rate, and it is the future research.

References

1. Das, D., Horst, H.T.: Recommender systems for TV. In: Proceedings of AAAI (1998)
2. Pin, R.: TV recommendation system based on confidence user preference model. Modern Electron. Technol. **6**, 30–33 (2014)
3. Palacio-Baus, K., Saquicela, V.: Semantic recommender systems for digital TV: from demographic stereotyping to personalized recommendations. Computer Aided System Engineering, pp. 392–396. IEEE (2015)
4. Paul, R., Varian, H.R.: Recommender systems. Commun. ACM **40**(3), 56–58 (1997)
5. Xia, X., Zhang, S., Li, X.: A Personalized recommendation model based on social tags. In: International Workshop on Database Technology and Applications, Wuhan, China, pp. 1–5 (2010)
6. Eck, D., Lamere, P., Bertin-Mahieux, T., et al.: Automatic generation of social tags for music recommendation. In: Conference on Neural Information Processing Systems, Vancouver, Canada, pp. 385–392 (2007)
7. Chen, T., Han, W., Wang, H., et al.: Content recommendation system based on private dynamic user profile. In: International Conference on Machine Learning and Cybernetics, pp. 2112–2118 (2007)
8. Lu, Y., Yu, S., Chang, T., et al.: A content-based method to enhance tag recommendation. In: IJCAI 2009, Proceedings of the International Joint Conference on Artificial Intelligence, Pasadena, USA, pp. 2064–2069 (2009)
9. BarragáNs-MartíNez, A.B., Rey-LóPez, M., Costa, Montenegro, E., et al.: Exploiting social tagging in a Web 2.0 recommender system. Internet Comput. IEEE **14**(6), 23–30 (2010)
10. Zhang, X., Jiang, S., Li, X., et al.: Hybrid recommendation algorithm based on network and tag. Comput. Eng. Appl. **51**(1), 119–124 (2015)
11. Chowdhury, C., Arefin, M.S., Morimoto, Y.: Developing a framework for recommending TV shows. In: 2017 ICIEV-ISCMHT, Himeji, Japan, pp. 1–6 (2017)
12. Parvathy, M., Ramya, R., Sundarakantham, K., et al.: Recommendation system with collaborative social tagging exploration. In: International Conference on Recent Trends in Information Technology. IEEE, pp. 1–6 (2014)

13. Pan, X., Yin, F., Chai, J.: Delayering tagging of television programs and association rule mining. In: 2014 IEEE 17th International Conference on Computational Science and Engineering (CSE), pp. 192–197 (2014)
14. Yin, F., Liu, X., Ding, W., et al.: Tag-based collaborative filtering recommendation algorithm for TV program. In: International Computer Conference on Wavelet Active Media Technology and Information Processing, pp. 47–52 (2016)

Research of Web Service Recommendation Using Bayesian Network Reasoning

Jianxiao Liu, Zonglin Tian, Yifei Liu, and Liang Zhao$^{(\boxtimes)}$

College of Informatics, Huazhong Agricultural University, Wuhan, China
zhaoliang323@mail.hzau.edu.cn

Abstract. How to recommend the atomic and a set of services with correlations to meet users' functional and non-functional requests is a key problem to be solved in the era of services computing. On the basis of organizing service clusters with different functions using the three-stage Bayesian network structure learning method. It uses the parameter learning method to obtain the conditional probability table (CPT) of all the nodes. The Bayesian network reasoning method (Gibbs Sampling) is used to recommend a set of service types that are interested to users. Finally, it selects a set of services in the specific service clusters to meet users' functional and QoS requirements. The case study and experiments are used to explain and validate the effectiveness of the proposed method.

Keywords: Bayesian network learning · Web service
Service recommendation · Gibbs sampling

1 Introduction

In the era of service-oriented computing, how to recommend the atomic service and a set of services with correlations to meet users' functional and non-functional QoS requirements is an important problem to be solved in the service-oriented software engineering [1].

There are a large number of Web services on the internet, and the most frequently used method is recommending services according to users' personal requirements. At present, there exists a lot of research work about service recommendation, such as collaborative filtering, using users' history usage information, QoS-aware method, latent semantic probabilistic model, Bayesian theory and some other approaches. The above research work mainly use certain approach to recommend services for users, and it mainly concentrates on the aspect of service function. However, there are a lot of services with similar function but have different QoS values on the internet. In addition, users usually need a set of services that can be composited to realize specific function. In order to solve the above problem, we can cluster services firstly, and then organize the service clusters to realize service organization network graph. Then we can recommend a set of service with correlations effectively and conveniently according to users' personal requirements. Bayesian network combines the acyclic graphs and probability theory, and it has solid foundation of probability theory. It has the advantages of constructing causal relationship, doing reasoning, mining the implicit

© Springer International Publishing AG, part of Springer Nature 2018
J. E. Ferreira et al. (Eds.): SCC 2018, LNCS 10969, pp. 19–35, 2018.
https://doi.org/10.1007/978-3-319-94376-3_2

knowledge, and so on. There are two kinds of Bayesian network structure learning methods: search score method and dependency analysis method [2]. This search score method uses the local or random search strategy. It is a combinatorial explosion problem as the number of nodes increases, and this leads to the efficiency of this method is too low. The efficiency of the dependency analysis method is relatively high, and it also can get the global optimal solution. The three-phase dependency analysis algorithm (*TPDA*) [3] is a commonly used dependency analysis method. Therefore, we mainly use the three-phase dependency analysis Bayesian network structure learning method to organize services and thus to construct the service organization network in this work. The main work is given as follows.

(1) It uses the three-stage Bayesian network structure learning method to organize Web services on the basis of using the service invocation history records. The Bayesian network parameter learning method is used to learn the conditional probability of all the nodes in the service organization network graph.

(2) On the basis of realizing service organization, it proposes a Web service recommendation method based on Bayesian network reasoning. The Gibbs sampling approach is used to calculate the conditional probability between particular service nodes. This method can recommend and help users to select the atomic and a set of services with the proper function and *QoS*.

(3) Experiments are conducted to validate the proposed methods, and the case study is used to do the Explanation.

2 Web Service Organization and Recommendation

2.1 Web Service Organization

The process of realizing *TPDA* method mainly includes three steps: *Drafting*, *Thickening* and *Thinning*.

(1) The first learning stage: *Drafting*

Algorithm 1. The first stage learning algorithm (*Drafting*)

Input: $Cluster=\{clusws_c, 1\leq c\leq cnum\}$, $clusws_c=\{ws_{cw}, 1\leq w\leq c_c\}$, $Rel_{ws}=\{rel_r: ws_{ij}\rightarrow ws_{mn}, 1\leq r\leq rnum, 0\leq i,m\leq cnum, 0\leq j\leq c_i, 0\leq n\leq c_m\}$

Output: *graph, R*

1: $c_1, c_2\leftarrow 0, S\leftarrow\varnothing, v_I\leftarrow 0, R\leftarrow\varnothing$
2: *Node*[] *nodes*←new *Node* [*cnum*]
3: *graph*←new *Graph(nodes,cnum)*
4: **for** *c*=1 **to** *cnum* **do**
5 *graph.nodes[c]*←*Cluster.clusws_c*
6: **end for**
7: **for** c_1=1 **to** *Cluster.cnum* **do**
8: **for** c_2=1 **to** *Cluster.cnum* **do**
9:   $v_I\leftarrow Imutual(clusws_{c1}, clusws_{c2}, Rel_{ws})$
10: **if**$(v_I>\varepsilon)$ **then**
11:    $S\leftarrow S\cup <clusws_{c1}, clusws_{c2,} v_I>$
12:   **end if**
13:**end for**
14:$S\leftarrow Sort(S)$//Sort *S* using $Imutual(clusws_{c1}, clusws_{c2}, Rel_{ws})$
15:**for all** $<clusws_{c1}, clusws_{c2,}Imutual(clusws_{c1}, clusws_{c2}, Rel_{ws})$ in *S* **do**
16: **if**$(ExistsPath(node_{c1}, node_{c2}))$ **then** //exists the open path
17:    $R\leftarrow R\cup <clusws_{c1}, clusws_{c2}>$
18: **else** *graph*.insert(new $Edge(clusws_{c1}, clusws_{c2}))$
19:**end for**
20:return *graph, R*

In Algorithm 1, the Rel_{ws} stores the service invocation information. The initial network graph will be constructed firstly using step 2–6. The $I(clusws_i, clusws_m, Rel_{ws})$ is used to calculate the mutual information between two service cluster nodes, and the concrete process can be seen in [5]. The edges whose nodes' mutual information is more than the threshold (ε) will be added into S. Then it will sort the node pair in S according to the value of mutual information, as seen in step 7–14. The node pair in S are judged in turn to see if there exists an open path between them. If there exists an open path, the node pair will be added into R. Otherwise, the edge of the node pair will be inserted into *graph*. Then the initial network diagraph will be constructed.

(2) The second learning stage: *Thickening*

The second stage firstly finds the cut set between two nodes when there is an open path between them in the network. Then the conditional mutual information about the two nodes and cut set will be calculated, and we will judge whether it is conditionally independent. If it is not independent, the corresponding edge will be added into the graph.

(3) The third stage: *Thinning*

In the third stage, for each edge e in the graph, it will be removed temporarily. Then we will find the minimum cut set between the nodes of e, and judge whether they are conditional independent or not. If they are conditional independent, e will be deleted. Otherwise, e will be added into the network again, and finally get the network.

2.2   Web Service Recommendation

According to users' personal requirements, we can recommend the atomic and a set of services with proper function and QoS in the organized services. This section uses the Bayesian network reasoning method to get the service cluster node that can meet users' functional requirements firstly. Then it selects a set of services with the proper QoS values in different service clusters for users in further.

Given specific network and evidence variable set, Bayesian network reasoning refers to calculate the posterior probability $P(X \mid E)$ of an event occurrence using the joint probability formula. It mainly includes two ways: causal reasoning and diagnostic reasoning. This section mainly introduces how to recommend a set of service types for users using Bayesian network causal reasoning method. These service types mean the service cluster nodes that are interested for users. Algorithm 2 gives the process of how to realize Web service recommendation based on Bayesian network reasoning method.

Algorithm 2. Web service recommendation based on Bayesian network Reasoning(*BRWSR*)
Input: *RE, graph, CPT, Cluster, Rel$_{ws}$*
Output: *wsnodes*
1: $v_r \leftarrow 0$, *wsnodes*$\leftarrow \varnothing$, *rnode*$\leftarrow \varnothing$, *pathnode*$\leftarrow \varnothing$
2: **for**i=1 to*graph.cnum***do**
3:   **if**(*matchreq(RE, clusws$_i$)*> α) **then**
4:       *rnodes*$\leftarrow$*rnodes* $\cup$ <*nodes[i]*, 1.0>
5:   **end if**
6: **end for**
7: **forall** *rnodes[r]* in *rnodes* **do**
8:   *wsnodes*$\leftarrow$*wsnodes* $\cup$ <*rnodes[r]*, 1.0>
9:   *pathnode*$\leftarrow$*getpathnode(rnodes[r])*
10: **forall** *pathnode[p]* in *pathnode* **do**
11:    $v_r \leftarrow p(pathnode[p] \mid rnodes[r])$
12:    **if**($v_r > \gamma$) **then**
13:        *wsnodes*$\leftarrow$*wsnodes* $\cup$ <*pathnode[p]*, v_r>
14:    **end if**
15:   **endfor**
16:   *pathnode*$\leftarrow \varnothing$
17:**endfor**
18:*wsnodes*$\leftarrow$*DelDuplicate(wsnodes)*
19:*wsnodes*$\leftarrow$*Sort(wsnodes)*
20:return*wsnodes*

In Algorithm 2, all the service clusters are done matching calculation according to users' functional requirements *RE* firstly. The service nodes whose matching degree are larger than the threshold will be found and recommended for users, and thus to form service cluster node set *rnodes*, as seen in step 2–6. Then all the nodes *rnodes[r]* in *rnodes* are judged in turn. It will add *rnodes[r]* and its matching degree (1.0) into the result node set *wsnodes*. It will also find the execution path *pathnode* of *rnodes[r]* in *graph*. The causal reasoning method is used to calculate the conditional probability p (*pathnode[p]* | *rnodes[r]*) of the related nodes in *pathnode*. When the conditional probability is larger than the threshold, we will add *pathnode[p]* and the matching degree into result node set *wsnodes*. Finally, the duplicate node in *wsnodes* will be removed, and all the nodes will be sorted according to the matching degree. Finally, return *wsnodes*.

The step 3 in Algorithm 2 is used to calculate the matching degree between users' request and services in service clusters considering of service interface and execution capability. The step 11 in Algorithm 2 is used to calculate the conditional probability between nodes. However, the complexity of precise reasoning is relatively high and the efficiency is too low for the large-scale and multi-connectivity Bayesian network. This leads to the inoperability for the large-scale Bayesian network, and it is a NP Hard problem. Therefore, it needs to use the approximate reasoning method. Markov Chain Monte Carlo (*MCMC*) method is a commonly used approximate reasoning method, including Gibbs sampling algorithm (Gibbs Sampling) and hybrid MCMC algorithms (Hybrid Monte Carlo Sampling) etc. This kind of algorithm is very effective when there is no extreme probability in the network. There is no extreme probability distribution between Web service cluster and Gibbs sampling algorithm using Markov chain theory (Markov coverage), it can ensure the results of the algorithm returns the convergence in real posterior probability. Therefore, we mainly use the approximate reasoning algorithm. Algorithm 3 is used to calculate the conditional probability $P(ws_{pi} \mid ws_{ej})$ between different services (like ws_{pi} and ws_{ej}) in specific service cluster node (like $node_p$ and $node_e$). Then we can calculate the conditional probability $p(node_p \mid node_e)$ of the corresponding service cluster node in further.

Algorithm 3. Service conditional probability calculation using Gibbs sampling (*GSWCP*)
Input: *graph, Cluster, Rel_{ws}, node_p, ws_{pi}, node_e, ws_{ej}*
Output: $p(node_p=ws_{pi} \mid node_e=ws_{ej})$
1: $m_q \leftarrow 0$, $Set_{sample} \leftarrow \varnothing$, $m \leftarrow 0$, $D[] \leftarrow \varnothing$, $nodes_{mb} \leftarrow \varnothing$, $val_{mb} \leftarrow \varnothing$, $nodes_{ne} \leftarrow graph.nodes-node_e$
2: $Set_{sample} \leftarrow Getsampleset(Cluster, Rel_{ws})$
3: $m \leftarrow Set_{sample}.length$
4: generate $D[1]$ with $node_e=ws_{ej}$ from Set_{sample} randomly
5: **if** ($D[1].node_p = = ws_{pi}$) **then**
6:     $m_q \leftarrow m_q+1$
7: **end if**
8: **for** i=2 **to** m **do**
9:     $D[i] \leftarrow D[i-1]$
10:    **forall** $nodes_{ne}[j]$ in $nodes_{ne}$ **do**
11:        $nodes_{mb} \leftarrow MB(nodes_{ne}[j])$ //getting Markov coverage nodes of $nodes_{ne}[j]$
12:        $val_{mb} \leftarrow D[i].nodes_{mb}$ // getting the value of Markov coverage nodes in $D[i]$
13:        $D[i].nodes_{ne}[j] \leftarrow Sampleing(p(nodes_{ne}[j].val \mid val_{mb}))$
14:    **endfor**
15:    **if** ($D[i].node_p = = ws_{pi}$) **then**
16:        $m_q \leftarrow m_q+1$
17:    **end if**
18:**endfor**
19:return m_q/m

In Algorithm 3, *m* in *Input* represents the sample size, $node_p$ and ws_{pi} represent the query variable node and the corresponding value. The $node_e$ and ws_{ej} represent the evidence variable node and the corresponding value. The $nodes_{ne}$ represents non-evidence variable node set, and $nodes_{mb}$ represents the Markov coverage nodes of a node. A node's Markov coverage nodes include the parent node, child node and other parent nodes of its child node. $MB()$ in step 11 is used to get the Markov coverage nodes of a particular node. Set_{sample} in step 2 represents sample set. Each sample can be got through constructing the exact match path between services in Rel_{ws}.

The step 4–19 in Algorithm 3 gives the process of how to calculate the conditional probability between nodes. It generates the sample $D[1]$ which is consistence with the evidence variable node ($node_e = ws_{ej}$) firstly. If $D[1]$ meets $node_p = ws_{pi}$, then m_q plus 1, as seen in step 4–7. Step 10–14 is used to operate on all the non-evidence variable node $nodes_{ne}[j]$ in turn according to the topological order. The Markov coverage nodes $nodes_{mb}$ of $nodes_{ne}[j]$ will be got firstly, then get val_{mb} of $nodes_{mb}$ in $D[i]$. Then it will calculate $p(nodes_{ne}[j] \mid val_{mb})$, sample and update the $nodes_{ne}[j]$ in $D[i]$ using the sample result. Step 15–17 is used to judge $D[i]$ whether it meets $node_p = ws_{pi}$ or not according to the sample result. If it meets the condition, m_q will be added 1. It will operate m times in turn using the above methods. Finally, it calculates m_q/m and return.

2.3   Web Service Selection of QoS

The service node set $wsnodes$ that can meet users' specific requirements can be got using Web service recommendation method. Each node can correspond to specific service cluster. Then it will select a set of services with better QoS values in different service clusters according to RE. We mainly use the following two approaches.

(1) On the basis of selecting services with proper function, the services with better QoS values will be selected. It mainly uses the following steps.
   (a) After calculating the conditional probability $p(node_m = ws_{mn} \mid node_i = ws_{ij})$ between specific service nodes using Gibbs sampling algorithm (Algorithm 3), we store the probability of recommending ws_{pi} in the condition of service ws_{ej}.
   (b) For specific service $node_e = ws_{ej}$, it sorts all the services in $node_p$ according to $p(node_p = ws_{pi} \mid node_e = ws_{ej})$.
   (c) The users' request RE and services will be done matching calculation from the functional level, service ws_{ij} in specific service cluster $clusws_i$ which can meet users' functional requirements can be got.
   (d) The service cluster $clusws_m$ of all the nodes in $wsnodes$ are operated in turn to get the probability $p(ws_{mn} \mid ws_{ij})$ of each service ws_{mn} in $clusws_m$. It sorts service ws_{mn} in the descending order, and calculates the matching value between $RE.ReQoS$ and $ws_{mn}.QoS$. When the matching value is larger than the threshold, it will recommend service ws_{mn} for users.
   (e) According to above methods, the services in service cluster $clusws_m$ of all the nodes in $wsnodes$ are judged in turn. Then the service set related to ws_{ij} can be got, thus it can recommend a set of services with better function and QoS values for users.
(2) Select a set of services with better QoS values from different service clusters directly

On the basis of getting service execution path node set $wsnodes$, this method will judge each service ws_{ij} in $clusws_i$ of $node_i$ in $wsnodes$. The matching value between RE.

ReQoS and $ws_{mn}.QoS$ will be calculated, and it will select the services with the largest *QoS* matching value.

3   Case Study

Example 1. *Cluster* = {$clusws_c$, $1 \leq c \leq 7$}. We use $A \sim G$ to express the service clusters, and it is denoted as $clusws_A \sim clusws_G$. The service number in $clusws_A \sim clusws_G$ is {5, 3, 6, 7, 7, 3, 5} respectively. We can see $clusws_A$ contains 5 services, $clusws_A$ = {ws_{Aw}, $1 \leq w \leq 5$}. Rel_{ws} = {rel_r: $ws_{ij} \rightarrow ws_{mn}$, $1 \leq r \leq 51$, $0 \leq i$, $m \leq 7$, $0 \leq j \leq c_i$, $0 \leq n \leq c_m$}. The relationship between services in Rel_{ws} is shown in Table 1.

Table 1. The relationship between services in Rel_{ws}

Service cluster	Rel_{ws}
$clusws_A$	$ws_{Aj} \rightarrow ws_{Bn}(clusws_B)$: $<A_0, B_0>$ $<A_0, B_1>$ $<A_0,B_2>$ $<A_1, B_0>$ $<A_1, B_1>$ $<A_1, B_2>$ $ws_{Aj} \rightarrow ws_{Cn}(clusws_C)$: $<A_0, C_3>$ $<A_1, C_4>$ $<A_1, C_5>$ $<A_2, C_4>$ $<A_2, C_5>$ $ws_{Aj} \rightarrow ws_{En}(clusws_E)$: $<A_0, E_0>$ $<A_1, E_1>$ $<A_2, E_2>$ $<A_3, E_3>$ $<A_4, E_1>$
$clusws_B$	$ws_{Bj} \rightarrow ws_{Cn}(clusws_C)$: $<B_0, C_0>$ $<B_1, C_1>$ $<B_2, C_2>$ $<B_1, C_3>$ $<B_0, C_4>$ $ws_{Cj} \rightarrow ws_{Dn}(clusws_D)$: $<C_1, D_4>$ $<C_3, D_6>$
$clusws_C$	$ws_{Cj} \rightarrow ws_{En}(clusws_E)$: $<C_1, E_1>$ $<C_5, E_5>$ $ws_{Cj} \rightarrow ws_{Fn}(clusws_F)$: $<C_0, F_0>$ $<C_1, F_1>$ $<C_2, F_2>$ $<C_3, F_2>$ $<C_4, F_1>$ $<C_5, F_0>$ $<C_4, F_2>$ $<C_1,F_0>$
$clusws_D$	$ws_{Dj} \rightarrow ws_{En}(clusws_E)$: $<D_0, E_0>$ $<D_1, E_1>$ $<D_2, E_2>$ $<D_3, E_3>$ $<D_4, E_4>$ $<D_5, E_5>$ $<D_6, E_6>$ $<D_4, E_4>$ $<D_2, E_1>$
$clusws_E$	$ws_{Ej} \rightarrow ws_{Gn}(clusws_G)$: $<E_0, G_0>$ $<E_1, G_1>$ $<E_2, G_2>$ $<E_3, G_3>$ $<E_2, G_4>$ $<E_1, G_3>$ $<E_0, G_2>$
$clusws_F$	–
$clusws_G$	$ws_{Gj} \rightarrow ws_{Fn}(clusws_F)$: $<G_4, F_1>$ $<G_4, F_2>$

(1)   Web service organization using TPDA

The concrete process of service organization can be seen in [5], and the initial graph will be got, as shown in Fig. 1(1). Using the third stage of *Thinning*, we can get the edges are not changed. The final network structure is shown in Fig. 1(2).

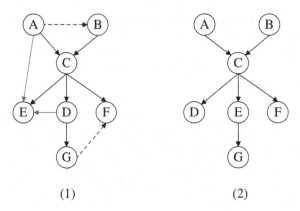

Fig. 1. The structure graph of service nodes

(2) **Web service recommendation based on Bayesian network reasoning**

   (a) Supposing *rnodes* = {*A*}, *wsnodes* ← *wsnodes* ∪ {<*A*, 1.0>} ⇒ *wsnodes* = {<*A*, 1.0>} through step 4 in Algorithm 2, the path is denoted by *getpathnode(rnodes[r])* = {{*A*, *C*, *D*}, {*A*, *C*, *E*, *G*}, {*A*, *C*, *F*}} ⇒ *pathnode* = {*A*, *C*, *D*, *E*, *F*, *G*}.

   (b) All the nodes in *pathnode* are done the calculation of *p(pathnode[p] | rnodes[r])* using step 10–15 in Algorithm 2. For example, when to calculate *p(E | A)* = 0.14283879, supposing $\gamma = 0.1$, we can get *p(E | A)* > γ, and *wsnodes* ← *wsnodes* ∪ <*E*, 0.14283879>. Then we can get *wsnodes* = {<*A*, 1.0>, <*C*, 0.13331947>, <*D*, 0.1428377>, <*E*, 0.14283879> <*F*, 0.3999311>, <*G*, 0.19997229>}.

   (c) All the nodes in *wsnodes* will be sorted using step 19 in Algorithm 2, and we can get *wsnodes* = {*A*, *F*, *G*, *E*, *D*, *C*}.

When to calculate *p(pathnode[p] | rnodes[r])* in above step (b), such as calculating *p(E | A)*, it can be got using Eq. (1). There are 5 services in the *clusws_E* of node *E*, and 7 services in the *clusws_A* of node *A*.

$$p(E \mid A) = \sum_{i=1}^{5} \sum_{j=1}^{7} p(ws_{Ei} | ws_{Aj}) \tag{1}$$

The *p(ws_Ei | ws_Aj)* in Eq. (1) can be calculated through Algorithm 3. For example, we use the following steps to calculate *p(ws_E2 | ws_A1)*.

(a) The service *ws_A1* in node *A* is evidence variable, and service *ws_E2* in node *E* is query variable. In Fig. 1(2), we can get non-evidence node *nodes_ne* = {*B*, *C*, *D*, *E*, *F*, *G*}.

(b) Using the given *Cluster* and *Rel_ws*, we can get *Set_sample*, and then *m* = 345.

(c) Generate *D[1]* whose evidence variable *node_e* is *ws_A1* in *Set_sample*, and *D[1]* = {*ws_A1*, *ws_B0*, *ws_C2*, *ws_D6*, *ws_E2*, *ws_F2*, *ws_G0*}. Then we can get *D[1]*. *node_p* = *ws_E2* ⇒ $m_q = m_q + 1$ ⇒ $m_q = 1$.

(d) $D[2] = D[1] \Rightarrow D[2] = \{ws_{A1}, ws_{B0}, ws_{C2}, ws_{D6}, ws_{E2}, ws_{F2}, ws_{G0}\}$. The nodes in $nodes_{ne}$ are operated using the following steps.

When $j = 0$, $nodes_{ne}[0] = B$, $nodes_{mb} \leftarrow MB(B) \Rightarrow nodes_{mb} = \{A, \quad C\} \Rightarrow val_{mb} = \{ws_{A1}, ws_{C2}\}$. Using step 13 in Algorithm 3, we can get $p(nodes_{ne}[0] \mid val_{mb}) = p(ws_{B0} \mid ws_{A1}, ws_{C2}) = 0.5$. Through the sampling calculation, the $D[2].B$ of node B in $D[2]$ will be updated to ws_{B1}. Then $D[2] = \{ws_{A1}, ws_{B1}, ws_{C2}, ws_{D2}, ws_{E2}, ws_{F2}, ws_{G0}\}$.

The calculation approach of $p(ws_{B1} \mid ws_{A1}, ws_{C2})$ is shown in Eq. (2), and $p(ws_{C2} \mid ws_{A1}, ws_{B1})$ can be got from *CPT* of node *C*.

$$p(ws_{B1} \mid ws_{A1}, ws_{C2}) = \frac{p(ws_{A1}, ws_{C2}, ws_{B1})}{p(ws_{A1}, ws_{C2})} = \frac{p(ws_{A1}) * p(ws_{B1}) * p(ws_{C2} \mid ws_{A1}, ws_{B1})}{p(ws_{C2} \mid ws_{A1}) * p(ws_{A1})}$$

(2)

When $j = 1$, then $nodes_{ne}[1] = C$, $nodes_{mb} \leftarrow MB(C) \Rightarrow nodes_{mb} = \{A, B, D, E, F\} \Rightarrow val_{mb} = \{ws_{A1}, ws_{B1}, ws_{D2}, ws_{E2}, ws_{F2}\}$. Using step 13 in Algorithm 3, we get $p(nodes_{ne}[1] \mid val_{mb}) = p(ws_{C2} \mid ws_{A2}, ws_{B1}, ws_{D2}, ws_{E2}, ws_{F2}) = 0.333$. Through the sampling calculation, the $D[2].C$ of node C in $D[2]$ is ws_{C2}. And its value is not changed. Then $D[2] = \{ws_{A1}, ws_{B1}, ws_{C2}, ws_{D2}, ws_{E2}, ws_{F2}, ws_{G0}\}$.

All the nodes in $nodes_{ne}$ are operated using above steps, we can get all the value of $D[i].D[2] = \{ws_{A1}, \quad ws_{B1}, \quad ws_{C2}, \quad ws_{D2}, \quad ws_{E2}, \quad ws_{F2}, \quad ws_{G0}\}$, and $D[2]$. $node_p = ws_{E2} \Rightarrow m_q = m_q + 1 \Rightarrow m_q = 2$.

(e) Then $D[3] = D[2]$. It will operate $345(m)$ times. And we can get $m_q = 87$, then $m_q/m = 0.2522$.

4 Related Work

At present, the research work about Web service recommendation includes the following approaches: collaborative filtering, using users' history usage information, *QoS*-aware, latent semantic probabilistic model, Bayesian theory and some other approaches. Most research work main uses the collaborative filtering method. Zheng et al. have proposed a *QoS*-aware Web service recommendation method by collaborative filtering [6]. The collaborative filtering method is used to predict the *QoS* values of Web services, and it mainly takes advantages of the past usage experiences of service users. In [7], a novel collaborative filtering algorithm is designed for large scale Web service recommendation. It mainly employs the characteristic of *QoS* and achieves considerable improvement on the commendation accuracy, and the recommendation visualization technique is also used as the auxiliary method. Nguyen *et al.* in [8] have proposed a collaborative filtering technique for Web service recommendation method based on user-operation combination. This method makes full use of the history usage records between users and operation, and it can recommend the services for users with the most similar service user preferences. Jiang *et al.* have proposed an effective Web service recommendation method based on personalized collaborative filtering [9]. It takes into account the personalized influence of services when computing similarity measurement between users and personalized influence of services. The personalized hybrid collaborative filtering (*PHCF*) technique by integrating personalized user-based algorithm and personalized item-based algorithm is proposed. Chen *et al.* have proposed a scalable hybrid collaborative filtering algorithm for personalized Web service recommendation [10], and their method can promote the personal Web service discovery. Kuang et al. have proposed a personalized services recommendation method based on context-aware *QoS* prediction [11]. This method refers the previous service invocation experiences under similar context with the current consumer. It clusters the service invocation records according to the similarity on context properties and selects the cluster that is most similar to the context of current consumer. And it predicts the *QoS* of an unused service for current consumer based on the filtered recommendation records by Bayesian inference. The above several mentioned methods mainly use the collaborative filtering method to recommend the proper services in the view of different aspects (such as *QoS*, users' operation, context, etc.). The services with different functions are organized in advance in our method, and the services are then recommended based on users' request information.

In addition, Kang *et al.* have proposed an active Web service recommendation (AWSR) [12] method based on usage history. It extracts users' functional interests and *QoS* preferences from his/her usage history. This method firstly calculates the similarity between users' functional interests and a candidate Web service. The hybrid new metric of similarity is used to combine functional similarity measurement and nonfunctional similarity measurement based on comprehensive *QoS* of Web services. The Top-K Web service list is recommended for users. This method can recommend the proper atomic service. However, our approach concentrates on recommending a set of services with correlations based on service organization in the view of function and *QoS*. In [13], a personalized Web service recommendation method based on latent semantic probabilistic model is proposed. It establishes the latent semantic relations among users, users' preferences and service situations. Then it uses the trained model to predict users' criteria preferences. Pan *et al.* have proposed a service classification and recommendation method based on software network [14]. The software network is used to describe the compositional strength between services, and the corresponding service algorithms have been proposed. Lee et al. have used the approach of member organization-based group similarity measures to realize service recommendation in Internet of Things environments [15]. Yu have proposed a framework named CloudRec to realize personalized service Recommendation in the Cloud. It exploits a user-centric strategy to achieve personalized QoS assessment of cloud services [16]. Kumara *et al.* have proposed a cluster-based Web service recommendation method [17]. It considers semantic similarity between services in the clustering process and the association between services. Cao *et al.* have proposed a mashup service recommendation method based on usage history and service network [18]. This approach firstly extracts users' interests from their Mashup service usage history and builds a service network based on social relationships information among Mashup services, APIs and their tags. Meng et al. mainly concentrate on the service recommendation for big data application [19]. This method aims at presenting a personalized service recommendation list and recommending the most appropriate services to users.

On the basis of organizing service from aspects of users' role, request goal and execution process, Liu *et al.* have proposed several service recommendation algorithms using users' different request information in [20, 21]. Wu *et al.* in [22, 23] have proposed a composite service recommendation method using Bayesian theory. They mainly analyze the service execution log, including service function, *QoS* record, etc. Based on the used service execution process that is generated manually or automatically, this approach calculates the service correlation probability using Bayesian theory, and recommend the optimal service sequence for users. The Bayesian theory is also used in our method. The difference is our method mainly concentrates on using the Bayesian structure learning theory to organize service clusters. Then users can firstly select the services that they are interested in, and thus use Bayesian network reasoning method to recommend services with correlations for users. This is different with the above method of recommending services based on the used service sequence. In addition, users will select the services with proper *QoS* values in different service clusters in further based on recommending different service types in our method.

5 Experiment

BN Toolkit(BNT) is a software development kit about Bayesian network learning using Matlab by Murphy [24]. This package does not support the algorithm of three-stage dependency analysis, and we implement this algorithm in this work. The experiment mainly compares our method with the algorithms of *K2*, hill-climbing (*HC*), greedy search (*GS*) and Markov chain Monte Carlo (*MCMC*) of realizing service organization. We denote these algorithms as *K2WS*, *HCWS*, *GSWS*, *MCMC* and *TPDA*. The experiment is carried out on the computer with the configuration of dual Intel (R) Core (TM)2 i5 CPU 760@ 2.80 GHz, and 4 G memory.

5.1 Web Service Organization Experiment

The experiment data is generated randomly. The *cnum* refers to the number of different service clusters, *snum* refers to the service numbers in different service clusters, *rnum* refers to number of service execution history records, as shown in Table 2.

Table 2. Experiment data

Type	Data									
cnum	5	10	15	20	25	30	35	40	45	50
snum	23	40	71	117	124	145	198	239	244	263
rnum	66	104	111	172	251	258	329	340	419	484

Experiment 1. Comparison of service organization accuracy.

We compare the common edge number, extra edge rate and loss edge rate of the standard network and the network using different methods, as shown in Figs. 2, 3 and 4.

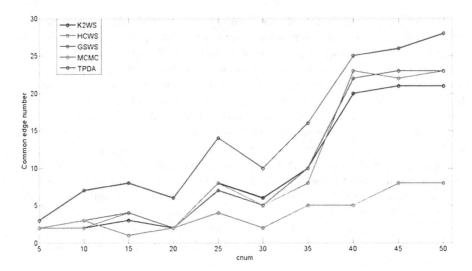

Fig. 2. Comparison of common edge number of different methods

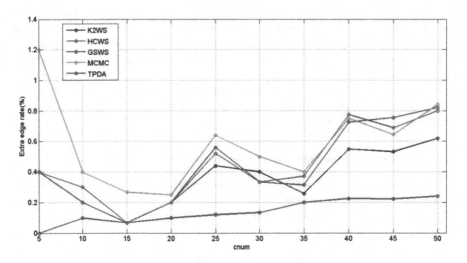

Fig. 3. Comparison of extra edge rate of different methods

The threshold in *TPDA* is set to 0.15. We can see the common edge number of *MCMC* method is the least of all, and its extra edge rate and loss edge rate is the largest. The learning effect of this approach is the worst. The extra edge rate and loss edge rate of our *TPDA* method is the least, it can learn the network with the better structure. The learning effect of *K2WS*, *HCWS* and *GSWS* is about same. The corresponding learning effect is better than *MCMC*, but it is less than *TPDA* method.

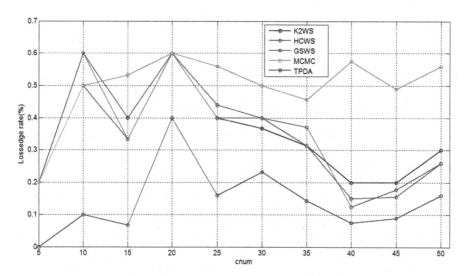

Fig. 4. Comparison of loss edge rate of different methods

5.2 Web Service Recommendation Experiment

Experiment 2. Comparison of service recommendation efficiency.

On the basis of realizing service organization using the methods of *K2WS*, *HCWS*, *GSWS*, *MCMC* and *TPDA*, we use three Bayesian network reasoning methods (*Variable Elimination, Join Tree, Gibbs Sampling*) to realize Web service recommendation respectively when to use two Bayesian network parameter learning approaches (*MLE* and *BE*). In the case of setting *cnum* to 4, 5, 6, 7, 8, 9, 10, 11, 12, 13 and 14, this experiment compares the service recommendation time of the above mentioned methods. The result is shown in Table 3.

Note: the time in Table 3 refers to the using time of recommending related nodes for all the nodes when we look the service cluster node as evidence node. And it is measured in seconds.

In Table 3, the service recommending time of all the approaches are becoming more as the service cluster number *cnum* increases. For the specific Bayesian network reasoning method, the recommending time of maximum likelihood estimation (*MLE*) parameter method is more than the Bayesian estimation method. For the specific Bayesian network structure learning method, the time of the three Bayesian network reasoning approaches is all about same. The time of Join Tree recommendation method is the least of all, and the time of Gibbs sampling method is the most. The time of variable elimination method is in the middle. In addition, the service recommendation time of *K2WS*, *HCWS*, *GSWS* and *MCMC* is about same, but it is less than the *TPDA* method.

Table 3. Comparison of service recommendation efficiency

cnum			4	5	6	7	8	9	10	11	12	13	14
Methods													
K2WS	Variable elimination	MLE	0.49	0.71	0.8	0.90	1.67	2.3	2.83	3.56	4.74	5.70	6.67
		BE	0.31	0.56	0.67	0.70	1.6	2.19	2.62	2.98	3.98	5.57	6.44
	Join tree	MLE	0.38	0.25	0.25	0.30	0.78	0.93	1.4	1.46	1.63	1.84	1.91
		BE	0.08	0.19	0.20	0.30	0.46	0.69	1.22	1.39	1.48	1.59	1.66
	Gibbs sampling	MLE	0.68	0.82	0.86	0.91	1.76	2.26	2.71	3.11	3.66	3.99	4.52
		BE	0.48	0.79	0.79	0.82	1.7	2.23	2.51	2.73	2.99	3.3	4.34
HCWS	Variable elimination	MLE	0.37	0.50	0.71	0.80	1.59	2.13	2.84	4.02	5.72	5.75	6.25
		BE	0.25	0.45	0.7	0.70	1.36	1.82	2.63	3.88	5.14	5.51	5.66
	Join tree	MLE	0.16	0.21	0.34	0.40	0.64	0.92	1.36	1.75	1.92	2.32	3.65
		BE	0.07	0.13	0.24	0.30	0.45	0.78	1.16	1.66	1.79	2.22	2.98
	Gibbs sampling	MLE	0.38	0.53	0.75	0.81	1.80	2.28	2.88	3.34	4.36	5.65	6.26
		BE	0.29	0.45	0.53	0.61	1.62	2.28	2.77	3.11	3.59	5.53	6.234
GSWS	Variable elimination	MLE	0.38	0.52	0.70	0.91	1.77	2.46	2.8	4.10	5.59	5.69	6.86
		BE	0.27	0.44	0.52	0.70	1.72	2.30	2.61	3.77	5.33	5.65	6.83
	Join tree	MLE	0.16	0.20	0.37	0.51	0.74	0.99	1.35	1.72	2.01	3.33	4.26
		BE	0.07	0.13	0.24	0.41	0.55	0.88	1.24	1.63	1.86	2.21	4.08
	Gibbs sampling	MLE	0.42	0.53	0.76	0.81	1.82	2.26	2.77	2.89	3.04	4.61	5.54
		BE	0.35	0.45	0.64	0.8	1.75	2.22	2.72	2.8	2.77	4.35	5.38
MCMC	Variable elimination	MLE	0.42	0.85	0.85	1.0	1.6	2.33	2.56	3.18	5.04	5.57	6.39
		BE	0.25	0.68	0.78	0.96	1.49	2.17	2.48	2.04	5.0	5.42	6.1
	Join tree	MLE	0.2	0.28	0.38	0.61	0.83	1.2	1.44	1.69	1.79	2.29	2.66
		BE	0.08	0.14	0.25	0.49	0.64	1.11	1.31	1.49	1.54	2.15	2.33
	Gibbs sampling	MLE	0.36	1.05	1.22	1.31	1.72	2.3	2.6	3.25	5.43	5.93	7.11
		BE	0.32	0.91	1.16	1.22	1.66	2.22	2.35	2.53	4.93	5.0	7.0
TPDA	Gibbs sampling	BE	2.01	2.16	5.2	7.55	11.1	13.9	15.9	21	24.5	28.1	31.3

Experiment 3. Comparison of service recommendation number of different methods.

On the basis of organizing services using *K2WS*, *HCWS*, *GSWS*, *MCMC* and *TPDA*, we use Gibbs sampling method to realize service recommendation. In the case of setting *cnum* to 4, 5, 6, 7, 8, 9, 10, 11, 12, 13 and 14, the number of recommending services using different methods is shown in Table 4.

In Table 4, for the several methods, the number of recommending service is different when setting *cnum* to different values. For specific *cnum*, the recommending service number of *MCMC* is the least of all, and *TPDA* method is the most. The methods of *K2WS*, *HCWS* and *GSWS* are in the middle.

Through Experiment 2 and 3, we can see the service recommendation time of *TPDA* is slightly larger than other methods. But this method can recommend the most number of services.

Table 4. Comparison of service recommendation number of different methods

cnum Methods	4	5	6	7	8	9	10	11	12	13	14
K2WS	10	7	8	15	10	15	16	19	25	28	27
HCWS	9	7	6	14	10	13	16	17	20	26	27
GSWS	9	6	6	10	8	13	12	14	17	20	18
MCMC	5	3	5	7	4	8	7	10	9	14	9
TPDA	10	9	11	19	12	20	18	22	32	33	34

Experiment 4. Comparison of service recommendation number of different thresholds.

In the case of setting different value of threshold γ in Algorithm 4, this experiment compares the service recommendation number using Gibbs sampling method in *TPDA*. It also analyzes the impact of threshold to service recommendation number. The result is shown in Table 5.

Table 5. Comparison of service recommendation number of different thresholds

cnum Thresholds	4	5	6	7	8	9	10	11	12	13	14
0.05	12	13	17	21	23	23	26	32	36	37	41
0.10	12	12	17	21	22	21	25	31	36	33	36
0.15	10	9	11	19	12	20	18	22	32	33	34
0.20	5	3	8	12	9	13	16	16	25	28	34
0.25	4	3	5	11	6	6	16	10	21	22	28
0.30	4	3	3	6	5	6	16	10	21	16	20
0.40	0	3	0	1	3	0	12	8	13	10	14
0.5	0	0	0	0	2	0	11	5	7	8	10

For the specific number of service cluster in Table 5, the service recommendation number is becoming less as the thresholds increases. The number of recommending service is becoming seldom when the threshold is set to 0.4. In addition, the number of recommending service shows the growing trend as the number of service clusters increases. The results are in good agreement with the experiment data.

6   Conclusion

In the era of service-oriented software engineering, how to effectively organize services and further to recommend a set of services for users is an urgent problem to be solved. In this work, we see different service clusters as nodes, and see the execution relationships between services as the edges between nodes in graph. We use the three-stage Bayesian network structure learning method to organize service clusters, and thus to form service cluster organization network graph. Two Bayesian network parameter learning methods (*MLE* and *BE*) are used to calculate the conditional probability of all the nodes, and thus to get the conditional probability table (CPT). The Bayesian network reasoning method (Gibbs sampling) is used to calculate the conditional probability and thus to realize Web service recommendation. A set of service type with correlations which can meet users' functional requirements will be recommended for users. On the basis of users' different QoS requirements, it will select services in further in different service clusters. Finally, the experiments and case study are used to do the validation. The next step research work mainly includes the following aspects: organizing Web services from the semantic level to improve the accuracy; optimizing the Bayesian network structure learning algorithm and improving the efficiency of service organization.

Acknowledgment. The authors are grateful to the valuable comments from the anonymous reviewers. This research is supported by the National Natural Science Foundation of China under Grant No. 31601078, the Natural Science Foundation of Hubei Province under Grant No. 2016CFB231, 2016CKB705. The Fundamental Research Funds for the Central Universities under grant No. 2662018JC030.

References

1. Papazoglou, P., Traverso, P., Dustdar, S., Leymann, F.: Service-oriented computing: a research roadmap. Int. J. Cooper. Inf. Syst. **17**(2), 223–255 (2008)
2. Liu, F.: Research on Bayesian Network Learning Algorithm. Doctoral Dissertation of Beijing University of Posts and Telecommunications, pp. 1–13 (2007)
3. Cheng, J., Grainer, G., Kelly, J., Bell, D., Liu, W.R.: Learning bayesian networks from data: an information-theory based approach. Artif. Intell. **137**, 43–90 (2002)
4. Zhang, Y.P., Zhang, L.: Machine Learning Theory and Algorithm. Science Press, pp. 246–269 (2012)
5. Liu, J.X., Xia, Z.H.: An approach of web service organization using bayesian network learning. J. Web Eng. **16**(3&4), 252–276 (2017)
6. Zheng, Z.B., Ma, H., Michael, R.L., King, I.: QoS-aware web service recommendation by collaborative filtering. IEEE Trans. Serv. Comput. **4**(2), 140–152 (2011)
7. Chen, X., Zheng, Z.B., Liu, X.D., Huang, Z.C., Sun, H.L.: Personalized QoS-aware web service recommendation and visualization. IEEE Trans. Serv. Comput. **6**(1), 35–47 (2013)
8. Ngoc Chan, N., Gaaloul, W., Tata, S.: Collaborative filtering technique for web service recommendation based on user-operation combination. In: Meersman, R., Dillon, T., Herrero, P. (eds.) OTM 2010. LNCS, vol. 6426, pp. 222–239. Springer, Heidelberg (2010). https://doi.org/10.1007/978-3-642-16934-2_17
9. Jiang, Y.C., Liu, J.X., Tang, M.D., Liu, X.Q.: An effective web service recommendation method based on personalized collaborative filtering. In: IEEE International Conference on Web Services, pp. 211–218 (2011)
10. Chen, X., Liu, X.D., Huang, Z.C., Sun, H.L.: RegionKNN: A scalable hybrid collaborative filtering algorithm for personalized web service recommendation. In: IEEE International Conference on Web Services, pp. 9–16 (2010)
11. Kuang, L., Xia, Y.J., Mao, Y.X.: Personalized services recommendation based on context-aware QoS prediction. In: IEEE 19th International Conference on Web Services, pp. 400–406 (2012)

12. Kang, G.S., Liu, J.X., Tang, M.D., Liu, X.Q., Cao, B.Q., Xu, Y.: AWSR: active web service recommendation based on usage history. In: IEEE 19th International Conference on Web Services, pp. 186–193 (2012)
13. Hu, Y., Peng, Q.M., Hu, X.H.: A personalized web service recommendation method based on latent semantic probabilistic model. J. Comput. Res. Develop. 51(8), 1781–1793 (2014)
14. Pan, W.F., Li, B., Shao, B., He, P.: Service classification and recommendation based on software networks. Chin. J. Comput. 34(12), 2355–2369 (2011)
15. Lee, J.S., Ko, I.Y.: Service recommendation for user groups in internet of things environments using member organization-based group similarity measures. In: IEEE International Conference on Web Services (ICWS), pp. 276–283 (2016)
16. Yu, Q.: CloudRec: a framework for personalized service recommendation in the cloud. Knowl. Inf. Syst. 43(2), 417–443 (2015)
17. Kumara, B.T.G.S., Paik, I., Siriweera, T.H.A.S., Koswatte, K.R.C.: Cluster-based web service recommendation. In: IEEE International Conference on Services Computing (SCC), pp. 348–355 (2016)
18. Cao, B.Q., Liu, J.X., Tang, M.D., Zheng, Z.B., Wang, G.R.: Mashup service recommendation based on usage history and service network. Int. J. Web Serv. Res. 10(4), 82–101 (2013)
19. Meng, S.M., Dou, W.C., Zhang, X.Y., Chen, J.J.: KASR: a keyword-aware service recommendation method on mapreduce for big data applications. IEEE Trans. Parallel Distrib. Syst. 25(12), 3221–3231 (2014)
20. Liu, J.X., He, K.Q., Wang, J., Yu, D.H., Feng, Z.W., Ning, D.: An approach of RGPS-guided on-demand service organization and recommendation. Chin. J. Comput. 36(2), 238–251 (2013)
21. Liu, J.X., Wang, J., He, K.Q., Liu, F., Li, X.X.: Service organization and recommendation using multi-granularity approach. Knowl. Based Syst. 73, 181–198 (2015)
22. Wu, J., Liang, Q.H., Jian, H.Y.: Bayesian network based services recommendation. In: IEEE Asia-Pacific Services Computing Conference, pp. 313–318 (2009)
23. Wu, J., Chen, L., Jian, H.Y., Wu, Z.H.: Composite service recommendation based on bayes theorem. Int. J. Web Serv. Res. 9(2), 69–93 (2012)
24. Murphy, K.P.: The bayes net toolbox for matlab (2001)

A Survey of Time-Aware Dynamic QoS Forecasting Research, Its Future Challenges and Research Directions

Yang Syu[1(✉)], Chien-Min Wang[1], and Yong-Yi Fanjiang[2]

[1] Institute of Information Science, Academia Sinica, Taipei City, Taiwan
{yangsyu, cmwang}@iis.sinica.edu.tw,
a29066049@gmail.com
[2] Department of Computer Science and Information Engineering,
Fu Jen Catholic University, New Taipei City, Taiwan
yyfanj@csie.fju.edu.tw

Abstract. The problem of time-aware (time series-based) dynamic quality of service (QoS) forecasting has attracted increased attention over the past decade. Developed forecasting approaches have been used to obtain the future values of dynamic QoS attributes for the support of the proactive decisions of various QoS-based applications (e.g., QoS-aware service selection and composition). Thus far, however, a comprehensive investigation and overview of the current research on this topic has yet to be produced. This paper proposes and introduces six assessment criteria which are then applied to the existing literature to produce a comprehensive comparison. Based on this analysis, we describe potential future challenges and research directions in this research area, focusing on gaps in the current literature. This survey provides a clear understanding of the current status of this research area with this paper; additionally, we also technically point out what have to be done by the researchers in this area for the advance of this research topic.

Keywords: Time-aware dynamic QoS attributes · Time series forecasting
Web services

1 Introduction

Many software systems rely on external Cloud/Web services to provide required functions or information, and new mobile applications increasingly incorporate existing services (e.g., the RESTful Web APIs exposed by Facebook, Google, and Instagram). The quality of these services (called quality of service, QoS) is an important concern to developers/engineers in service-oriented software engineering (SOSE) and researchers in service computing (SC). Among current QoS-related research topics and concerns, particular attention has focused on the prediction of dynamic QoS properties, such as service response time.

In both SOSE and SC, QoS is mostly just a general and conceptual term covering many different concrete properties and attributes, such as availability, throughputs, reputation (these are domain-independent, general QoS properties), and various

© Springer International Publishing AG, part of Springer Nature 2018
J. E. Ferreira et al. (Eds.): SCC 2018, LNCS 10969, pp. 36–50, 2018.
https://doi.org/10.1007/978-3-319-94376-3_3

domain-specific QoS attributes. A detailed introduction and explanation to QoS in the context of Web services can be found in Sect. 2 of [1]. For disparate QoS properties and attributes, a binary classification categorizes them into *static QoS* and *dynamic QoS*. The values of the former type of QoS are fixed or rarely changed. However the values of dynamic QoS could vary with one of the QoS dynamic factors discussed below. Because the real values of dynamic QoS are uncertain and unknown, a prediction method is needed, and several attempts have been made.

Our survey of the relevant literature finds that, when calling/using the same service, two factors have been identified as causing QoS value variation: *disparate service consumers* and *different invoking times* [2]. When invoking a service, it is likely to receive different dynamic QoS values for different service consumers because of the heterogeneity of their internal and external environments, as demonstrated and discussed in [3]. Furthermore, actual QoS values could even be changeable and dynamic in the case of the same user using a single service at different times. We identify and consider the predictions for these two factors as two different research areas (i.e., *consumer-aware* dynamic QoS prediction and *time-aware* dynamic QoS forecasting). This paper focuses on the later, namely, the research efforts targeting time-aware QoS variations and their forecasting.

Our survey identifies a number of relevant findings, but there is currently no systematic review or analysis of these works to provide an informative comparison of the properties and inadequacies of the various proposed approaches. This paper first conducts a detailed review and analysis of current time-aware (time series-based) dynamic QoS forecasting research, comparing various approaches in terms of the six identified criteria. Based on these observations, we then propose and discuss future challenges and research directions that must be considered and addressed to further advance this research area.

The first contribution of this paper is a detailed comparison and discussion of current time-aware QoS forecasting studies. This comparison allows the reader to quickly understand the current status of this research area, the pros and cons of each reviewed work, and the concerns that must be considered and addressed for this research topic. For our comparison, six common characteristics are identified as criteria for comparison: (1) year published, (2) problem specifications defined and addressed, (3) forecasting methods proposed/employed and methods used for performance comparison, (4) measures considered for performance evaluation, (5) dynamic QoS datasets tested, and (6) QoS-aware applications combined. These criteria can be viewed as key research concerns for this topic and researchers working on this problem should consider them carefully. The second contribution is to identify future research directions and challenges in this area, including (1) the collection of a large-scale, real-world dynamic QoS time series dataset from modern Web/cloud services, (2) a formal and detailed analysis of dynamic QoS data for understanding their intrinsic characteristics and specialties, (3) an investigation on the use of innovative machine-learning (ML) techniques (e.g., Markov chain models and recurrent neural networks, RNNs) and different statistical strategies (e.g.,, cross-approach selection and combination strategies), and (4) the efficient integration of a QoS forecasting approach with its application.

The remainder of this paper is organized as follows. Section 2 presents a survey of the existing research, including an explanation for the assessment criteria identified and adopted, along with a comparison table showing the existing studies in terms of the proposed criteria, and a description and discussion of the cited works. Section 3 lists and discusses potential future work and research challenges in this area. Conclusion are drawn in Sect. 4.

2 A Survey of Time-Aware Dynamic QoS Forecasting

This section reviews current research on time-aware (time series-based) dynamic QoS forecasting to produce a detailed comparison table. Published works are reviewed and carefully analyzed to extract and identify a number of common properties as the fundamental criteria for comparison and discussion. Below, we first introduce the identified criteria and then apply them to the collected studies for comparison, followed by a discussion of the comparison and the cited works.

2.1 Criteria

Each study to be compared is identified in terms of *the names of its authors* and *the year* it was published. We consider the publication date because SC research and the service industry are developing rapidly, and results from only a few years ago may already be out of date. For example, research performed on an obsolete time-aware dynamic QoS dataset is less relevant than from a recently collected dataset. However, some recent works have performed experiments on ancient QoS datasets [2, 4, 5]. In this case, it would be ideal to consider both the time that a work was reported and when its experimental QoS dataset was made.

Even though the works cited in this paper all focus on time-aware dynamic QoS forecasting, their detailed problem specifications still differ in many ways. Many of the surveyed works consider their studied problem as a case of time series forecasting of which there are many variations, such as univariate prediction and multivariate prediction as well as one-step-ahead forecasting and n-step-ahead forecasting (i.e., the length of forecasting horizon). Thus, one cannot say that the reviewed works all study exactly the same problem. Due to its complexity, we divide the second criterion, *the problem specifications*, into three sub-concerns to accurately differentiate between the reviewed works. The first sub-criterion indicates whether *the formal (mathematical) problem definition* has been presented in the original paper. The second sub-criterion is that the problem defined to study or the experimental results reported comprises *both modeling and forecasting stages or only covers the later*. The last sub-concern is *the forms of the studied problem in terms of time series research*. Due to the diversity of problem specifications, if a formal definition for the studied problem is not provided in the original paper (according to the first sub-criteria), it is difficult to determine its detailed specification (the forms of the studied problem, namely, the third sub-criterion) and to reproduce its (experimental) results for impartial comparison.

The third criterion regards the solutions developed and considered in each work. This criterion is also divided into two sub-criteria, namely, *the approach proposed by the authors in a work* and *the methods that are considered for a comparison with the proposed approach.* Note that, among the reviewed works, a few empirical studies just employ a number of well-developed, long-standing (e.g., time series and/or machine learning) techniques to compare their performance on a time-aware QoS dataset. For these works, there would not be any proposed approach for them in our comparison.

Most time-aware QoS forecasting research focuses on numerical QoS attributes (e.g., response times, throughputs, and availability), and determining the performance of the proposed approaches and methods considered for comparison, requiring *a way to quantitatively evaluate and present their results.* Many of the reviewed studies just intuitively adopt some common measures of accuracy in time series research as their metrics, such as mean absolute errors (MAEs) and mean absolute percentage errors (MAPEs). However, some QoS-specific metrics have also been considered, such as the rate at which QoS violations can be correctly predicted. Aside from accuracy, time cost is also a common concern of many existing studies, primarily the time consumed for training/fitting a predictor (predictor generation time, PGT) or for yielding a forecasting value (forecast production time, FPT).

In addition to prediction approaches, another indispensible element for time-aware dynamic QoS forecasting research is *QoS time series datasets used for practical evaluations (experiments).* Most of the work reviewed for our study consider a real-world, time-aware QoS dataset, with some collecting original real world QoS data, while others rely on publicly available datasets. Note that, as previously mentioned, the age of the QoS dataset is an important concern.

Our final consideration is *whether the applications are combined and used with the proposed QoS forecasting approaches.* For QoS forecasting approaches, actually, it is not meaningful in practice; to be useful, a QoS forecasting approach should be integrated with a QoS-aware application that needs future QoS values to proactively and reliably perform make decisions and/or perform operations, such as design-time QoS-aware service selection/composition and runtime service adaptation (i.e., dynamic binding). In the column for this criterion, we list the application in each reviewed work, and the entry would be empty if the study in question only focuses on the forecasting problem.

2.2 Comparison

Given the criteria proposed and discussed in the previous section, the results of our survey on existing time-aware dynamic QoS forecasting approaches are presented in Table 1, ordered by date of publication.

2.3 Discussion

Based on Table 1, this section discusses current time-aware dynamic QoS forecasting research in terms of the six proposed criteria. Note that, in this section, we also discuss what concerns must be considered, addressed, and presented (i.e., the contents that must be shown for the reader to read and understand) in a paper to be considered referable and valuable research.

Table 1. The survey of time-aware dynamic QoS forecasting research in terms of the criteria proposed.

Author	Year published	Problem specifications			Approaches	Models/methods compared	Evaluations	Time-aware dynamic QoS datasets	QoS-aware applications combined
		Formal definitions	Stages covered	Problem forms	Models/methods proposed				
Yang et al. [4]	2017	Provided	Forecasting	Univariate, one-step-ahead, and single-predictor mode	None	Baseline approaches (Average, three Naïve methods, Drift, six Regression models), TS approaches (ARIMA family, ES family, two SETAR models, and GARCH family), and ML approaches (ANNs and GP)	Accuracy (MAE and MAPE) and time (PGT and FPT)	Two response-time time series in the dataset provided by [6]	None
Fanjiang et al. [2]	2016	Provided	Forecasting	Univariate, one-step-ahead, and single-predictor mode	GP	Baseline approaches (Random search, Average, three Naïve methods, Drift, and six Regression models), TS approaches (ARIMA models and ES models), and one ML approach (ANNs)	Accuracy (MAE and MAPE) and improvement (RPAI)	One response-time time series in the dataset provided by [6]	None
Ye et al. [7]	2016	Provided	Forecasting	Multivariate, N-step-ahead (long-term), and single-predictor mode	Multivariate ARIMA or Multivariate Holt-Winters, depending on their univariate RMSE modeling accuracy	VAR, (univariate) ARIMA models, and (univariate) Holt-Winters method	Accuracy (RMSE)	A set of short (28 observations only) response-time and throughput time series for 100 real-world cloud services	QoS-aware cloud service composition (selection) based on long-term QoS time series similarity
Nourikhah et al. [5]	2015	None	Forecasting	Difficult to define	ARFIMA	Naïve, Average, and ARIMA	Accuracy (MAE and MAPE) and improvement (RPAI)	The dataset provided by [6]	None
Rehman et al. [8]	2014	None	Modeling and Forecasting	Difficult to define	None	ARIMA and ES	Accuracy (MAE, RMSE, and MASE) and residual diagnosis	Amazon cloud service data provided by CloudClimate (no longer available)	None
Leitner et al. [9]	2013	None	Forecasting	Difficult to define	None	ML approaches (DTs for nominal attributes and ANNs for numerical attributes) and TS approach (ARIMA models)	Accuracy (training/modeling data correction, MAE, and SD of absolute errors for numerical data and precisions and recalls for nominal attributes) and time (PGT and FPT)	The historical execution data of the sub-flow of a real-world business process	Theoretically, proactive detection for SLA violation (i.e. SLA prediction)

(continued)

Table 1. (*continued*)

Author	Year published	Problem specifications			Approaches	Models/methods compared	Evaluations	Time-aware dynamic QoS datasets	QoS-aware applications combined
		Formal definitions	Stages covered	Problem forms	Models/methods proposed				
YunNi et al. [10]	2013	None	Forecasting	Difficult to define	ARMA	None	None (overall dependability of a composite service)	The QoS time series collected from eight services	Dependability prediction for WS-BPEL-based composite services
Amin et al. (a). [11]	2012	None	Forecasting	Difficult to define	ARIMA-GARCH (both sequentially combined)	ARIMA	Accuracy (MAPE), improvement (RPAI), and time (PGT and FPT)	The dataset provided by [6]	Simulated proactive detection for QoS violation (i.e. SLA prediction)
Amin et al. (b). [12]	2012	None	Forecasting	Difficult to define	ARIMA or SETARMA (selected based on linearity using statistical test)	ARIMA	Accuracy (MAPE), improvement (RPAI), and time (PGT and FPT)	The QoS time series collected from 800 real-world services	None
Senivongse et al. [13]	2011	None	Forecasting	Difficult to define	ANNs	None	None (not revealed)	The QoS time series collected from 39 real-world/self-made services	QoS-aware service selection with varying granularity
Yilei et al. [14]	2011	Provided	Forecasting	Time-aware and consumer-aware QoS prediction (tensor filling)	Tensor Factorization	Three other less sophisticated tensor factorization approaches	Accuracy (MAE and RMSE)	A 142 × 4532 × 64 (consumes × services × times) QoS data tensors	None
Zadeh et al. [15]	2010	Not well-defined	Modeling and Forecasting	Difficult to define	ANNs	None	Accuracy (MAE, MSE, and percentage of correctly predicted trends)	Not clearly mentioned	Theoretically, designed for replacing QoS monitoring
Cavallo et al. [6]	2010	None	Forecasting	Difficult to define	None	Average, Last Observation (Naive), Linear Regression, and ARIMA	Accuracy (MAPE and SD of percentage errors)	The QoS time series collected from ten real-world services	Simulated detection for QoS violation

(*continued*)

Table 1. (*continued*)

Author	Year published	Problem specifications				Approaches			Evaluations		Time-aware dynamic QoS datasets	QoS-aware applications combined
		Formal definitions	Stages covered	Problem forms		Models/methods proposed	Models/methods compared		Evaluations			
Godse et al. [16]	2010	None	Forecasting	Difficult to define		ARIMA	None		None (only an unclear program execution result was presented)		The QoS time series collected from two real-world services	Theoretically, designed to be combined with QoS-aware service selection
Mu et al. [17]	2009	Provided (but difficult to understand)	Forecasting	Difficult to define		Structural Equation Modeling	None		Accuracy (MAPE)		The QoS time series data collected from self-made services	QoS-aware service selection

The oldest study reviewed in Table 1 dates back almost ten years (i.e., Mu et al. [17] in 2009), and new studies have been published each year since.

Regarding the problem specifications, except for a few of recent works (i.e., Yang et al. [4] in 2017 and Fanjiang et al. [2] and Ye et al. [7] in 2016), most studies did not formally define or present their addressed problem (or they are difficult to understand due to the poor definition or presentation, such as those in Zadeh et al. [15] and Mu et al. [17]). We consider that this lack of formal definition is a series defect for such quantitative research because the lack of clear definitions makes it difficult to infer the research assumptions or to understand the work in details sufficient to reproduce the experimental results for an impartial comparison with newly proposed forecasting approaches. Second, regarding the covered problem stages, only one work (Zadeh et al. [15]) reported the modeling accuracy of their proposed/applied forecasting approach (ANNs). Even though forecasting performance is definitely the most important concern of any time series forecasting task, it could be helpful to also report corresponding modeling/training performance to understand the fitting/modeling capability of the considered approaches/models and for analysis of the original data and forecasting results (e.g., exploring the relationships between the modeling and forecasting performance of an approach/model to assist the development of strategies for cross-approach/model selection or combination). Finally, in terms of the problem forms, lack of formal definitions in most of the reviewed papers (as indicated in the first sub-criterion) makes it difficult to fully realize the problem specifications in forms of time series forecasting. Among papers without any formal definitions, some provided a brief text description of their problem form (e.g., they performed one-step-ahead forecasting). However, we consider such information to be incomplete and partial for the inference of a full specification. According to our survey, most of the reviewed studies were assumed to perform univariate, one-step-ahead forecasting, which is the most basic form for the problems in time series research. One exception is Ye et al. [7], in which the authors demonstrated that the correlations between the different dynamic QoS attributes of the same service can sometimes help to improve forecasting accuracy (i.e., performing multivariate prediction), and cloud service consumers raise the need for long-term QoS information (which can be obtained by using N-step-ahead forecasting). Yilei et al. [14] is another exception in that the study problem definition also includes another dynamic QoS factor, namely, different consumers (consumer-aware). The difference in the problem studied in Yilei et al. [14] also results in a different type of the employed solution, as discussed below.

Aside from the tensor factorization used in Yilei et al. [14] and the structural equation modeling adopted in Mu et al. [17], the approaches considered here can be categorized into three different classes, namely, the baseline approaches (including Random Search, Average, Naïve, Drift, and Regressions methods), the statistical time-series methods (Auto-Regressive Integrated Moving Average, Auto-Regressive Fractionally Integrated Moving Average, Exponential Smoothing, Generalized Autoregressive Conditional Heteroskedasticity, and Self-Exciting Threshold Auto-Regressive models), and the machine-learning techniques (Genetic Programming, Decision Trees, and Artificial Neural Networks). In time series research, the baseline approaches were mostly used as the bottom for a comparison with sophisticated approaches that the proposed approach must be at least superior to (i.e., more accurate than) the baseline approaches; otherwise, it is useless and meaningless [18]. According to our survey, in most studies that have compared TS and/or ML approaches with the baseline approaches (including Yang et al. [4], Fanjiang et al. [2], Nourikhah et al. [5], and Cavallo et al. [6]), the TS and ML approaches generally surpass the baseline approaches in terms of forecasting accuracy. Regarding the comparison between the TS approaches and the ML techniques, recent studies (e.g., Yang et al. [4] and Fanjiang et al. [2]) demonstrated that the ML approach GP is superior to the other TS and ML approaches in terms of forecasting accuracy; however, GP raises a tradeoff because it takes more time to train and evolve a predictor (i.e., increased predictor generation time, PGT). As indicated in Yang et al. [4], to reach a compromise between forecasting accuracy and time cost, it is worth considering using the two most widely used TS approaches, namely, ARIMA models and ES methods. Finally, most surveyed works follow a single-approach strategy to address the problem (e.g., using GP or ARIMA models to predict future QoS values regardless of the characteristics of historical QoS data). However, there are also a few exceptions that use a cross-approach selection strategy (Ye et al. [7] and Amin et al. [12]) or a model combination strategy (Amin et al. (a). [11]), with experimental results that suggest these strategies can further improve forecasting accuracy.

For evaluation, forecasting accuracy is the most common and important concern in this research area. The existing research considers a number of time-series measures of accuracy, including mean absolute error (MAE), mean absolute percentage error (MAPE), and root mean squared error (RMSE). Based on these measures, to quantitatively calculate the improvement of a proposed approach over the others in terms of forecasting accuracy, most studies adopt relative prediction accuracy improvement (RPAI) as a numerical indication, including Fanjiang et al. [2], Nourikhah et al. [5], Amin et al. (a). [11], and Amin et al. (b). [12]. Basically, MAE, MAPE, and RMSE (and the other measures of accuracy in time series research, as listed and introduced in [19]) calculate the overall accuracy of a measured approach, integrating and expressing it as a single number for quick comprehension and comparison. To assess the forecasting stability of an approach, some studies, such as Leitner et al. [9] and Cavallo et al. [6], also calculate the standard deviations (SDs) of their original forecasting point errors. Finally, except for accuracy, as shown in Table 1, the cost of time is also an important concern in many of the reviewed studies. Mostly, they consider the time that is required to train, fit, and produce a predictor (i.e., predictor generation time, PGT) and to obtain a set of forecast values through the predictor (forecast production time, FPT).

For time-aware dynamic QoS forecasting, most studies used real-world QoS data to perform their empirical evaluation and experiments. Thus far, the QoS time series dataset collected and provided by Cavallo et al. [6] is most widely used, with application in the early research Cavallo et al. [6] and Amin et al. [11] along with more recent work in Nourikhah et al. [5], Fanjiang et al. [2], and Yang et al. [4]. The other authors performed experiments on original dynamic QoS datasets. These self-collected QoS datasets show no consistency in terms of properties, such as the number of observed services and dynamic QoS attributes or the length of gathered QoS time series. In fact, no widely acceptable standard or consensus exists for the features of a valid time-aware dynamic QoS dataset, and we this may cause problems for research validity. In addition, these self-collected datasets are typically not publicly available, making it difficult or impossible to reproduce the experimental results for comparison with newly proposed forecasting approaches. This lack of a large-scale, widely-acceptable QoS dataset (benchmark) is further discussed in the next section.

Finally, as indicated in Table 1, some research exclusively focuses on forecasting problems, while the others seek to integrate an QoS-aware application with the developed/applied forecasting approaches. A number of the latter works only theoretically describe or discuss the combining of both types of QoS-based approaches, without providing any practical implementation or evaluation, while the others have integrated and tested both types of approaches and reported their performance to demonstrate the usage and influences of time-aware dynamic QoS forecasting approaches. Among the combined QoS-aware applications, most are approaches to provide proactive detection (prediction) for SLA violations and automated service selection (composition). We consider these applications as demonstrating the usefulness and value of time-aware dynamic QoS forecasting approaches.

3   Future Challenges and Research Directions

Despite nearly a decade's work on the time-aware (time series-based) dynamic QoS forecasting problem, there are still a number of challenges and issues that must be addressed:

3.1   Time-Aware Dynamic QoS Datasets

Aside from various forecasting approaches, another indispensable component for any prediction research is the use of a valid and referable dataset (benchmark) for performance evaluation and comparison. However, we consider the QoS datasets used in the current work to be somewhat defective in several different aspects. First of all, as mentioned in the previous section, many of the time-aware QoS datasets are not retrievable, and thus do not allow for the reproduction of experimental results. Second, Cavallo et al.'s QoS dataset [6] and other self-collected datasets are outdated and most likely to not represent current QoS status. For example, a paper published in 2010 uses the Cavallo et al. dataset [6] was recorded and gathered in 2006, thus the underlying data is over a decade old. Most datasets, such as those used in Cavallo et al. [6], Amin et al. [12], Senivongse et al. [13], and Yilei et al. [14], were produced by gathering QoS values from a set of SOAP/WSDL-based Web services. However, currently the RESTful style [20] is the most popular and prevalent form of cloud/Web services. These two types of services have many intrinsic differences; thus, the QoS values obtained from SOAP/WSDL-based Web services may not be representative of today's services. Finally, the properties of certain QoS datasets are not suitable for large-scale experiments. For example, in the dataset used in Ye et al. [7], for each recorded service, its QoS history is 6 months old and has only 28 time slots (i.e., observations, thus the length of a QoS time series is 28). Thus it has too few observations and too long a time interval (6 months/28). Another issue in many datasets is that the number of their QoS time series samples (i.e., the number of services observed) are poor. For example, in the dataset provided in Cavallo et al. [6], only the data from ten real-world services were recorded, which may raise doubts about this dataset's validity because currently there are hundreds of thousands of services available in the real world. Experimental results based on poor quality datasets may not be reliable (i.e., their generality could be questioned).

A time-aware (time series-based) dynamic QoS dataset without the above issues must be considered and developed to offer a robust basis for studies and experiments in this research area. When gathering QoS data for the production of such a dataset, its collection time and duration, the number of observed services and dynamic QoS attributes, and the type of services must be carefully considered in terms of the dataset's validity; otherwise, the dataset must be easy to retrieve or publicly available. A referable time-aware QoS dataset is the third dataset reported and studied in [20] (namely, the dataset used in Yilei et al. [14]). However, this dataset suffers from several shortcomings including its relative age (the data were collected in March 2011), the type of services used (SOAP/WSDL-based Web services), and the length of each QoS time series (only 64 observations). In addition to forecasting performance, we believe that a large-scale, modern QoS time series dataset would also be very useful for understanding the current status of cloud/Web services and networks, as discussed in the next section.

3.2   Statistical Analysis to QoS Time Series

According to our survey, most current research presents empirical studies, without applying formal, statistical analytics to the targeted QoS data processing, modeling, and prediction. For the most part, the forecasting approaches and QoS data were simply tested for performance comparison to other approaches. In other words, the studied QoS time series were block boxes being used as a benchmark to test various approaches, and their intrinsic natures and characteristics remain unclear. A few studies briefly explored the processed QoS data; for example, in the approach proposed in [12], the authors used the Hanset test to check the linearity of the QoS data: the Engle test to verify volatility in [11], and the Hurst exponent to test the existence of long memory in [5]. However, this type of one-sided analysis mainly serves to support or verify of an authors' assumptions regarding the QoS time series and are thus insufficient to provide comprehensive insight into the QoS data.

The characteristics of time-aware QoS data differ from many other types of time series (e.g., financial time series). For example, the response-time time series of real-world Web services feature sudden peaks (i.e., very long response times), potentially caused by short-term network congestion or server problems. But such phenomenon are very rare in financial time series, such as the overall index of a stock market. In the time series of stock market indexes, major fluctuations (i.e., exceeding ten percent of the previous value) are extremely rare, but such oscillations are common in response-time QoS time series due to service and network instability.

An insightful and comprehensive analysis is required of QoS time series focusing on identifying their unique characteristics and specialties (the differences from the other types of time series). We believe that such knowledge would be very helpful in developing dedicated modeling and forecasting approaches for QoS time series, taking advantage of the presented findings (for example, in developing a sophisticated criterion for the cross-approach model selection strategy, as discussed in the next section), and in answering various questions, such as why the machine learning approach GP can outperform conventional time series methods in this kind of forecasting task [2, 4]. Analyzing and exploring a large-scale, modern QoS dataset might also help indicate the current status of services and networks. For example, observing the QoS variations of the services in a given region or from a single provider may indicate stability and usability (i.e., service and/or network conditions).

3.3   Forecasting Approaches and Strategies

According to the relatively recent work by Yang et al. [4] and Fanjiang et al. [2], the ML approach GP has superior forecasting accuracy than the other methods. Another common ML approach, ANNs, is also widely considered in the existing research. We believe that this demonstrates the potential and superiority of ML approaches for such forecasting problems. However, several ML approaches applicable to time series modeling and forecasting have yet to be considered, including support vector machines (SVMs), Markova chains, and some more complicated ANNs developed and used in deep learning (e.g., recurrent neural networks, RNNs). A complete performance evaluation and comparison including all applicable approaches would be informative for this research area.

As noted in Table 1, most studies follow the single-approach strategy (applying only an individual forecasting method to address the problem). Two exceptions are Ye et al. [7] and Amin et al. [12]; the former selects between ARIMA models and the Holt-Winters method based on their modeling/fitting accuracy, and the later chooses between ARIMA models and SETARMA models according to the linearity of QoS data. However, they suffer defects in terms of the poor number of candidate approaches and the non-robust selection criterion. In time series research, each forecasting method has its own rationale and most suitable data type. When selecting the most suitable approach, one would ideally take more approaches into account (as shown in [4], many statistical and ML approaches can perform time series forecasting). On the other hand, thus far, a well-developed, sophisticated selection criteria have not been identified for QoS time series forecasting; the two above-mentioned examples only choose based on a single process data property and lack comprehensive and insightful consideration of the data. A more complex and robust selection criterion, such as a rule-based guidance, would be useful.

In addition to the single-approach and cross-approach selection strategies discussed above, another common strategy is to combine the forecasting results of different approaches (i.e., the cross-approach combination strategy). For example, the authors of [21] reported that a combination of the forecasting results of their top three individual approaches can effectively increase forecasting accuracy for cloud workload. However, our survey finds no instance of this strategy being applied to this kind of forecasting task. Overall, in terms of the three different strategies for time series forecasting (namely, the single-approach, the cross-approach selection, and the cross-approach combination strategies), the existing studies are somehow insufficient.

3.4 Integration

Without a QoS-aware (QoS-based) application to be integrated and used with the developed dynamic QoS forecasting approach, the forecasting approach is actually useless (and even meaningless). Despite several instances of viable integration, a more efficient way to combine both types of approaches is still needed. For example, most surveyed forecasting approaches use single-predictor mode, thus a trained and fitted predictor is used for prediction for long periods (e.g., the next 100 future time points) without any update. However, in the real world, as time passes, new QoS values can be observed and recorded, and these new QoS values should be incrementally and efficiently applied to maximize predictor performance because more recent values are more valuable and referable for the performance of the training and fitting task of a predictor). A simple way to ensure the most recent data is used is to re-train a new predictor each time a newer QoS value becomes available. However, this entails repetitive costs for training and fitting. For example, if we consider using the most suitable approach for time-aware QoS forecasting (i.e., GP), each time it must wait for GP to evolve and then search for a new predictor from scratch. GP's biggest problem is its very long training time, as demonstrated in [4]. To overcome this problem, we would suggest using the dynamic GP approach demonstrated in [22], which is specifically developed for the performance of continuous time series forecasting with lower evolving costs and higher forecasting accuracy. In [22], the authors proposed several techniques for the progressive evolution and searching of a set of expression-based predictors for prediction at consecutive future time points. Using this approach, it is no longer necessary to start the evolution and searching from scratch each time the prediction moves in time, and it can produce a set of predictors adapted to different data generation processes. We consider that the integration, development, or searching of such a relatively efficient approach would be useful in addressing the problem.

4 Conclusion

Because the values of time-aware dynamic QoS attributes vary over time, considerable research attention has focused on predicting such attributes. The present paper provide a comprehensive survey, comparison, and discussion of relevant studies over the past decade, and proposes challenges and research directions that should be carefully considered for future research efforts.

Six general criteria were used for comparison, including year of publication, the problem specification addressed in each work, the approaches proposed and/or considered for comparison, method of performance evaluation, the QoS dataset adopted for empirical experiments, and finally the type of application for which a forecasting approach was developed. Insufficiencies in the existing research were categorized into four groups: improper current time-aware QoS datasets, lack of an insightful and comprehensive analysis to QoS time series data (i.e., to the QoS dataset), incompleteness in the approaches and strategies developed, and finally a more efficient way to integrate a QoS forecasting approach and its application. Examples and possible solutions are proposed for each.

Acknowledgement. This research is partially sponsored by the Ministry of Science and Technology (Taiwan) under the Grant MOST106-2811-E-001-003 and MOST106-2221-E-001-007-MY2.

References

1. Kritikos, K., Plexousakis, D.: Requirements for QoS-based web service description and discovery. IEEE Trans. Serv. Comput. **2**(4), 320–337 (2009)
2. Fanjiang, Y.-Y., Syu, Y., Kuo, J.-Y.: Search based approach to forecasting QoS attributes of web services using genetic programming. Inf. Softw. Technol. **80**, 158–174 (2016)
3. Zheng, Z., Lyu, M.R.: Personalized reliability prediction of web services. ACM Trans. Softw. Eng. Methodol. **22**(2), 1–25 (2013)
4. Syu, Y., Kuo, J.-Y., Fanjiang, Y.-Y.: Time series forecasting for dynamic quality of web services: an empirical study. J. Syst. Softw. **134**, 279–303 (2017)
5. Nourikhah, H., Akbari, M.K., Kalantari, M.: Modeling and predicting measured response time of cloud-based web services using long-memory time series. J. Supercomput. **71**(2), 673–696 (2015)
6. Cavallo, B., Penta, M.D., Canfora, G.: An empirical comparison of methods to support QoS-aware service selection. In: Proceedings of the 2nd International Workshop on Principles of Engineering Service-Oriented SystemsCape Town, South Africa, pp. 64–70. ACM (2010)
7. Ye, Z., Mistry, S., Bouguettaya, A., Dong, H.: Long-Term QoS-aware cloud service composition using multivariate time series analysis. IEEE Trans. Serv. Comput. **9**(3), 382–393 (2016)
8. Rahman, Z.U., Hussain, O.K., Hussain, F.K.: Time series QoS forecasting for management of cloud services. Presented at the Proceedings of the 2014 Ninth International Conference on Broadband and Wireless Computing, Communication and Applications (2014)
9. Leitner, P., Ferner, J., Hummer, W., Dustdar, S.: Data-driven and automated prediction of service level agreement violations in service compositions. Distrib. Parallel Databases **31**(3), 447–470 (2013)
10. Xia, Y., Ding, J., Luo, X., Zhu, Q.: Dependability prediction of WS-BPEL service compositions using petri net and time series models. In: 2013 IEEE 7th International Symposium on Service Oriented System Engineering (SOSE), pp. 192–202. IEEE, Redwood City (2013)
11. Amin, A., Colman, A., Grunske, L.: An approach to forecasting QoS attributes of web services based on ARIMA and GARCH models. In: 2012 IEEE 19th International Conference on Web Services (ICWS), Honolulu, HI, pp. 74–81. IEEE (2012)
12. Amin, A., Grunske, L., Colman, A.: An automated approach to forecasting QoS attributes based on linear and non-linear time series modeling. In: Proceedings of the 27th IEEE/ACM International Conference on Automated Software EngineeringEssen, Germany, pp. 130–139. ACM (2012)
13. Senivongse, T., Wongsawangpanich, N.: Composing services of different granularity and varying QoS using genetic algorithm. In: Proceedings of the World Congress on Engineering and Computer Science 2011. Lecture Notes in Engineering and Computer Science, San Francisco, CA, USA, pp. 388–393 (2011)
14. Yilei, Z., Zibin, Z., Lyu, M.R.: WSPred: a time-aware personalized QoS prediction framework for web services. In: 2011 IEEE 22nd International Symposium on Software Reliability Engineering (ISSRE), Hiroshima, pp. 210–219. IEEE (2011)

15. Zadeh, M.H., Seyyedi, M.A.: Qos monitoring for web services by time series forecasting. In: 2010 3rd IEEE International Conference on Computer Science and Information Technology (ICCSIT), vol. 5, Chengdu, pp. 659–663. IEEE (2010)
16. Godse, M., Bellur, U., Sonar, R.: Automating QoS based service selection. In: 2010 IEEE International Conference on Web Services (ICWS), Miami, FL, pp. 534–541. IEEE (2010)
17. Mu, L., Jinpeng, H., Huipeng, G.: An adaptive web services selection method based on the QoS prediction mechanism. In: IEEE/WIC/ACM International Joint Conferences on Web Intelligence and Intelligent Agent Technologies, WI-IAT 2009, Milan, Italy, pp. 395–402. IET (2009)
18. Hyndman, R.J., Athanasopoulos, G.: Forecasting: principles and practice. OTexts (2014)
19. Hyndman, R.J., Koehler, A.B.: Another look at measures of forecast accuracy. Int. J. Forecast. **22**(4), 679–688 (2006)
20. Zheng, Z., Zhang, Y., Lyu, M.: Investigating QoS of real-world web services. IEEE Trans. Serv. Comput. **PP**(99), 1 (2012)
21. Engelbrecht, H.A., v. Greunen, M.: Forecasting methods for cloud hosted resources, a comparison. In: 2015 11th International Conference on Network and Service Management (CNSM), pp. 29–35 (2015)
22. Wagner, N., Michalewicz, Z., Khouja, M., McGregor, R.R.: Time series forecasting for dynamic environments: the DyFor genetic program model. IEEE Trans. Evol. Comput. **11**(4), 433–452 (2007)

Efficient Web Service Composition via Knapsack-Variant Algorithm

Shi-Liang Fan[1,2], Yu-Bin Yang[1(✉)], and Xiao-Xuan Wang[2]

[1] State Key Laboratory for Novel Software Technology, Nanjing University,
Nanjing 210023, China
`dyyslfan@smail.nju.edu.cn`, `yangyubin@nju.edu.cn`
[2] Science and Technology on Information System Engineering Laboratory,
Nanjing 210007, China

Abstract. Since the birth of web service composition, the minimization of the number of web services in the resulting composition while satisfying user requests has been a significant perspective of research. With the increase in the number of services released across the Internet, efficient algorithms for this research area are urgently required. In this paper, we present an efficient mechanism to solve the problem. For a given request, a service dependency graph is first generated with the relevant services selected from an external repository. Then, the searching process of the minimal composition over the graph is divided into several steps, and each search step is transformed into a dynamic knapsack problem by mapping services to items, the volume and cost of which are changeable, after which a knapsack-variant algorithm is applied to solve each problem in order. When the final search step has been completed, the minimal composition that satisfies the request can be obtained. Experiments on eight public datasets proposed for the Web Service Challenge 2008 demonstrate that the proposed mechanism outperforms the state-of-the-arts by generating solutions containing the same or a smaller number of services with much higher efficiency.

Keywords: Web service composition · Minima · Efficient · Knapsack

1 Introduction

Web services are platform-independent applications that are released, discovered, and invoked over the web using open standards such as UDDI [1], SOAP [2], and WSDL [3]. As software modules published on servers and consumed across the Internet, web services transmit their communication data over the network expediently, which leads to their loosely coupled nature. The characteristics of loose coupling pave the way for easier and wider-ranging integration and interoperability among systems, and thus, web service technology is used extensively in enterprises. It is clear that web services have provided the support technology for the swift development of the IT-based services economy.

© Springer International Publishing AG, part of Springer Nature 2018
J. E. Ferreira et al. (Eds.): SCC 2018, LNCS 10969, pp. 51–66, 2018.
https://doi.org/10.1007/978-3-319-94376-3_4

The complex requirements of businesses cannot be met by a single service in most cases. However, there has been a sharp increase in the number of web services, and the composition of web services provides a means of solving the problem. Web service composition is the process of building a more complex, functional workflow by combining a collection of single services, to satisfy the inputs and outputs provided by users. Two main types of approaches exist for addressing the web service composition problem. Some researches transform the composition problem into a planning one by mapping services to actions [4–6], which is known as the AI-based technique, whereas others constructed a graph to express the relationship of services and aimed to extract a reachable path from the graph [7,8], which is called the graph-based technique.

A phenomenon exists that a growing number of services own a similar or identical functionality. Therefore, it is easy to understand that for a given request, the composition process of massive services may generate many possible solutions comprising a differing number of services. Minimization of the number of services of the resulting composition while satisfying the user request is significant for brokers, customers, and providers [9]. From the brokers' viewpoint, a composition result with fewer services could facilitate maintenance and management work; from the customers' point of view, a smaller composition ordinarily means that a lower payment is demanded for the services. Thus, a decrease in the number of services included in the composition may greatly increase the success rate of achieving the desired responses to the requests of customers. From the service providers' viewpoint, solutions with fewer services could save resources and costs for the same task.

Till date, several studies have been conducted on web service composition that take the optimization of the number of services into consideration. Nevertheless, as the repositories contain a substantial number of services, existing methods take an excessive amount of time to obtain an optimal solution because of the huge search space. Thus, these approaches are not sufficiently efficient to allow their application in large-scale and real-time environments. In this paper, we present a mechanism to efficiently solve the web service composition problem. The main contributions are as follows.

- An equivalent transformation approach that transforms the search steps on the service dependency graph into dynamic knapsack problems by mapping services to items having changeable volume and cost.
- A knapsack-variant algorithm that guarantees efficient generation of the composition with a minimal number of services by means of solving each dynamic knapsack problem in order.
- A strategy to reduce the spatial complexity of the above algorithm.

Furthermore, a full validation of our mechanism on eight datasets of Web Service Challenge 2008 was conducted. The experimental results demonstrate that it performs better than the state-of-the-arts in terms of both quality and efficiency.

The rest of this paper is organized as follows. Section 2 reviews some related work, Sect. 3 describes the background and formalizes the web service composition problem, and then illustrates the motivation of this research.

Section 4 introduces the proposed mechanism, Sect. 5 presents the experimental results, and Sect. 6 provides final remarks.

2 Related Work

The effective combination of a minimal number of services distributed over the web to build enterprise-class services that satisfy given requirements was the goal of this study. A survey of web service composition shows that several studies have been conducted from this perspective, and each has its own merits.

A heuristic A* search algorithm was proposed in [7] for the automatic web service composition. For a given request, a digraph called a service dependency graph is constructed first with a part of the original services chosen from an external repository. Certain techniques are then applied to reduce the number of redundant nodes in the graph. Then, a heuristic-based search algorithm named A* is executed over the optimized graph to seek the minimal composition that fulfills the user request. Although it can obtain compositions with a minimal number of services when applied to WSC-2008's datasets, the algorithm may show a poor performance in large-scale and real-time environments. On the one hand, the application of different types of optimizations on the service dependency graph may be very time consuming; on the other hand, a large number of iterations of an A* search algorithm is incompatible with real-time scenarios.

A scalable and approximate mechanism was presented in [10] to obtain the near-minimal compositions against time. The authors proposed an on-the-fly strategy to construct a path of only the auxiliary graph instead of the complete graph. Additionally, a deterministic and a probabilistic approach were discussed to find the path with the minimal number of services, which is the final result of the composition. Although the service composition time of the algorithm is superior to that of other algorithms, the greedy strategy adopted always gets stuck in local optima. As a result, it always generates compositions with more services than other algorithms; that is, it performs well in terms of efficiency, but leaves room for improvement in terms of the quality of its solutions.

Rodriguez-Mier et al. [11] presented a composition framework integrating a fine-grained I/O service discovery strategy and an optimal composition search algorithm. To improve the efficiency of the generation of a layered service composition graph, the discovery and matchmaking phases are optimized using indexes and a cache. When the graph has been generated, many optimizations are applied to reduce the graph size. Then, a search, which is modeled as a state-transition system, is performed over the graph to find the minimal composition among all the possible compositions that satisfy the users request. Their experimental results show the scalability and flexibility of the composition framework. However, similarly to the mechanism in [7], although many optimizations are used to improve the optimal composition search performance, considerable additional time is spent on this step. However, the search algorithm is not sufficiently efficient to allow its application in large-scale and real-time environments.

In summary, despite the existence of the above algorithms to optimize the number of services, there is a lack of approaches to minimize the number of services in the composition both effectively and efficiently. In this paper, an effective and efficient mechanism is proposed that strives to find compositions with a minimal number of services in large-scale and real-time scenarios.

3   Preliminaries and Motivation

3.1   Preliminary Knowledge

Web service composition is a well-studied problem of which web services are the foundation. In this paper, a *web service* is formally defined as follows [12–14].

Definition 1. *Given a set of concepts, Con, a web service ("service" for short) is defined as a tuple $s = \{In_s, Out_s\}$, where $In_s = \{in_s^1, \ldots, in_s^n\}$ is the set of inputs required to invoke the web service s and $Out_s = \{out_s^1, \ldots, out_s^n\}$ is the set of outputs generated by executing service s. Each element of In_s and Out_s is in fact a semantic concept belonging to the set Con, namely, $In_s \subseteq Con$ and $Out_s \subseteq Con$.*

Individual services can be combined by connecting their matched inputs and outputs to construct compositions [15,16].

Lemma 1. *Given an output $out_s \in Out_s$ of a service s, as well as an input $in_{s'} \in In_{s'}$ of another service s', if out_s and $in_{s'}$ are equivalent concepts or out_s is a sub-concept of $in_{s'}$, out_s matches $in_{s'}$, i.e., $in_{s'}$ is matched by out_s.*

Two main types of structures of these compositions exist: sequential and parallel. The services organized as a sequential structure are invoked in order, whereas those organized as a parallel structure are invoked synchronously. A *composition* can be described as follows.

Definition 2. *A composition containing the set of services $S = \{s_1, \ldots, s_n\}$ is defined as $\Omega_S = s_1, \ldots, s_n$. If the services are chained in sequence, the composition is expressed as $\Omega_S^{\rightarrow} = s_1 \rightarrow \ldots \rightarrow s_n$; if in parallel, it is expressed as $\Omega_S^{\parallel} = s_1 \parallel \ldots \parallel s_n$. The set of services involved in Ω_S is defined as $Servs(\Omega_S) = S$. Moreover, the length of a composition Ω_S is defined as $Len(\Omega_S) = |S|$, namely, the number of services in Ω_S.*

The aim of the service composition problem is to automatically select the minimal composition of available services to fulfil a user request, which is defined as follows.

Definition 3. *A user request is defined as a tuple $R = \{In_R, Out_R\}$, where $In_R = \{in_R^1, \ldots, in_R^n\}$ is the set of inputs provided by the user ($In_R \subseteq Con$), and a second element $Out_R = \{out_R^1, \ldots, out_R^n\}$ represents the set of expected outputs ($Out_R \subseteq Con$).*

On the basis of the above concepts, the precise definition of the *web service composition problem* is given as follows.

Definition 4. *A web service composition problem is defined as, for a given composition request R, to seek a composition Ω_S fulfilling R with the optimization objective of $\mathbf{min|S|}$; namely, Ω_S contains the minimal number of services.*

3.2   Motivating Example

Graphs are a natural and intuitive means of expressing the complex interaction relations between entities. A *service dependency graph* is a digraph used to describe services and the matching relations among them [8], [10], [12]. For a given request $R = \{\{in_1, in_2\}, \{out_1, out_2\}\}$, an example of a service dependency graph is shown in Fig. 1. Each service is represented as a rectangle and the inputs and outputs of a service are represented as circles. Furthermore, the matching relations among services are represented as edges connecting two circles.

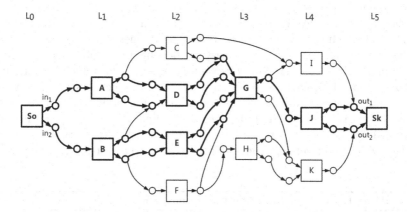

Fig. 1. Example of a service dependency graph; the optimal composition is highlighted.

As can be seen in Fig. 1, the highlighted composition, which can be represented as $\Omega = s_o \rightarrow ((A \rightarrow D) \parallel (B \rightarrow E)) \rightarrow G \rightarrow J \rightarrow s_k$, contains eight services in total (including s_o and s_k). Several other compositions also satisfy the same user request R, such as $\Omega' = s_o \rightarrow ((A \rightarrow C \rightarrow I) \parallel (B \rightarrow F \rightarrow H \rightarrow K)) \rightarrow s_k$; however, the number of their services is without exception greater than eight. Therefore, composition Ω highlighted in the graph is the optimal one having the smallest number of services.

In large-scale scenarios, the dependency graph may be exceedingly complex, which leads to a huge search space. As a consequence, it is a formidable task to extract the optimal composition from the graph. Undoubtedly, an exhaustive combinatorial search can guarantee the optima, but it will take an unacceptable amount of time to generate the compositions and is not applicable in real-time environments. In summary, we should pay attention not only to the quality of the resulting composition but also to the efficiency of the composition algorithm.

4   Detailed Methodology

In this section, an efficient mechanism is proposed for the problem of web service composition. Given a composition request $R = \{In_R, Out_R\}$ and a service repository S_r, a service dependency graph is first constructed containing the relevant services for the request. Then, the search steps on the graph are transformed into dynamic knapsack problems. A knapsack-variant algorithm is proposed to solve each dynamic knapsack problem. Finally, an optimization strategy is adopted to reduce the spatial complexity of the knapsack-variant algorithm.

4.1 Service Dependency Graph

As shown in Fig. 1, a service dependency graph is a layered digraph. The first layer contains only one dummy service, $s_o = \{\varnothing, In_R\}$; similarly, there is only a dummy service, $s_k = \{Out_R, \varnothing\}$, in the last layer, while the specific services in the other layers are selected from S_r. Moreover, each layer contains the services, the inputs of which are all matched by the outputs generated by previous layers.

The generation process of a service dependency graph is shown in Algorithm 1. Given request R and repository S_r, s_o is first added to the first layer, L_0, after which each following layer, L_i, is constructed with the services having inputs that are all matched by the outputs generated by previous layers. s_k is added to the final layer if the set of expected outputs Out_R is included in Out_{all}. Finally, unused services that do not contribute to Out_R are removed from the graph by traversing from the final layer to the first layer.

Algorithm 1. Construction of Service Dependency Graph

Input: R, S_r
Output: L
1   $i \leftarrow 0$, $L_i \leftarrow \{s_o\}$, $i \leftarrow i + 1$, $Out_{all} \leftarrow In_R$
2   **repeat**
3   **for** service $s \in S_r$ **do**
4   **if** $s \notin L_j (\forall j < i)$ and $In_s \subseteq Out_{all}$ **then**
5            $L_i \leftarrow L_i \cup \{s\}$
6            $Out_{all} \leftarrow Out_{all} \cup Out_s$
7      $i \leftarrow i + 1$
8   **until** $Out_R \subseteq Out_{all}$;
9   $tot \leftarrow i$, $L_{tot} \leftarrow \{s_k\}$, $j \leftarrow tot$, $In_{all} \leftarrow Out_R$
10 **while** $j \geq 0$ **do**
11   **for** service $s \in L_j$ **do**
12   **if** $Out_s \cap In_{all} = \varnothing$ **then**
13            $L_j \leftarrow L_j - \{s\}$
14   **for** service $s \in L_j$ **do**
15         $In_{all} \leftarrow In_{all} \cup In_s$
16      $j \leftarrow j - 1$
17 **return** L

4.2 Dynamic Knapsack Problem

When the service dependency graph has been completed, the composition problem is regarded as searching for a reachable path from s_o to s_k. Each search step on the graph is defined as determining the optimal *precursors* of each service.

Definition 5. *The set of precursors of a service $s \in L_i$ is defined as $Pre(s) = \{s' \mid s' \in L_j(\forall j < i) \land In_s \cap Out_{s'} \neq \varnothing\}$. In particular, $Pre(s_o) = \varnothing$.*

The search step of service G is shown in Fig. 2. Note that the minimal composition starting from service s_o and ending with service s is expressed as Ω^s, and c_i in the figure represents an input or output concept of services. Assuming that the minimal compositions ending with the precursors of G, i.e., Ω^C, Ω^D, Ω^E, and Ω^F, have been determined in advance, the search step of G is defined as selecting the optimal subset of $\{\Omega^C, \Omega^D, \Omega^E, \Omega^F\}$ to compose Ω^G, which is in fact a greedy strategy. On the basis of the greedy strategy, an equivalent transformation approach is proposed to transform each search step similar to that shown in Fig. 2 into a **dynamic knapsack problem**.

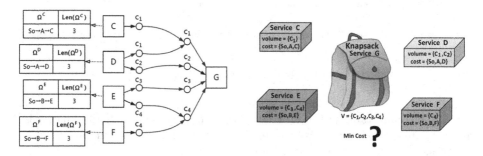

Fig. 2. Search step on the graph.   **Fig. 3.** Dynamic knapsack problem.

As shown in Fig. 3, assuming that the optimal precursors of a service s must be determined, s is abstracted into a knapsack having a capacity of In_s (the set of inputs of service s). Each precursor of s is spontaneously regarded as an item with a **dynamic** *volume* and *cost*. The problem is to minimize the sum of the cost of the items in the knapsack so that the sum of the volume is equal to the knapsack's capacity. The volume of an item $s' \in Pre(s)$ is relevant to $Out_{s'}$ (the set of outputs of service s'), and the cost of s' is measured with $Servs(\Omega^{s'})$ (the set of services involved in the composition $\Omega^{s'}$), which is too inconvenient to be applied to the following composition algorithm. Therefore, an approach is presented to quantify the volume and cost of each item.

Quantization of Volume. First, all the subsets of In_s are obtained by using Algorithm 2 in a certain order. Then, on the grounds of the returned subsets

---

Algorithm 2. Generation of Subsets

Input: In_s
Output: $Subs$
1   $Subs \leftarrow \{\varnothing\}$, $upper\_bound \leftarrow 2^{|In_s|}$
2   **for** $index = 0$; $index < upper\_bound$; $index{+}{+}$ **do**
3      $i \leftarrow 0$, $tmp \leftarrow index$, $subset \leftarrow \{\}$
4   **while** $tmp > 0$ **do**
5   **if** $(tmp \bmod 2) > 0$ **then**
6            $subset \leftarrow subset \cup \{In_s[i]\}$
7         $tmp \leftarrow tmp$ div 2, $i \leftarrow i + 1$
8      $Subs[index] \leftarrow subset$
9   **return** $Subs$

Table 1. Mapping table

Index	0	1	2	3	4	5	6	7
Subs[index]	∅	$\{c_1\}$	$\{c_2\}$	$\{c_1,c_2\}$	$\{c_3\}$	$\{c_1,c_3\}$	$\{c_2,c_3\}$	$\{c_1,c_2,c_3\}$
Item/Knapsack		C		D				
Volume	0	1	2	3	4	5	6	7
Index (binary)	0000	0001	0010	0011	0100	0101	0110	0111
Index	8	9	10	11	12	13	14	15
Subs[index]	$\{c_4\}$	$\{c_1,c_4\}$	$\{c_2,c_4\}$	$\{c_1,c_2,c_4\}$	$\{c_3,c_4\}$	$\{c_1,c_3,c_4\}$	$\{c_2,c_3,c_4\}$	$\{c_1,c_2,c_3,c_4\}$
Item/Knapsack	F				E			G
Volume	8	9	10	11	12	13	14	15
Index (binary)	1000	1001	1010	1011	1100	1101	1110	1111

$Subs$, a mapping table is constructed to quantify the volume of the knapsack and each item. Taking the problem in Fig. 3 as an example, the mapping table used to support the volume quantization is shown as Table 1.

By means of Table 1, the volume of the knapsack and each item can be quantified as follows.

- The capacity of knapsack s is quantified as the upper bound of the *index*, namely, $|Subs| - 1$.
- Assuming that service s' provides the set of outputs $Out \subseteq Out_{s'}$ for service s, the volume of s' is quantified as the value of the *index* that satisfies the condition that $Subs[index] = Out$.

Taking the problem in Fig. 3 as an instance, the capacity of the knapsack G is $V_{cap} = 15$ after quantization. Two different feasible solutions of the dynamic knapsack problem are shown in Fig. 4. As can be seen from the solution I, *Service D* provides the set of outputs $\{c_1, c_2\}$ for *Service G*, and thus, the volume of the item D is quantified as $volume_D = 3$ according to Table 1. In addition, $volume_E = 4$, because *Service E* provides the set of outputs $\{c_3\}$ for G. Similarly, $volume_F = 8$. It is not difficult to observe that $volume_D + volume_E + volume_F = 3 + 4 + 8 = V_{cap}$, and hence, knapsack G can be filled with the set of items $\{D, E, F\}$, which indicates the effectiveness of the quantization.

The volume of an item is changeless in the 0-1 knapsack problem, whereas it is changeable in the dynamic knapsack problem. For example, let us discuss solution II shown in Fig. 4(b). Despite the fact that the set of outputs of *Service D* is $\{c_1, c_2\}$, D provides only $\{c_2\}$ for G, given that $\{c_1\}$ is provided by *Service C*, which leads to the change of *volume*$_D$ from 3 to 2. Meanwhile, *volume*$_C$ + *volume*$_D$ + *volume*$_E$ + *volume*$_F$ = $1 + 2 + 4 + 8 = V_{cap}$. The outputs provided by service s' for service s are uncertain before decision making, and hence, the volume of item s' cannot be determined in advance.

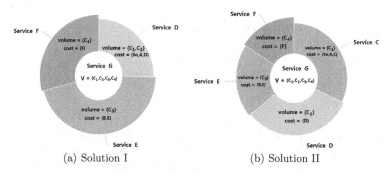

(a) Solution I   (b) Solution II

Fig. 4. Two different feasible solutions to fill G.

Quantization of Cost. Considering that the goal of this study was to minimize the number of services involved in the resulting composition, the cost of an item s' is designed as the minimal number of services that must be invoked to generate the outputs of service s'. As a result, the cost of each item is quantified as follows.

- Assuming that Ser represents the set of services that belong to $Servs(\Omega^{s'})$ and have not yet been invoked, the volume of item s' is quantified as the size of $Ser \cup \{s'\}$.

Taking the solution I shown in Fig. 4(a) as an example, suppose that the set of items $\{D, E, F\}$ are put into knapsack G in order of the name $(D \rightarrow E \rightarrow F)$. We have already assumed that the minimal compositions ending with the precursors of G have been determined in advance. Figure 2 reveals that $\Omega^D = s_o \rightarrow A \rightarrow D$, $\Omega^E = s_o \rightarrow B \rightarrow E$, and $\Omega^F = s_o \rightarrow B \rightarrow F$. Because D is included in knapsack G before E, the set of services $\{s_o\}$ has been invoked in advance. As a result, only $\{B\}$ should be invoked before E, which leads to $cost_E = 2$. Similarly, $cost_D = 3$ and $cost_F = 1$, and the total cost of the solution I is calculated as $cost_D + cost_E + cost_F = 3 + 2 + 1 = 6$.

The cost of an item is changeable also in the dynamic knapsack problem. As shown in solution II (assume that the items are put into the knapsack G in the order $C \rightarrow D \rightarrow E \rightarrow F$), the set of services $\{s_o, A\}$ has been invoked when putting item C into the knapsack. Consequently, D can be invoked directly, which leads to a change in $cost_D$ from 3 to 1.

In summary, only by ingeniously determining the dynamic volume and cost of an item can we solve the dynamic knapsack problem.

4.3   Knapsack-Variant Algorithm

The dynamic knapsack problem aimed at determining the optimal precursors of a service s can be described as follows. Given a knapsack s, the capacity of which is V_{cap}, and a set of items $Pre(s) = \{s_1, s_2, \ldots, s_N\}$, where $N = |Pre(s)|$ represents the number of items, each with a dynamic volume $volume_i$ and a dynamic cost $cost_i$, some items are selected from $Pre(s)$ to fill knapsack s with the objective

$$\begin{aligned}
\text{minimize} & \sum_{i=1}^{N} cost_i \cdot x_i \\
\text{subject to} & \sum_{i=1}^{N} volume_i \cdot x_i = V_{cap}, \\
& x_i \in \{0, 1\}.
\end{aligned} \tag{1}$$

where x_i represents the number of item i to be included in the knapsack. Unlike in the 0-1 knapsack problem, all $volume_i$ and $cost_i$ are uncertain here, which leads to the inapplicability of the *0-1 knapsack algorithm*. In this section, a **knapsack-variant algorithm** is proposed for solving the problem by determining the volume and cost of each service dynamically.

Let $C[i][v]$ represent the minimal cost of selecting items from $\{s_1, s_2, \ldots, s_i\}$ $(1 \le i \le N)$ to fill a temporary knapsack, the capacity of which is v $(1 \le v \le V_{cap})$, and $I[i][v]$ the set of items selected to minimize $C[i][v]$. Then,

$$\begin{aligned}
C[i][v] & = \min \{C[i-1][v], C[i-1][v - volume_i] + cost_i\} \\
\text{where} & \quad volume_i = \mathbf{DV}(s_i, In_s, Subs, v), \\
& \quad cost_i = \mathbf{DC}(s_i, I, i, v, volume_i).
\end{aligned} \tag{2}$$

$volume_i$ and $cost_i$ are determined dynamically in the process of the dynamic programming, which is the quintessence of the knapsack-variant algorithm.

The function DV in Algorithm 3 is used to dynamically calculate the volume of an item. For the given temporary knapsack with capacity v, the outputs provided by service s_i for the knapsack are determined as $Out_{s_i} \cap Subs[v]$. Thus, the volume of item s_i can be quantified by the quantization approach proposed in Sect. 4.2. Inspired by the one-to-one match between the *index (binary)* and the *Subs[index]* in Table 1, a binary method is applied to determine the *index* that satisfies $Subs[index] = Out_{s_i} \cap Subs[v]$, namely, $volume_i$.

For the given temporary knapsack with capacity v, the reason why the outputs provided by s_i for the knapsack are determined as $Out_{s_i} \cap Subs[v]$ is as follows. The knapsack with capacity v corresponds to a temporary service s_v with the inputs $Subs[v]$. Therefore, the largest set of outputs provided by service s_i for s_v is obviously $Out_{lar} = Out_{s_i} \cap Subs[v]$. However, if a smaller one $Out_{sma} \subset Out_{lar}$ is provided for s_v, $Out_{lar} - Out_{sma}$ may need to be provided by additional services selected from $\{s_1, s_2, \ldots, s_{i-1}\}$, which causes the loss of the local optimum, as well as the global optimum.

Algorithm 3. Determination of Volume of Items

$\quad$ **Input:** s_i, In_s, $Subs$, v
$\quad$ **Output:** $DV(s_i, In_s, Subs, v)$
1 $\quad map \leftarrow \{\}$, $volume \leftarrow 0$, $Out \leftarrow Out_{s_i} \cap Subs[v]$
2 $\quad$ **for** $index = 0; index < |In_s|; index{+}{+}$ **do**
3 $\qquad c \leftarrow In_s[index]$
4 $\qquad map[c] \leftarrow index$

5 $\quad$ **for** concept $c \in Out$ **do**
6 $\qquad index \leftarrow map[c]$
7 $\qquad volume \leftarrow volume + 2^{index}$

8 $\quad DV(s_i, In_s, Subs, v) \leftarrow volume$
9 $\quad$ **return** $DV(s_i, In_s, Subs, v)$

Moreover, the function DC shown in Algorithm 4 is applied to determine the cost of an item s_i. Since the items that have been included in the knapsack are cached in the data structure I, the set of services $Ser \subseteq Servs(\Omega^{s_i})$ that have not been invoked can be obtained by drawing support from I, after which the cost of item s_i is quantified as $|Ser| + 1$.

Algorithm 4. Determination of Cost of Items

$\quad$ **Input:** s_i, I, i, v, $volume_i$
$\quad$ **Output:** $DC(s_i, I, i, v, volume_i)$
1 $\quad Union \leftarrow \{\}$
2 $\quad$ **for** service $s \in I[i-1][v - volume_i]$ **do**
3 $\qquad Union \leftarrow Union \cup Servs(\Omega^s)$

4 $\quad Inter \leftarrow Servs(\Omega^{s_i}) \cap Union$
5 $\quad Ser \leftarrow Servs(\Omega^{s_i}) - Inter$
6 $\quad DC(s_i, I, i, v, volume_i) \leftarrow |Ser| + 1$
7 $\quad$ **return** $DC(s_i, I, i, v, volume_i)$

According to the optimization model in (2), by systematically increasing the values of i (from 1 to N) and v (from 1 to V_{cap}), composition Ω^s with the minimal number of services will be finally obtained when $i = N$ and $v = V_{cap}$.

$$Len(\Omega^s) = C[N][V_{cap}] + 1. \tag{3}$$

Therefore, the time complexity of the search step is $O(NV_{cap})$, so is the spatial complexity. However, the spatial complexity of (2) can be further optimized.

Considering that $C[i][v]$ is relevant only to $C[i-1][v']$ ($1 \leq v' \leq v$), $C[i][v]$ can be replaced by a one-dimensional array $C[v]$. Then,

$$
\begin{aligned}
C[v] \;&= \min\; \{C[v], C[v - volume_i] + cost_i\} \\
\text{where} \quad volume_i &= DV(s_i, In_s, Subs, v), \\
cost_i &= DC(s_i, I, i, v, volume_i).
\end{aligned}
\tag{4}
$$

Algorithm 5. Knapsack-Variant Algorithm

    Input: L

    Output: $Len(\Omega^{s_k})$

1 $Servs(\Omega^{s_o}) \leftarrow \{s_o\}$, $Len(\Omega^{s_o}) \leftarrow 1$

2 **for** $index = 1; index < |L|; index{+}{+}$ **do**

3   **for** service $s \in L_{index}$ **do**

4          $pres \leftarrow Pre(s)$, $N \leftarrow |pres|$

5          $Subs \leftarrow$ all subsets of In_s, $V_{cap} \leftarrow |Subs| - 1$

6          $C[0..V_{cap}] \leftarrow +\infty$, $C[0] \leftarrow 0$, $I[0..N][0..V_{cap}] \leftarrow \{\}$

7   **for** $i = 1; i <= N; i{+}{+}$ **do**

8              $s_i \leftarrow pres[i]$

9   **for** $v = V_{cap}; v > 0; v{-}{-}$ **do**

10                 $volume_i \leftarrow DV(s_i, In_s, Subs, v)$

11                 $cost_i \leftarrow DC(s_i, I, i, v, volume_i)$

12   **if** $C[v - volume_i] + cost_i < C[v]$ **then**

13                    $C[v] \leftarrow C[v - volume_i] + cost_i$

14                    $I[i][v] \leftarrow I[i-1][v - volume_i] \cup s_i$

15   **else**

16                    $I[i][v] \leftarrow I[i-1][v]$

17          $Servs(\Omega^s) \leftarrow \{\}$

18   **for** service $item \in I[N][V_{cap}]$ **do**

19              $Servs(\Omega^s) \leftarrow Servs(\Omega^s) \cup Servs(\Omega^{item})$

20          $Len(\Omega^s) \leftarrow C[V_{cap}] + 1$

21 **return** $Len(\Omega^{s_k})$

The problem can be solved by systematically increasing the values of i (from 1 to N) and decreasing v (from V_{cap} to 1), and hence, the spatial complexity is reduced from $O(NV_{cap})$ to $O(V_{cap})$.

The knapsack-variant algorithm is shown in Algorithm 5. The search steps on the graph are executed layer by layer. Each search step depends on the optimization results of the search steps in the previous layers and is transformed into a knapsack problem that can be solved by (4). After completing the final search step of s_k, the expected composition with length $Len(\Omega^{s_k})$ can be obtained.

5 Experimental Results

To evaluate the performance of the proposed composition algorithm, we conducted a group of experiments using eight public repositories from the Web Service Challenge 2008. The services in each repository are defined on a WSDL file, and inputs and outputs are semantically described in an XML file called an ontology.

Table 1 shows the detailed characteristics of each dataset. The number of services and concepts in the ontology of each dataset are shown in rows *#Services* and #*Concepts* respectively. Row #*Sol.Services* indicates the number of services for the optimal solution provided by the WSC'08 (Table 2).

Table 2. Characteristics of the datasets

WSC-2008's datasets	D-01	D-02	D-03	D-04	D-05	D-06	D-07	D-08
#Services	158	558	604	1041	1090	2198	4113	8119
#Concepts	1540	1565	3089	3135	3067	12468	3075	12337
#Sol.Services	10	5	40	10	20	40	20	30

To validate our composition algorithm, we compared our approach with three different approaches in the same experimental environment. For each dataset, we focused mainly on the number of services in the composition result (#*C.Services*) and the execution time to extract the solution from the service dependency graph (*C.Time*). The results are shown in Table 3.

Table 3. Comparison of proposed approach with other approaches

Datasets		D-01	D-02	D-03	D-04	D-05	D-06	D-07	D-08
Method in [7]	#C.Services	10	5	40	10	20	35	20	30
	C.Time (ms)	47	78	1028	54	1295	137	243	191
Method in [10]	#C.Services	14	5	48	12	34	47	20	36
	C.Time (ms)	1	1	2	1	2	2	3	2
Method in [11]	#C.Services	10	5	40	10	20	35	20	30
	C.Time (ms)	61	52	176	122	156	855	193	304
Our method	#C.Services	10	5	40	10	20	35	20	30
	C.Time (ms)	6	10	21	13	22	61	33	20

As can be seen in Table 3, compared with other approaches, our approach can generate compositions with the same or a smaller number of services. On the dataset *D-06*, our approach succeeds in finding a better composition than the solution provided by the WSC'08 (35 versus 40). The execution time of the approach in [10] is no more than 3 ms for all datasets, which proves that the method is sufficiently efficient to solve the service composition problem. However, it always generates compositions containing more services than the other methods. Considering that all the methods, except that in [10], can find the minimal compositions, we compare our method with those methods in terms of the execution time.

Figure 5 shows that our algorithm takes considerably less time to generate solutions than the other two. The dotted lines in blue and orange represent the average execution time of the methods in [7] and [11], respectively, while

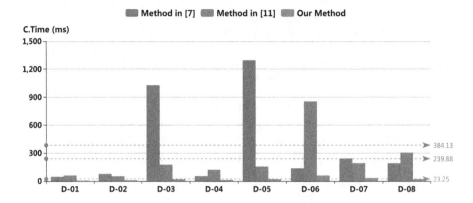

Fig. 5. Efficiency comparison. (Color figure online)

Table 4. Comparison considering the service dependency graph

Datasets		D-01	D-02	D-03	D-04	D-05	D-06	D-07	D-08
Method in [7]	G.Size	17	19	60	31	62	95	89	78
	G.Time (ms)	37	43	872	219	4861	536	7533	4761
	Tot.Time (ms)	84	121	1900	273	6156	673	7776	4952
Method in [11]	G.Size	13	13	40	25	52	75	70	58
	G.Time (ms)	138	297	553	472	618	891	1253	1374
	Tot.Time (ms)	199	349	729	594	774	1746	1446	1678
Our method	G.Size	60	61	104	43	101	170	140	124
	G.Time (ms)	5	12	62	15	62	181	403	576
	Tot.Time (ms)	11	22	83	28	84	242	436	596

the green line represents the average time of our algorithm. It appears that our algorithm is more than 10 times faster than that in [7] and nearly 17 times faster than that in [11] on average, which is a significant improvement.

We further compared our method with those in [7,11] taking the generation of the service dependency graph into account. As shown in Table 4, the size of the graph ($G.Size$) generated by the methods in [7,11] is smaller than that of ours, because many optimizations are applied to reduce the graph size in these two methods, which leads to the time that they take to generate the graph ($G.Time$) being longer than the time that our method takes. Therefore, our knapsack-variant algorithm is executed over a larger graph, but is still more than 10× faster than the other two algorithms, which sufficiently indicates the efficiency of our composition algorithm. Even when $G.Time$ is taken into consideration, the total time ($Tot.Time = G.Time + C.Time$) of our mechanism is still considerably less than that of the other mechanisms. As a result, our mechanism is more applicable to the large-scale or real-time scenarios.

6   Conclusions

In this paper, we proposed an effective and efficient mechanism to automatically generate the minimal service composition over a service dependency graph. Each search step on the graph is ingeniously transformed into a dynamic knapsack problem, after which the proposed knapsack-variant algorithm is executed to minimize the number of services by solving each dynamic knapsack problem. Moreover, a full validation performed on eight different datasets from Web Service Challenge 2008 demonstrates that our algorithm outperforms the state-of-the-art methods as its execution is much faster while the minimal composition results are retained and that it is applicable to large-scale or real-time scenarios.

Acknowledgment. This work is funded by the Natural Science Foundation of China (No. 61673204), National Key R&D Program of China (No. 2018YFB1003800), State Grid Corporation of Science and Technology Projects (Funded No. SGLNXT00DKJS1700 166), and the Program for Distinguished Talents of Jiangsu Province, China (No. 2013-XXRJ-018).

References

1. Bellwood, T., Bryan, D., Draluk, V., Ehnebuske, D., Glover, T., Hately, A.: UDDI version 2.04 API specification. UDDI Committee Specification, OASIS (2002)
2. Hadley, M., Mendelsohn, N., Moreau, J., Nielsen, H., Gudgin, M.: SOAP version 1.2 part 1: messaging framework. W3C REC REC-soap12-part1-20030624, pp. 240–8491, June 2003
3. Chinnici, R., Gudgin, M., Moreau, J.J., Schlimmer, J., Weerawarana, S.: Web services description language (WSDL) version 2.0 part 1: core language. W3C working draft 26 (2004)
4. Sirin, E., Parsia, B.: Planning for semantic web services. In: Semantic Web Services Workshop at 3rd International Semantic Web Conference, pp. 33–40. Springer, Hiroshima (2004)
5. Klusch, M., Gerber, A., Schmidt, M.: Semantic web service composition planning with OWLS-Xplan. In: Proceedings of the 1st International AAAI Fall Symposium on Agents and the Semantic Web, pp. 55–62 (2005)
6. Akkiraju, R., Srivastava, B., Ivan, A.A., Goodwin, R., Syeda-Mahmood, T.: Semaplan: combining planning with semantic matching to achieve web service composition. In: International Conference on Web Services, ICWS 2006, pp. 37–44. IEEE (2006)
7. Rodriguez-Mier, P., Mucientes, M., Lama, M.: Automatic web service composition with a heuristic-based search algorithm. In: IEEE International Conference on Web Services (ICWS), pp. 81–88. IEEE (2011)
8. Rodriguez-Mier, P., Mucientes, M., Vidal, J.C., Lama, M.: An optimal and complete algorithm for automatic web service composition. Int. J. Web Serv. Res. (IJWSR) **9**(2), 1–20 (2012)
9. Rodriguez-Mier, P., Mucientes, M., Lama, M.: Hybrid optimization algorithm for large-scale QoS-aware service composition. IEEE Trans. Serv. Comput. **10**(4), 547–559 (2017)

10. Chattopadhyay, S., Banerjee, A., Banerjee, N.: A scalable and approximate mechanism for web service composition. In: IEEE International Conference on Web Services (ICWS), pp. 9–16. IEEE (2015)
11. Rodriguez-Mier, P., Pedrinaci, C., Lama, M., Mucientes, M.: An integrated semantic web service discovery and composition framework. IEEE Trans. Serv. Comput. **9**(4), 537–550 (2016)
12. Xia, Y.M., Yang, Y.B.: Web service composition integrating QoS optimization and redundancy removal. In: IEEE 20th International Conference on Web Services (ICWS), pp. 203–210. IEEE (2013)
13. Yan, Y., Chen, M., Yang, Y.: Anytime QoS optimization over the PlanGraph for web service composition. In: Proceedings of the 27th Annual ACM Symposium on Applied Computing, pp. 1968–1975. ACM (2012)
14. Chen, M., Yan, Y.: Redundant service removal in QoS-aware service composition. In: IEEE 19th International Conference on Web Services (ICWS), pp. 431–439. IEEE (2012)
15. Paolucci, M., Kawamura, T., Payne, T.R., Sycara, K.: Semantic matching of web services capabilities. In: Horrocks, I., Hendler, J. (eds.) ISWC 2002. LNCS, vol. 2342, pp. 333–347. Springer, Heidelberg (2002). https://doi.org/10.1007/3-540-48005-6_26
16. Rodriguez-Mier, P., Mucientes, M., Lama, M.: A hybrid local-global optimization strategy for QoS-aware service composition. In: IEEE International Conference on Web Services (ICWS), pp. 735–738. IEEE (2015)

Security-Aware Passwords and Services Usage in Developing Countries: A Case Study of Bangladesh

Rasib Khan[1(✉)] and Ragib Hasan[2]

[1] Department of Computer Science, Northern Kentucky University,
Highland Heights, KY, USA
`khanr2@nku.edu`

[2] Department of Computer Science, University of Alabama at Birmingham,
Birmingham, AL, USA
`ragib@uab.edu`

Abstract. Users from developing nations, such as Bangladesh, had a rather late entry into the information highway and may not be equally aware of the different secure practices on the Internet. Such behaviors include awareness of security technologies, having similar/dissimilar passwords, frequency of changing passwords, saving passwords on browsers, and verifying authenticity of visited websites. The category of services being accessed as well as the type of devices being used may implicate the level of exposure to identity theft threats. Unfortunately, users never behave in the expected manner in terms of practicing secure technologies. In this paper, we present a study on security-aware usage of passwords and Internet-based services for users from Bangladesh. We conducted an online survey on a total of 1682 Bangladeshi Internet users in English and Bengali language. We analyzed the survey statistics to study the general trend of behavior, practices, and expectations pertaining to secure Internet usage and identity preservation. We posit that such a study can help researchers identify the weakest-link of Internet safety and focus on building secure technologies to protect users from online crimes in developing countries.

Keywords: User study · Developing country · Security awareness
Case study · Bangladesh

1 Introduction

The rate of Internet penetration in developing countries is increasing everyday. Each of these users on the Internet has their personal behavior and practices [16,27]. Unfortunately, a lack of IT-education in such developing countries result in a lower level of awareness and cognizance of secure Internet practices and is a crucial concern in terms of protecting their digital identities [11].

© Springer International Publishing AG, part of Springer Nature 2018
J. E. Ferreira et al. (Eds.): SCC 2018, LNCS 10969, pp. 67–84, 2018.
https://doi.org/10.1007/978-3-319-94376-3_5

Bangladesh is a South Asian country with a population of approximately 156.6 million and a growth rate of 3.6% as of 2013 [29]. The IT infrastructure is progressive with a mobile penetration rate of 56% as of 2011 and increasing every year [28]. The number of mobile subscribers and Internet users were 121.9 million ($\approx$77.8%) and 42.7 million ($\approx$27.3%) as of January 2015 [3]. Advancement of the IT infrastructure has significantly affected the way people use their personal information on the Internet and has been misused in developed countries since the beginning [9,13,30]. We posit that a lack of Internet security awareness in developing countries as Bangladesh may result in increased e-crimes with this exponential increase in the number of Internet users. Various studies have been conducted on users from developed countries [7,12,17]. However, to the best of our knowledge, this is the first time a study on security-oriented practices of Internet users from developing countries has been performed.

The frequency of accessing the Internet and the types of services being used can imply the susceptibility of the users. Secure password policies aim to ensure safety of the users [10,25]. Unfortunately, complicated policies result in degraded usability and reduced memorability [32]. Usable technologies, such as, saving of passwords on mobile devices and/or web browsers, provide users with various tools and services to manage and use their personal information [7,20,24]. Unfortunately, the different types of devices, such as smartphones, which are being used to access the Internet, are exposed to different levels of threat, resulting in compromised private information [2].

Such incidents are quite often the result of unawareness of users towards secure technology usage. Password habits of users do not comply to the secure practices suggested by security experts [27]. Moreover, enforced security does not always guarantee proper behavior [10]. There had been numerous research which illustrate the inability of general users to apply secure technologies in commonplace activities, such as risk evaluation, secure emailing, and web surfing [6,8,26]. Researchers have also attempted to tie information security with the psychology of Internet users in various contexts [1]. Therefore, the security of devices and services on the Internet must be designed to address the security holes created due to the users' behaviors and practices [25]. However, most of such studies have been performed on users from the developed world. In this study, we bring these perspectives on the behavioral aspects of Internet users from Bangladesh. In the context of developing countries as Bangladesh, the lack of awareness on secure practices makes the situation complicated with a greater risk of exploitation of Internet users.

Contributions: In this paper, we present the results of an online survey on security-oriented usage of passwords and services for 1682 Internet users from Bangladesh. The survey data reveals crucial information regarding the weakest-links in Internet security: the practices of the users. We performed a cross-analysis of password and service usages to identify the security-critical aspects in online behavior. We posit that such a study can greatly help researchers to design Internet-enabled services with a guided knowledge of the users' behavior and ensure greater security in developing countries.

The rest of the paper is organized as follows. We present the related work in Sect. 2 and our survey methodology in Sect. 3. The results from the study and a discussion on the presented work are presented in Sect. 4 and Sect. 5 respectively. Finally, we conclude in Sect. 6.

2   Related Work

A lot of people fall victims to Internet scams every day [4,13]. Susceptibility of naive Internet users being victims of malware and viruses is not new [12,18,23]. The number of identity theft cases have increased from 12 million in 2012, which was a 13% increase from 2010, to 13.1 million in 2013 [17,21]. Unfortunately, one-third of such victims do not take any further actions to prevent future exploitation [19]. With a high Internet and mobile penetration rate in Bangladesh [3,28], the aspects of secure Internet practices is a crucial field of study with respect to such developing parts of the world.

Hull et al. [9] analyzed the contextual privacy issues on Facebook and the way social media effects privacy issues. User behavior regarding disclosing the identity on micro-blogs and the relative factors have been studied by Lee et al. [16]. Wagner et al. [30] presents an interesting work on malware infected Twitter users and their actions, and categorizing them based on the users' level of susceptibility. According to most studies, the primary factors influencing the behavior of users on the Internet are age, education, gender, technology experience, content creation and sharing, online activities, income group, amount of leisure time, and the type of job.

Kumaraguru et al. [14,15] presented a qualitative study based on 20 individual interviews, focus group discussions, and a widely circulated survey on privacy-oriented practices in India. Pew Research Center published a report [22] on Internet usage and psychology of users from developing countries while using various services. Chen et al. [5] discussed the security perceptions in Ghana from an interview survey of 193 participants. However, our study focuses on the analysis of security-aware practices and the overall safe/unsafe behaviors of users on the Internet in such developing countries.

Stanton et al. [27] presented an analysis of user behavior based on a two-factor taxonomy for classification. A large-scale study on the use and re-use of web passwords was presented by Florencio et al. [7]. A survey on the usability of passwords enforced by password creation policies was presented by Inglesant et al. [10]. The reasons why people generally maintain Internet anonymity was studied by Kang et al. [11]. Most of such studies focus mainly on developed countries. However, Internet trends in developing countries are different than that in developed counties. Additionally, our study intends to unfold the generalized aspect of security-oriented behavior for Internet usage in developing countries.

3   Survey Methodology

Survey Questionnaire: The survey consisted of two demographic questions, and 18 information-oriented questions. We inquired the age and geographic location of the respondent and no other private information (e.g. name, IP address) were asked/stored. The survey was conducted using a publicly accessible online form. The survey was available in two languages: Bengali and English. The translation of the questionnaire from English to Bengali was performed by four volunteer Bengali native-speakers. The survey agreement stated that no personally identifiable information would be asked or stored, and the published research will only include aggregated results. The agreement also specified that the storage of all collected data will be within secure physical perimeter within the research institution. The responses for each of the questions were qualified with pre-specified options. All questions were provided with an explanatory sub-text and examples (e.g. *changing passwords of your account is a complex operation, website authenticity can be validated by the secure lock symbol at the corner of your browser*) to ensure clarity of understanding for both language versions.

Population Recruitment: The survey population of 1682 users were all voluntary participants. The survey questionnaire was promoted via social media networks (Facebook, LinkedIn, Twitter, Google+), personally, as well as in different social and professional groups. The survey included a consent form, upon agreeing to which, the user was taken to the survey page. The survey data was collected over a period of three months between September 2014 and December 2014.

Limitations: The primary target of the survey was to collect preferential and behavioral data from Bangladeshi Internet users regarding secure password and service usage. Due to the nature of publicity, the collected data may have a certain bias towards the behavior of users who are active in social networks. The participation in the survey was not controlled and was completely voluntary. The authors' social network connections and community groups were utilized for publicity.

4 Survey Results

In this section, we present the summary of the findings from the security survey on the Internet users from Bangladesh.

4.1 Survey Demographics

The survey included respondents over the age of 19 in five different age groups and excluded minors (18 and below). The box-plot of the respondents in five different age groups is shown in Fig. 1. The median age was between the ages 25 to 29 years with the interquartile range between ages

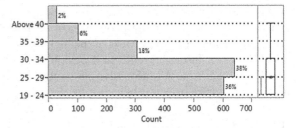

Fig. 1. Age group distribution

19 and 29 years. The age distribution shows that most of the users who participated in the online survey were rather young and active on the Internet and can be considered as the tech-savvy generation of users. The data was collected using survey forms in Bengali and English languages. Table 1 summarizes the response distribution for the two languages.

4.2   Usage Frequency Vs. Security Knowledge

We surveyed the frequency of Internet access of the users, varying from more than once a day to at least once a month. Majority (96%) of the users claimed they were very frequent Internet users, accessing the Internet at least once a day. Hence, we were assured that the study emphasized on the behaviors of the most frequent Internet users.

Table 1. Distribution for Bengali and English responses

Language	Count	Percentage
Bengali	1507	89.59
English	175	10.41
Total	**1682**	**100**

We asked the level of (self-proclaimed) knowledge the respondents had in security. Only 16% of the users felt that they have a high level of (self-proclaimed) security-oriented knowledge on the Internet. On the other hand, 65.1% and 18.7% of users responded to have moderate or low level knowledge of Internet security respectively.

We were also interested to see the variation of (self-proclaimed) Internet security knowledge with respect to the frequency of access to the Internet. Figure 2 shows the distribution of users for different levels of knowledge for varying Internet access frequencies. The frequencies are shown in numbers (1 to 7) with decreasing frequency, based on the different options from 'more than once a day' to as few as 'at

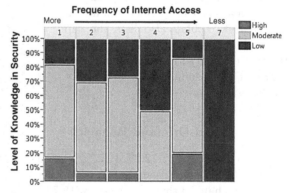

Fig. 2. Frequency of Internet access vs. (self-proclaimed) Knowledge of Internet security

least once a month'. We observed an overall trend of moderate level of security awareness among the users regarding Internet safety, varying within 63% and 68% among most frequency groups with at least 1% of total user responses.

4.3   Security Knowledge Vs. Language

We further investigated the (self-proclaimed) knowledge of security on the basis of the response language (Bengali and English). A higher percentage of English language respondents (24%) compared to the Bengali language respondents (15.34%) claimed to have 'high' level of knowledge of Internet security. The statistical test displayed heterogeneity of the proportions among the two groups (chi-Square $\chi^2 = 8.119$, Degrees of Freedom (DF) = 2, p-value = 0.0173). We believe that there might be two probable reasons for this particular observation. First, the fact that 55.5% of contents on the Internet till today are in English, which creates a general obstacle for self-awareness among other Internet users [31]. The second probable reason might be that non-native English speakers in developing countries, such as Bangladesh, might be considered more educated than the rest of the population.

4.4 Popularity of Internet Services

We surveyed the users regarding their usage of online services, such as email, social networks, messaging, and media streaming. The summary of the results is presented in Table 2. Online social networks were the most popular service among the users (98.9%). However, social media was one of the major channels of our survey publicity and might have created a certain bias in the result. The second-most popular service is emails (95.4%), which is followed by the rest. Table 2 also lists the top 6 combinations (above 4%) of popular Internet-enabled services. We found that 25.5% of the respondents were users of all the listed services.

Table 2. Popularity of Internet-enabled services

Internet-enabled services	% Users
Social networks	98.9%
Email	95.4%
Messaging	68.1%
Streaming	79.5%
Maps and navigation	66.2%
Finance management	43.0%
Bill payments	42.9%
Top 6 combinations of popular Internet-enabled services	% Users
All services	25.5%
Emails, social networks, messaging, streaming, maps & navigation	15.1%
Emails, social networks, messaging, streaming	7.3%
Email, social networks	5.2%
Email, social networks, streaming	5.0%
Email, social networks, streaming, maps & navigation	4.5%

4.5 Password-Oriented Behavior

The data showed that 72.2% (23.7% + 48.5%) of the users had all or at least some of their passwords similar to each other. 7.7% of them also responded that they never changed their passwords with 74.1% rarely changing their passwords. We performed a cross-variance analysis for the two variables. As seen from the heat map in Fig. 3, the largest class of users are those who had all or some of their passwords similar to each other and rarely changed the credentials (37.4%). Given the current scenario of online account breaches and similar attacks, the behavior of users for password-oriented practices poses as a critical security issue in terms of identity thefts. The behavior of users regarding similar passwords and frequency of changing passwords were homogeneous for the two language groups (*Similar passwords*: $\chi^2 = 0.247$, $DF = 2$, p-value = 0.8839; *Changing passwords*: $\chi^2 = 3.121$, $DF = 2$, p-value = 0.2101).

4.6   Logging-In Practices

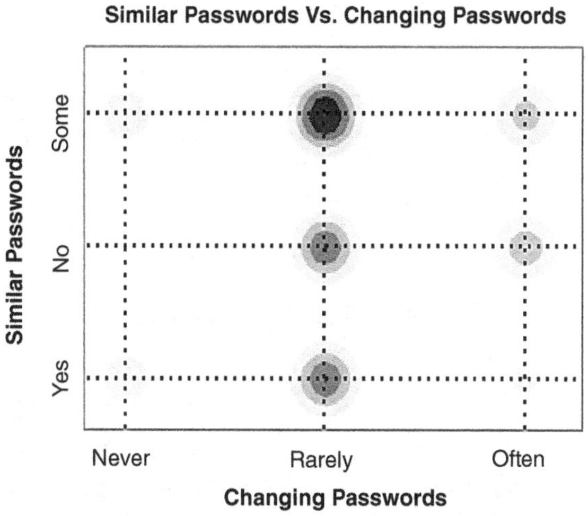

The survey included three questions to extract the behavioral practices pertaining to logging-in to online services. We observed that 62.5% (19.6% + 42.9%) of users saved most or at least some of their passwords on web browsers. Additionally, 57.9% of users preferred automated sign-in with 44.6% using Single-Sign-On (SSO) services. We analyzed the cross-variance in terms of the preference for automated sign-in for both saved passwords and SSO services. Among the users who preferred auto-

Similar Passwords Vs. Changing Passwords

Fig. 3. Usage of similar passwords vs. changing passwords

mated sign-in (44.6%), as shown in Fig. 4, 82.5% (32.1% + 50.4%) actually saved most or some of their passwords on the web browsers. Interestingly, many users (34.8%) still saved passwords on their browsers even though they did not prefer automated sign-in.

For users who preferred automated sign-in (44.6%), as illustrated in Fig. 5, 53.3% of users were using SSO for automated sign-in. However, we also observed that many users (32.5%) also used SSO even though they did not prefer automated sign-in. We drilled down further to observe the effects of saved passwords and SSO on the preference of using automated sign-in. We created a nominal logistic model and a generalized linear model to fit the data for the corresponding classes. Both models performed similarly with p-value < 0.001 and maximal standard error 0.095 for the two intercepting variables. The result implied a high correlation between the preferences for automated sign-in with saving passwords and using SSO services.

4.7   Third-Party Applications

Third-party applications, such as Facebook apps, require authenticated access to personal accounts. Surprisingly, only 34.3% of the users responded that they do not allow these applications access to their accounts. This is a positive indication of a good number of online users being aware of their privacy. However, 65.6% (2.1% + 63.5%) of users, always, or at least sometimes, grant such applications the access rights to their personal accounts. For the people who saved most or at least some of their (probably the most frequently used) passwords on web browsers (62.4%), 70.1% of the users (which is 43.8% of the total sample

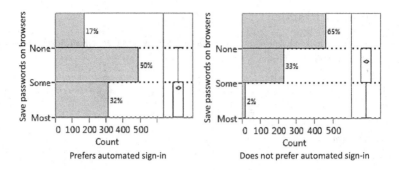

Fig. 4. Saving passwords on browsers vs. preference for automated sign-in

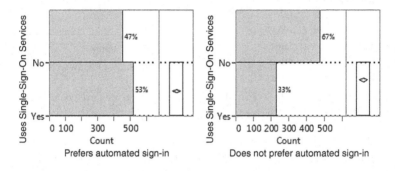

Fig. 5. Using Single-Sign-On services vs. preference for automated sign-in

population) always or at least some times allowed third-party applications to access their personal information. On the other hand, among the users who never saved their passwords on web browsers (37.5%), 41.7% of them never allowed third-party applications to have access to their accounts. Therefore, the distribution of users allowing third-party applications with respect to saving their passwords was heterogeneous ($\chi^2 = 26.402$, $DF = 4$, p-value < 0.001).

4.8   Usage History Vs. Anonymity

Usage history is commonly utilized for augmenting online services, such as, search results, recommendations, advertising, and financial activity detection. Overall, 88.1% (36.2% + 51.9%) of users felt strongly, or at least to some degree, that, usage history is useful in identifying them on the Internet. On the other hand, 52.2% of users responded that anonymous authentication is useful for them while accessing Internet services. 26.7% of the users felt that anonymous access might be something which is useful to them, even though they weren't completely sure about it.

As shown in the heat map in Fig. 6, almost 39% of the users were inclined towards benefiting from usage history but still preferred anonymity while accessing the services. However, we observed a heterogeneous distribution for the preference of usage history with respect to anonymity ($\chi^2 = 24.781$, $DF = 4$, p-value < 0.0001). This was due to the fact that a total of 62.2% of the survey sample were probably confused or unsure regarding their preference for either usage history or anonymity. We found that usage history and anonymity were heterogeneously distributed among the Bengali and English language respondents (*Usage history*: $\chi^2 = 11.475$, $DF = 2$, p-value $= 0.0032$; *Anonymity*: $\chi^2 = 17.391$, $DF = 2$, p-value $= 0.0002$).

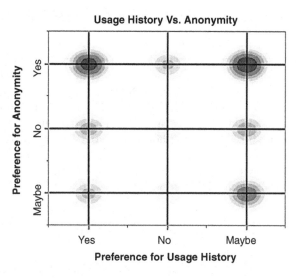

Fig. 6. Expectation of users regarding usage history vs. anonymous access

4.9 Usage of Internet-Enabled Devices

The type of devices that the users utilize to access the Internet can imply a lot on Internet-safe behavior. Our survey inquired the users on the different types of devices that they use. The summary of the different types of Internet devices is presented in Table 3. The most popular devices are personal laptops (77.7%) and smartphones (75.5%). Table 3 also shows the top 7 combinations (above 5%) for the combinations of Internet-enabled devices owned by the survey respondents. We observed that 22.4% of the respondents used both laptops and smartphones. The survey results showed that 82.9% of the users were using at least two devices to access the Internet and online services.

Table 3. Popularity of devices

Internet-enabled devices	% Users
Personal laptop	77.7%
Smartphone	75.5%
Personal desktop PC	54.3%
Tablet	22.6%
Public desktop PC	11.7%
Top 7 Combinations of popular Internet-enabled devices	% Users
Personal laptop and smartphone	22.4%
Personal desktop PC, personal laptop, smartphone	15.4%
Personal desktop PC, smartphone	10.3%
Personal desktop PC, personal laptop, smartphone, tablet	9.3%
Personal laptop	8.8%
Personal laptop, smartphone, tablet	6.0%
Personal desktop PC	5.8%

4.10   Complex Operations from Portable Devices

Given the popularity of portable devices, as shown in Table 3, we inquired if the respondents accessed complex operations, such as changing passwords and making secure transactions, from their smartphones and tablets. Such statistics are important to evaluate the scenario of privileged operations which the users perform on such portable mobile devices, and is summarized in Fig. 7. The results were similar between tablets and smartphones. We observed that 51.8% (17.2% and 34.6%) of smartphone users and 58.6% (18.7% and 39.8%) of tablet users accessed such operations on a regular basis or at least some times. Respondents who owned both smartphones and tablets had a higher percentage (61.1%) of privileged usage with both devices.

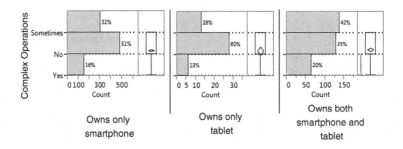

Fig. 7. Accessing complex operations from portable devices

4.11   Effective Re-authentication

A lot of Internet-enabled services require users to re-enter the authentication credentials for enhanced security. We found that 51.6% of the users were actually happy that they are being secure. Interestingly, 28.6% of the users seemed irritated with re-entering information, with 19.9% only doing it because they are asked for it. However, re-entering credentials does not carry any meaning if the users actually never changed their passwords, saved their passwords on the browsers, or were accessing privileged operations from their portable devices. We investigated the data using two approaches for modeling the mentality of users regarding re-authentication credentials.

In the first case, we utilized the responses for password-oriented behaviors, logging-in practices, and accessing privileged operations from smartphones/tablets to create a nominal logistic model. The model gained an Akaike Information Criterion (AIC) of 3146.53 (χ^2 = 328.886, DF = 20, p-value < 0.0001). The primary effects were introduced by the preference for saving passwords on web browsers and automated sign-in (p-value < 0.001), followed by frequency of changing passwords (p-value = 0.0089) and having similar passwords (p = 0.0157). Next, we created a generalized linear model using the same response variables. However, we enforced a binomial distribution on for people who were happy to be secure versus the others. The model reached an AIC of 2086.65 ($\chi^2 = 264.195$, $DF = 10$, p-value < 0.0001) with the same primary indicators.

Given the outcome of the models, we were interested to investigate the cross-variance of responses for re-entering credentials with the responses for saving passwords on browsers and preference for automated sign-in. We observed that among the users who were irritated to re-enter authentication credentials for secure logins and preferred automated sign-in (23.8% of total survey population), 85.8% saved at least some of their passwords on web browsers. Only 20.9% of users who were happy to be secure by re-entering their credentials but preferred automated sign-in did not save any passwords.

4.12   Privacy Awareness

Careless web browsing, especially, providing private information and not using privacy settings, may be considered a critical issue to address the increasing rate of e-crimes. 76.9% (37.8% + 39.1%) of the users responded that they never or only sometimes check the authenticity of websites prior to providing any private information. However, 64.8% of users mentioned that they use privacy settings, with 9.9% users who never use any privacy settings. A heat map of the two behavioral aspects is illustrated in Fig. 8.

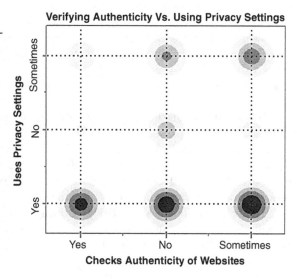

Fig. 8. Verifying authenticity of websites and using privacy settings on Internet

The cross-validation revealed that 71.4% (33.1% + 38.3%) of the users never or only some times checked the authenticity of the visited websites even though they were using privacy settings. We found that only 18.5% of the survey population used privacy settings and verified the authenticity of websites. Unfortunately, 67.7% of the users who did not use privacy settings did not check the authenticity of the websites at all. Additionally, 87.3% (38.2% + 49.1%) of respondents with sparing use of privacy settings mentioned that they were also not always aware of the authenticity of the websites.

4.13 Exploitation Victims

Internet users may be victims of various forms of e-crimes. We inquired if the respondents had the experience of hacked online accounts or misused shared online contents. 13.3% of the users reported that they had the experience of having their account(s) hacked with 16.4% of users who shared online contents which were later misused. A total of 25.7% of the users either had an experience of having their accounts hacked or their shared contents misused. A cross-variance analysis revealed that 24.3% of users who had experiences with content abuse also had their account(s) hacked.

We studied different models to fit the class of users with account breaches. We performed a stepwise iteration model generation approach to minimize the AIC. The model converged with AIC 1278.64 with 5 indicator variables ($\chi^2 = 57.661$, $DF = 7$, p-value < 0.0001). The model also had a lack-of-fit p $= 0.5339$. Experience of previous shared-content misuse played the major indicating role (p-value < 0.0001). The age of the user was the next key indicator (p-value $= 0.0111$). We observed that users who preferred anonymity were one of the other major indicators of prior victims of account breaches (p-value $= 0.0231$). The other indicator variables were users who allowed third-party applications to access their personal accounts (p-value $= 0.0328$) followed by the frequency of Internet usage (p-value $= 0.0442$).

Given that information misuse was the primary indicator of account breaches, we performed a stepwise model generation for information misuse victims. The model converged with AIC 1461.5 and had a different set of primary indicators ($\chi^2 = 61.955$, $DF = 10$, p-value < 0.0001) and a lack-of-fit p $= 0.4429$. The type of services accessed, the devices used to access the Internet, and the preference of usage history had dominant effects (p-value < 0.009). Additionally, the frequency of Internet usage (p-value $= 0.0106$), allowing access to third-party applications (p-value $= 0.0.0141$), and performing complex operations from portable devices (p-value $= 0.0155$) had significant effects on the outcome variable.

5 Discussion

We were able to gain insightful information regarding the security-oriented behaviors, practices, experiences, and usability preferences of Internet users from Bangladesh who are mainly active on social networks. The key findings from our study are summarized in Table 4. The survey population comprised of considerably active Internet users with varying frequencies for different types of services and moderate (self-proclaimed) level of security knowledge. Unfortunately, we still found that the users are not exercising proper behaviors in terms of password usage and security-awareness. Unfortunately, the preference for seamless authentication experience probably drives a lot of users towards 'unhealthy' practices. Users are quite often trusting third-party applications to have access to their personal accounts, which is inherently a risky behavior. Some users prefer anonymity while using the Internet, but which somewhat contradicts with their preference for usage history based services.

Table 4. Summary of key findings from the security-oriented survey

Key Findings
Participation: 74% of participation was between ages 19 and 29 with 91% of the respondents claiming to be frequent Internet users.
Awareness: Moderate Internet security awareness varies within 63% and 68% among all frequency groups, and was heterogeneously distributed within Bengali and English language respondents.
Service Usage: Above 95% of respondents used online social networks (98.9%) and email (95.4). 25.5% of respondents were users of all of the listed services. Low penetration of e-commerce in Bangladesh is a probable reason for only 43.0% and 42.9% respondents using financial services.
Password Usage: 72.2% of users had similar passwords for online services. 81.8% of users never or rarely changed their passwords. 37.4% of users had both similar passwords and rarely changed the credentials.
Logging-in Practices: Among the users who preferred automated sign-in, 82.5% of users saved passwords on web browsers and 53.3% used SSO services. Among users who did not prefer automated sign-in, 34.8% still saved passwords on the web browsers and 30.2% used SSO.
Third-party Application Access: 65.6% of users always or at least some times allowed third-party applications to access their personal accounts. 70% of users who saved their passwords on web browsers allowed third-party applications to access their personal information.
Anonymity and Usage History: 38.3% of users wanted anonymity with usage history. 49.6% of users did not feel the necessity for usage history, but still wanted anonymity. 62.2% of the users were unsure about the implications and applications of usage history and anonymity.
Internet-enabled Devices: Personal laptops (77.7%) and smartphones (75.5%) were the most popular Internet devices. 22.4% of respondents used both devices. 51.8% of smartphone owners, 58.6% of tablet owners, and 61.1% of both device owners accessed privileged operations from their portable devices.
Re-Authentication: Saving passwords on web browsers, preference for automated sign-in, accessing privileged operations from portable devices, changing credentials, and using similar passwords had influence on users in terms of re-entering authentication credentials for secure logins.
Privacy Awareness: 76.9% of users do not check website authenticity. 9.9% of respondents never use any privacy settings. 71.4% of users with privacy settings do not always verify website authenticity. 67.7% of users without privacy settings never verify website authenticity. 87.3% of users with sparing use of privacy settings are also not always aware of the authenticity of the visited websites.
Exploitation Victims: 13.3% and 16.4% of users had their account hacked or shared contents abused. Victims of shared content misuse, age, preference for anonymity, allowing access to third-party applications, and frequency of Internet usage had dominant effects in determining account hack victims. 24.3% of the content abuse victims had their accounts hacked. Type of services and devices, preference for usage history, frequency of Internet access, allowing access to third-party applications, and performing complex operations from portable devices had dominant effects in determining victims of content misuse.

The choices of Internet-enabled devices were considerably high for portable devices. Unfortunately, a high percentage of users performed privileged operations from such devices. As a result, this puts the users into the risk of identity thefts in case of a stolen device. Re-authentication mechanisms enforced by service providers are supposed to enhance the security. However, a considerable segment of users were irritated with the process. Therefore, such users are inclined towards insecure practices which questions the overall effectiveness of the two-factor procedure. We also observed a general lack of awareness regarding the authenticity of websites and privacy settings when presenting personal information. Users who were victims of account hacks and information misuse had dominant effects on other behavioral aspects. However, some of the factors might be the reason why they were the victims, such as age and type of service/devices used, while some may have evolved as an effect of being prior victims, such as preference for anonymity and usage history.

5.1 Security Implications

Our key findings from the online survey can be leveraged by security researchers and service providers for designing security technologies and to ensure the safety of the Internet users. Moreover, educators can utilize the identified opportunities to deliver awareness messages for addressing the particular insecure practices.

Observation 1 (Language): Even though a developing nation, the high percentage of responses in Bengali from the younger tech-savvy generation shows the predominant interest for contents in their native language. This creates a concern, given that 55% of contents on the Internet are, in fact, available only in English [31]. As a result, security-news, tutorials, and similar contents are being circulated in a limited context. Therefore, contents on security-awareness should be available in native languages to gain the attention from such Internet user groups.

Observation 2 (Education Methods): We found that the knowledge on Internet security was not generally high irrespective of the frequency of Internet usage. Moreover, research works have suggested that self-proclaimed evaluations tend to be higher than collective comparison. In practice, many of the respondents claiming to be moderately well-aware of Internet security may actually be less educated than expected. As a result, a tendency of overconfidence usually leads to people being reluctant towards learning and being careless. The critical mass requires innovative and passive security education methods without the requirement of active involvement. Moreover, the majority of the educational institutions in Bangladesh have a Bengali medium of instruction. This provides us with an opportunity to leverage the role of such educational components to deliver security-awareness on the Internet from the grass-roots of the society.

Observation 3 (Service Channels): Users are regularly accessing different types of services, and therefore, all of them should be the focus of enhanced security. Moreover, the variety of service usage also provides us with opportunities to deliver security-awareness education via multiple channels. The high popularity of social networks and messaging is a direct implication of the younger generation being more active on the Internet. Therefore, the younger user group should be addressed with a higher concern for ensuring the security and privacy awareness on such social Internet-based services.

Observation 4 (Passwords): Majority of the users are vulnerable to insecure password-oriented practices. Users having similar passwords are evident in most Internet user groups. However, the reluctance to changing the passwords creates an incremental threat for such users. As a result, a stolen identity for one account can lead to the revelation of multiple accounts for the given user. Users can be educated on developing useful password setting techniques, which are both easy to remember and not similar across all the online accounts. Service providers are also required to instigate the password changing process for their users to ensure greater protection.

Observation 5 (Usable Security): Internet users have a tendency to prefer usability over security. Users were generally inclined towards experiencing automated and seamless authentication for Internet services. This is implied with the high percentage of users who usually saved their passwords to avoid typing in their passwords every time. As a result, this creates a weak link to ensure the security of such users and may be easily targeted by phishing and cross-site scripting attacks. The results signify the importance of usable security designs for services, and the impact such technologies can have on the security of Internet users.

Observation 6 (Relative Knowledge): Users allowing access to third-party applications may be the target of malicious advertisers and app developers. Client-side scripts and malicious applications can easily exploit the users in terms of privacy of their personal data using the saved credentials on the web browsers. We found that a general lack of security awareness can have relative effects on multiple insecure practices. On the other hand, users being educated on a particular security aspect may also learn to be aware of other secure practices by induction. Security educators can leverage the transitional knowledge application to create better awareness among the Internet users.

Observation 7 (Privacy): There is a limited rising awareness of users in terms of anonymity and privacy protection. However, a significant number of respondents were unsure regarding their preferences, showing the general lack of privacy issues on the Internet. Moreover, the heterogeneity for Bengali and English language respondents may be related to the limited security education, language barrier, and predominant English language contents on the Internet [31], as discussed earlier in observations 1 and 3.

Observation 8 (Device Usage): Users are logging into online websites from various devices and locations. Majority of the users are preferring portable devices (laptops and smartphones). However, mobility comes with the inherent risk of theft and loss. Therefore, users being prone to saving passwords on their devices (observation 6) are putting them under the risk of losing their credentials along with the loss or theft of a personal device. Security educators are therefore required to highlight the risks of using portable devices and the associated security concerns.

Observation 9 (Service Access): Users are performing complex operations from their hand-held devices while accessing Internet services. Public usage of devices puts the users at risk of shoulder-surfing attacks. Accessing such services also results in an increased risk of user security and privacy. Unfortunately, the users are not being aware of the associated risks. Institutions and device sellers can be a channel to deliver awareness messages to the end users to not use such devices for complex and secure operations.

Observation 10 (Effective Security): The negative impact in the experience of users while re-authenticating was primarily driven by the reduced usability of the system. Users require intuitive and highly usable interfaces for properly utilizing security enforcing technologies. Conventional models simply burden the users with repetitive tasks and result in insecure practices. The general users are saving passwords on their browsers and opting for automated sign-ins, and thus, making the security ineffective for re-authentication. As a result, requirement engineering for Internet security technologies should be highly behavior and usability driven.

Observation 11 (Web Browsing): We observed a lack of awareness in web browsing, which is highly correlated to the privacy-unaware usage of online services. While some users claimed using privacy settings, most users were not aware of the authenticity of the websites. However, security of a system is only as strong as the weakest link. Such contradictory behavior puts the users at risk of phishing and exploitation attacks, irrespective of the active privacy settings. Online service providers generally display privacy concern for users due to the legal aspects of protecting the users' personal information. Unfortunately, a victim of a phishing attack is not the service providers' legal responsibility. Hence, security education for general users must thus focus on the importance of verified websites with corresponding implications.

Observation 12 (Victimology): Victims of identity thefts and misused shared contents had a high dependency on each other. However, we are unsure of the cause-and-effect relationship between the two cases. Our results show that users are inducing the threat upon themselves based on various combinations of behavioral practices. Such information can be highly leveraged to design user-oriented technologies for greater Internet safety and security. Researchers and developers should carefully study such cases of exploitation and design secure solutions based on the behavior of the users.

6 Conclusion

Proliferation of the Internet had also brought along various threats on the users. Secure technologies aim to protect the users, but often reduce the usability and force the users to incline towards insecure practices. The developing world had a slower start but is catching up to the tech-trends on the information highway. In this paper, we summarized the various implications based on the study on security-oriented practices, expectations, behaviors, and usability preferences of 1682 Internet users from Bangladesh. Our findings reflect that users do not behave in the ideal way that security experts believe that they should.

Expectations such as hassle-free and seamless authentication, drive behaviors and practices such as using SSO services. Moreover, degraded user experiences for increased security, such as, while re-authenticating, create inclination towards ineffective practices, such as, saving the passwords to avoid re-typing. We believe that security technologies should evolve from behavioral aspects and security comprehensibility of users, rather than only focusing on attacker models. Unfortunately, in today's world, Internet users circumvent the security and safety of technologies using improper practices, or simply suffer from degraded user experience. We provided a set of observations and the ways we can leverage the aspects of user behavior for providing security-awareness education. We believe, that, such a study can greatly help security researchers in designing effective, yet usable, and non-obtrusive technologies, to ensure the safety of Internet users from developing countries.

Acknowledgment. This research was supported by the National Science Foundation CAREER Award CNS-1351038, ACI-1642078, and DGE-1723768.

References

1. Anderson, R., Moore, T.: Information security: where computer science, economics and psychology meet. Philos. Trans. R. Soc. A Math. Phys. Eng. Sci. **367**(1898), 2717–2727 (2009)
2. Auchard, E.: Smartphones at Risk: Vulnerable to Stolen Passwords, Data Theft, August 2014. http://www.carriermanagement.com/news/2014/08/05/127054.htm
3. Bangladesh Telecommunication Regulatory Commission: Internet Subscribers in Bangladesh, January 2015. http://www.btrc.gov.bd/content/internet-subscribers-bangladesh-january-2015
4. Bureau of Justice Statistics: Identity Theft Supplement (ITS) to the National Crime Victimization Survey (2012). http://www.bjs.gov/content/pub/pdf/vit12.pdf
5. Chen, J., Paik, M., McCabe, K.: Exploring internet security perceptions and practices in Urban Ghana. In: Proceedings of SOUPS. Usenix (2014)
6. Cybenko, G.: Why Johnny can't evaluate security risk. IEEE S&P **4**(1), 5 (2006)
7. Florencio, D., Herley, C.: A large-scale study of web password habits. In: Proceedings of WWW. ACM (2007)
8. Herzberg, A.: Why Johnny can't surf (safely)? Attacks and defenses for web users. Comput. Secur. **28**(1–2), 63–71 (2009)
9. Hull, G., Lipford, H.R., Latulipe, C.: Contextual gaps: privacy issues on Facebook. Ethics Inf. Technol. **13**(4), 289–302 (2011)
10. Inglesant, P.G., Sasse, M.A.: The true cost of unusable password policies: password use in the wild. In: Proceedings of SIGCHI. ACM (2010)
11. Kang, R., Brown, S., Kiesler, S.: Why do people seek anonymity on the internet? Informing policy and design. In: Proceedings of SIGCHI. ACM (2013)
12. Khan, R., Hasan, R.: The story of naive alice: behavioral analysis of susceptible users on the internet. In: Proceedings of COMPSAC. IEEE (2016)
13. Khan, R., Mizan, M., Hasan, R., Sprague, A.: Hot zone identification: analyzing effects of data sampling on spam clustering. JDFSL **9**(1), 67–82 (2014)

14. Kumaraguru, P., Cranor, L.: Privacy in India: attitudes and awareness. In: Danezis, G., Martin, D. (eds.) PET 2005. LNCS, vol. 3856, pp. 243–258. Springer, Heidelberg (2006). https://doi.org/10.1007/11767831_16

15. Kumaraguru, P., Sachdeva, N.: Privacy in India: attitudes and awareness v 2.0. Available at SSRN 2188749 (2012)

16. Lee, S., Kim, Y., Lee, B.G.: Determinants of voluntary self-disclosure in the usage of micro-blog. In: Proceedings of ICONI, December 2010

17. Lipka, M.: Rise in Identity Fraud Tied to Smartphone Use, February 2012. http://www.reuters.com/article/2012/02/22/us-idtheft-javelin-idUSTRE81L16520120222. Reuters

18. Moore, T., Clayton, R., Anderson, R.: The economics of online crime. J. Econ. Perspect. **23**(3), 3–20 (2009)

19. National Consumers League: The consumer data insecurity report: examining the data breach - identity fraud paradigm in four major metropolitan areas. Technical report, Javelin Strategy & Research (2014)

20. Oh, H.K., Jin, S.H.: The security limitations of SSO in OpenID. In: Proceedings of ICACT (2008)

21. Pascual, A.: Identity fraud report: card data breaches and inadequate consumer password habits fuel disturbing fraud trends. Technical report, Javelin Strategy & Research (2014)

22. Poushter, J., Carle, J., Bell, J., Wike, R., Cuddington, D., Devlin, K., Keegan, M., Parker, B., Simmons, K., Stokes, B., Deane, C., Drake, B., Kent, D., Schwarzer, S., Smith, B., Zainulbhai, H.: Internet seen as positive influence on education but negative on morality in emerging and developing nations. Pew Research Center Studies, March 2015

23. Reynolds, J.K.: RFC1135: The Helminthiasis of the Internet, December 1989. http://tools.ietf.org/html/rfc1135

24. Ross, B., Jackson, C., Miyake, N., Boneh, D., Mitchell, J.C.: Stronger password authentication using browser extensions. In: Proceedings of Usenix Security (2005)

25. Shay, R., Komanduri, S., Kelley, P.G., Leon, P.G., Mazurek, M.L., Bauer, L., Christin, N., Cranor, L.F.: Encountering stronger password requirements: user attitudes and behaviors. In: Proceedings of SOUPS. ACM (2010)

26. Sheng, S., Broderick, L., Koranda, C.A., Hyland, J.J.: Why Johnny still can't encrypt: evaluating the usability of email encryption software. In: Proceedings of SOUPS. Usenix (2006)

27. Stanton, J.M., Stam, K.R., Mastrangelo, P., Jolton, J.: Analysis of end user security behaviors. Comput. Secur. **24**(2), 124–133 (2005)

28. The World Bank: Bangladesh - leveraging ICT for governance, growth, and employment project (2012)

29. United Nations: World population prospects: the 2012 revision, highlights and advance tables. Economics and Social Affairs (2013)

30. Wagner, C., Mitter, S., Körner, C., Strohmaier, M.: When social bots attack: modeling susceptibility of users in online social networks. In: Proceedings of MSM. Citeseer (2012)

31. W^{3}Techs Web Technology Surveys: Usage of Content Languages for Websites, January 2015. http://w3techs.com/technologies/overview/content_language/all

32. Yan, J.J., Blackwell, A.F., Anderson, R.J., Grant, A.: Password memorability and security: empirical results. IEEE S&P **2**(5), 25–31 (2004)

Research Track: Services Linkage

Data Service API Design for Data Analytics

Yun Zhang[1,2(✉)], Liming Zhu[1,2], Xiwei Xu[1,2], Shiping Chen[1,2],
and An Binh Tran[1]

[1] School of Computer Science and Engineering, UNSW, Sydney, Australia
[2] Data 61, CSIRO, Sydney, Australia
{yun.zhang,liming.zhu,xiwei.xu,shiping.chen}@data61.csiro.au

Abstract. Data service APIs provide uniform and filtered interfaces for data analysts to retrieve data. However, existing RESTful data services do not serve data analytics well because most of them are designed based on the underlying data schema rather than aligning with the requirements of data analytics. First, the API representations only support *one-off* communication, which lacks analytic semantics to guide analysts to continuously explore and retrieve data. Second, the current data service design does not support re-usage of data exploration processes and derived data generated from data analysts.

In this paper, we propose an analytics-focused API design for data services. First, we introduce a service architecture and its resource APIs to realize core functions of data retrieval. Second, we design a navigation model for analysts to navigate resource APIs more efficiently. Third, we extend and leverage data package technique to provide context information about the origin, scope, and historical manipulations on a certain dataset. This mechanism allows the analysts to share and reuse historical data exploration process and derived data. We evaluate our approach using a case study and compare our approach against the conventional data APIs. The evaluation shows that our approach has advantages over traditional data service APIs in maturity, interoperability, discoverability, and reusability.

Keywords: Data analytics · Data service · REST · API
Data package

1 Introduction

Large amounts of data are increasingly being published on the web. For example, on Twitter, more than three million tweets are published every 10 min[1]. Another example is open data platforms provided by governments, like data.gov.au[2], which already published over twenty thousands of datasets for free. How to

---

[1] http://www.internetlivestats.com/twitter-statistics/.
[2] https://data.gov.au.

© Springer International Publishing AG, part of Springer Nature 2018
J. E. Ferreira et al. (Eds.): SCC 2018, LNCS 10969, pp. 87–102, 2018.
https://doi.org/10.1007/978-3-319-94376-3_6

properly and efficiently retrieve these data for data analytics is becoming a hot issue [1].

To analyze a dataset, data analysts often start by exploring data before knowing exactly what they are looking for. It is not pragmatic to download the whole large dataset before performing any exploratory analysis. Instead, it is desirable to allow analysts to have a glimpse into the data through a sequence of exploratory queries before the retrieval for further analysis [2]. Data exploration, which is an interactive process to retrieve data, allows the analysts issue a query, receive a response, and then iteratively interact with the data system to refine their query based on the response from the system and domain knowledge [3].

Since data exploration is labor-intensive and repetitive, it would be beneficial for analysts if the value-added data derived from the exploration stage could be shared and reused in future. Data analysts can share the results from the earlier exploration to better streamline the data analytics pipeline. To enable more efficient data sharing and reuse, it is very important to provide provenance information of data source so that data consumers are informed about what sort of earlier manipulations have been done to the data.

Data services provide uniform, scalable, and filtered interfaces for data analysts to retrieve data [4]. Many companies and platforms, like Twitter, Google, and CKAN[3] offer data service APIs that provide simple and easy-to-use access to some of their resources. Data services allow third-parties to easily integrate the data resource into their applications. However, these conventional interfaces fall short on supporting responsive, interactive, and comprehensive data retrieval for analytics. First, the existing data services are designed to answer questions according to the underlying database schema and pre-assembled index, rather than being driven by the requirement of data retrieval for data analytics [5]. Second, the current data services only support *one-off* queries, which are isolated, static and of not analytics semantics. Data analyst have to blindly request data services many times to understand underlying data. Third, there is no standard mechanism to provide context information about the origin, scope, and usage of the data in data services. Data analysts cannot be informed about what data exists, how the data is derived and used, and as a result, they cannot infer whether these processed data can be reused.

In this paper, we propose a data service API design driven by the requirements of data analytics. Our contributions include (1) a new data service architecture with a set of analytic APIs (2) a navigation model to help discover and generate data service API dynamically, and (3) a mechanism that extends *data package* to share data processing scripts and data context information associated with data. We evaluate the proposed API design through a real case study and discuss quality attributes. The evaluation shows that our approach has advantages over conventional data service APIs in maturity, interoperability, discoverability, and reusability.

The remainder of this paper is organized as follows. Section 2 describe a brief background and some related work. Section 3 gives three research requirements

---

[3] https://ckan.org/.

derived from a scenario of human resource data analytics. Section 4 introduces our approach with the service architecture, the navigation model and the application of data package. Section 5 uses a case study to evaluate our API design and discuss the contribution. Section 6 concludes the paper and extended work.

2   Background and Related Work

REST (REpresentational State Transfer) [6] is an architectural style for designing web applications. Following REST design principles, a data service is identified by a URI as a resource. Client applications interact with data services through using request-response messages. Protocols and Structures for Inference (PSI)[4] specification defines a RESTful architecture for presenting concepts used in machine learning as RESTful web services. The data source is wrapped as data service, named relation. However, the relation does not indicate how to discover a related data service for data exploration.

Database-as-a-Service (DaaS) has emerged as a new paradigm in the cloud computing environment. Many commercial databases, like Amazon SimpleDB[5], provide accessible data service APIs to their data stores. HTSQL[6] enables accessing SQLServer via HTTP arbitrarily, which is an advanced query language on the web. However, the design of these CRUD-based data services are merely based on the underlying database schemas and pre-assembled indexes without referring to the domain application protocol.

To build a domain application protocol over HTTP, which is domain agnostic in the web application, additional explicit semantics are needed [7]. In the Semantic Web, semantics are described by ontologies written in RDFS and OWL, while RESTful implementations encode semantics by annotating hypermedia with link relations [8]. Hypermedia as the Engine of Application State (HATEOAS) is a constraint applied to hypermedia. HATEOAS requires that the service embed links in its responses. The links represent the next possible actions that clients can take [6].

However, there is a semantic gap for the clients to be navigated by hyperlink automatically. To remedy this design flaws in HATEOAS implementation, some hypermedia specifications such as AtomPub[7] and OpenSearch[8] are tailored to achieve the specific application goals. However, the semantics of these domain-specific media types are implicit and generic [9]. AtomPub is designed to cover all the collection-based APIs but cannot reflect different application semantics. Microsoft's Open Data Protocol (OData)[9] is derived from AtomPub. OData defines the protocol semantics for filtering and sorting a collection of data, using a query language similar to SQL, but the semantics of the relationship between

---

[4] http://psi.cecs.anu.edu.au/.
[5] http://aws.amazon.com/simpledb/.
[6] http://htsql.org/.
[7] https://bitworking.org/projects/atom/rfc5023.html.
[8] http://www.opensearch.org/Home.
[9] http://www.odata.org/.

resources focus on data instead of analytics operations, and the related metadata services only present limited description documents [10].

Our approach fills this semantic gap by specifying the domain application protocol for data exploration in analytics and using this protocol for the implementation of our services following HATEOAS principle.

In REST architecture, metadata provides self-describing information about web resources, which enable automatic processing of web resources [11]. However, the metadata is sent in the header of HTTP messages and restricted to provide information about the syntax used in the resource representation. In addition, the semantics of the origin, scope, and usage of the data is less considered. Ground [12] is a data context service that supports collecting, publishing and querying the metadata information from applications, behavior, and change of data context, but it is implemented as a system without consideration of RESTful API presentation. A data package is a collection of datasets, metadata information and other data files. Data package protocol[10] defines an open standard for the format of a package, which guides users to share and manage distributed dataset using data package. However, there is no guidance on how to apply data package for exchanging metadata in RESTful services.

3   Scenario and Requirements

To explore the potential of our data services, we describe a practical human resource analytics scenario in which the data services can aid in data exploration and facilitate better collaboration between data analysts.

The purpose of the analysis is to help a company understand why some of their most experienced employees are leaving prematurely and predict who will leave in future.

Analyst Bob first requests the data service to investigate the sum, average, min, max, and medium of numeric attributes respectively. Then he makes the second request to discover a correlation between each pair of attributes. The results show that on average, employees who left the company have lower satisfaction levels. After knowing all the features of employees who have left, Bob request data service to retrieve the data about valuable but left employees with an evaluation result above average performance, or spend at least four years in the company, or were working on more than five projects at the same time and still left the company. Later, Bob will use these data to conduct an analysis model to predict who will leave. After Bob completes the explorative analysis, this value-added data and his explorative process could be shared by another analyst named Alice. Alice can use Bob's data to do a further analytic activity without preparing the data from scratch. She also can reproduce Bob's exploration process to verify his result. Even, she can extend and construct her operation based on Bob's. Afterward, Alice's data exploration process and derived data can be shared with another analyst.

---

[10] https://specs.frictionlessdata.io/data-package/.

From this scenario, we can derive three main requirements for building data services to explore and retrieve data.

R1. The data service should be grounded on data explorative operations. An analyst should be able to interact with the data services in the same manner as client side data analysis tools.

R2. The data services should be able to guide analysts to discover the related resources based on their specific requirements. An analyst should be able to navigate resource APIs to understand underlying data efficiently.

R3. The data services should allow data analysts to share and reuse the result of the explorative analysis. An analyst should be able to replay the shared process based on the provided context information about who, when and what operations have been performed on the data.

4   Service Design

The requirements described above motivate us to design a new data service that fills the gap in current data services. First, we introduce a RESTful service architecture including key resources to facilitate data operations in data exploration. Second, we propose a navigation model to describe the relationship of the main resources in the domain of data analytics and illustrate how to use this model to guide analysts to explore data. Finally, we customize and leverage data package into our data services and showcase its usage and advantages for building a data analysis sharing environment.

4.1   Service Architecture

As shown in Fig. 1, the main resources in our architecture are *gateway, filter, aggregator, sampler, function supplier* and *packager*. A request from user or web client is sent to *gateway*, which responds with a roadmap of all resource categories provided by the data service. Each resource category contains a set of RESTful resource APIs that map a category of functions used in data exploration and retrieval. The resources are interconnected via hyperlink whereby the

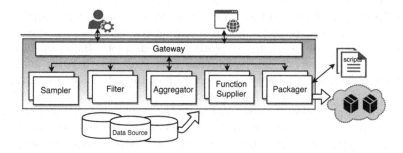

Fig. 1. Data service architecture

user can navigate among resource APIs to explore data. After explorative data analysis done, *packager* created a data package which contains the derived data, processing scripts, and context information. Specifically, the properties of this architecture are in the following:

Gateway is a self-describing resource that exposes the metadata defining data schema and other information like type of data source(e.g. dynamic, static), data size and description about this dataset, which helps the data analyst have an initial understanding about the dataset. Data analysts interact with Gateway to discover the resources related to the dataset.

Filter allows the data analysts to filter the dataset based on dimensions and measures which are presented based on non-numeric attributes and quantitative attributes. Dimensions represent which attributes of data that can be extracted while measures represent the query schema that is used to extract the subset or transformation of the dataset.

Aggregator allows the data analysts to have a summary statistics of the data without extracting original data items. It can perform aggregation function over one attribute's values and group by the attribute's name. The aggregation queries have constraints based on the numeric or non-numeric data attribute.

Sampler provides diverse sampling methods to allow data analysts to quickly build and test their models within a sample of data that can fit into their memory. The sample size and specific sample methods are defined by users.

Function Supplier provides a set of statistics functions, which effectively assist data analysts to discover the relation, general trend, and outlier of the data as auxiliary means. For example, *correlation* is for understanding the relationship between attributes; *isnull* is used to check for the missing value to help analysts estimate the data quality.

Packager retrieves the data, wraps them with optional primitive operations which are presented as scripts into the package, and then stores them in external storage. Using the packager resource, the data consumer can acquire a targeted subset of a dataset in batch along with the optional scripts provided by the data publisher. These scripts can be used to pre-process the data and accelerate the forthcoming analysis work. We will discuss more detail in Sect. 4.3.

4.2   Navigation Model

The resources in the service architecture are interconnected to each other according to the context of the data analytics. A navigation model which defines the domain application protocol for data exploration is designed to assist clients to form their queries for interactive exploring large datasets. Based on the navigation model, data service can recommend next steps for the data analyst in the query session, and provide the information of the relationship between the resources in the context of data analytics.

The navigation model is shown in Fig. 2. The circles represent the resources introduced in the Sect. 4.1, while arrows correspond to the connections between the resource API templates. The relationships across resources are categorized into four types, including *narrow down, summary, relate* and *wrap up*. Specifically, *narrow down* means zoom into the data from less detail to more detail. Users could be guided to the *filter* API template by the *narrow down* link to query detailed data from summarized data based on the data distribution or extreme value provided by the *aggregator* or the *sampler*. Conversely, users can zoom out the data that are of little interest to discover other attributes through *sampler* or *aggregator* API template guided by the *summary* link. The *relate* link presents auxiliary services, for example, some statistic functions like correlation, standardization and distribution. During the process of data exploration, *wrap up* appears in every stage to refer users to the *packager* API template when the returned data are too large for the client memory or the users wants to download the whole data with previously recorded data exploration track.

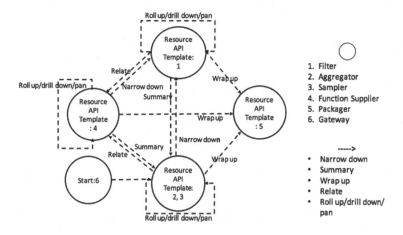

Fig. 2. Navigation model

When focusing on one resource, the user can send a sequence of requests to the resource API template adjusting the parameter values until she is satisfied with the results. Alternatively, such a query session could be accelerated by our navigation model through parameter prediction—parameter values can be used to instantiate the API templates through analyzing the past parameters provided by user. We generalize three types of relationship based on users navigation activates including *Roll up, drill down* and *pan*. Concretely, *drill down* provides a more detailed view by either stepping down a hierarchy within a dimension or introducing additional dimensions through changing the parameters. For example, when viewing the salary data of Australia, a *drill down* link provides the service querying the data of different states like NSW (New South Wales), QLD (Queensland), etc. A further *drill down* on NSW may display data of Sydney. It also can restrict the results in *aggregator* by tweaking the conditions. *Roll up* is the reverse of *drill down*: it means climbing up a concept hierarchy for a dimension, reducing the dimensions or relieving the conditions in a measure.

Pan allows users to change the angle they observed by changing the dimensions of data or the operations used.

The navigation model incorporates the analytics domain semantics into HATEOAS. Specifically, the `links` property is used to represent all the actions and resources related to each resource. Users can select one of the `links` to follow as the next step. `links` is defined as an array of Linked Description Objects (LDOs) in JSON Hyper-Schema[11], which obeys HATEOAS principle and assists discovering all the related resource API templates with the current resource API. Each LDO at least contains one `href` property, which is the target of the link, and a `rel` property indicating the relationship between the linked resource and the current resource. Users could effectively make a data exploration by following `links` embedded in the representation to access the next useful resource.

The navigation model involves both dynamical discovery and generation, which enables users to dynamically discover the resource API templates and automatically generate the parameters of API templates based on the previous input from the client. We present their schemas of Links separately in Listings 1.1 and 1.2.

```
{        "$schema": "http://json-schema.org/draft-04/schema#",
         "title": "Schema defining links between resources",
         "type": "array",
         "items": {
         "links": [{
                  "rel": "narrow down",
                  "href": "/filter",
                  "method": "GET"
         },{
                  "rel": "summary",
                  "href": "/aggregator",
                  "method": "GET"
         },{
                  "rel": "relate",
                  "href": "/functionSupplier",
                  "method": "GET"
         },{
                  "rel": "wrap up",
                  "href": "/packager",
                  "method": "POST",
                  "schema": {}
         }]}}
```

Listing 1.1. HyperSchema of links for dynamical discovery

```
{        "$schema": "http://json-schema.org/draft-04/schema#",
         "title": "Schema defining links within one resource",
         "base": "/{resource}?{measures,dimensions}",
         "type": "array",
         "links": [{
```

---

[11] http://json-schema.org/latest/json-schema-hypermedia.html.

```
            "rel": "drill down",
            "href": "/{resource}?{measures,added_dimensions}",
            "method": "GET"
    },{
            "rel": "roll up",
            "href": "/{resource}",
            "method": "GET"
    },{
            "rel": "pan",
            "href": "/{resource}?{new_measures,new_dimensions}",
            "method": "GET" }]}...
```

Listing 1.2. HyperSchema of links for dynamical generation

As shown in Listing 1.1, each `links` comprises of `rel` that presents the meaning of related action, and `href` that points to the location of resource. The value of `rel` can be *relate, summary, narrow down* and *wrap up*. `rel` is used for the dynamic discovery of resource APIs. The `method` and `schema` properties specify the HTTP method and data format for the input. Client can send a HTTP OPTIONS request to acquire further assistance on how to form a specific API.

Listing 1.2 defines the schema of `links` for generating the specific resource APIs. According to the different semantics of `rel`, the new parameters can be generated based on the measures and dimensions in the `base`, and form a new resource API as a `href` property for client. The value of `rel` can be *roll up, drill down* and *pan*. `rel` is used for resource APIs dynamic generation.

4.3 Data Package

To allow users to share and reuse the data exploration process, our data services adopt data package as a media type, which has an flexible and extensive data structure to include various data.

Figure 3 gives an overview of the data format of the extended data package, which may contain (1) **data** such as tables and files stored remotely in cloud storage or internally in the package. Data is classified into source data, result data, query data according to their purposes, (2) **scripts** processing and analyzing data, which are written by the data provider or generalized by the data service in any cross-platform languages like Python or Java, and (3) **metadata** describing the structure and the content of the package, as well as the relationship between the data and scripts and other data context information. Specifically, a metadata includes but not is limited to following properties:

- *Resources* describe and locate all packaged data. The descriptor could be in JSON or XML format while the paths could be a local path within a package (inline) or URLs pointing to remote storage (non-inline).
- *Scripts* indicate the location and purposes of data processing scripts on the datasets and specify the correlation among scripts and data. This property helps analysts specify what operations have been done on which datasets.

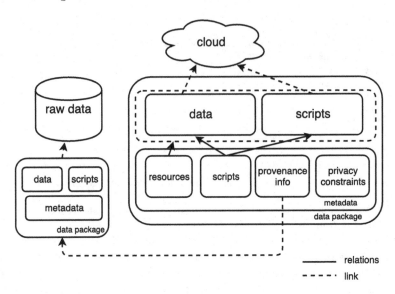

Fig. 3. Data package structure

- *Provenance information* is a sequence of links pointing to the previous data packages from which current package is generated. After acquiring a data package, analysts can modify the package content and create a new package. A *package chain* is formed when this activity is repeated. Analysts can trace the data usage back to the original dataset through the package chain.
- *Privacy constraints* record the privacy constraints imposed on the data in the package. When data providers apply privacy-enhancing techniques to generate anonymous data or expose their data partially, the operations they used to preserve data privacy are informed to analysts so that they can take corresponding tactics in their analysis.
- *Other descriptor* includes data schema, author, contributor, version, etc.

A simplified data package example in JSON is shown in Listing 1.3. The required properties are listed, others are omitted due to length limitation.

```
{       "name": "dataPackage",
        "id": "",
        "sources": [{
               "title":"hr-analytics dataset",
               "path": "https://www.example .com/datasets/hr-analytics"
        }],
        "resources": [{
               "path": "http:/www.example.com/hr-analytics.csv",
               "schema": "{...}"
        }],
        "scripts": [{
               "name": "retreive_good_employee_who_left",
               "path": "",
               "type": "python",
               "resources": ["good_employees_left", ".."]
```

```
    }],
    "provenanceLogs": [{
            "lastPackage": "",
            "created_in": "06/12/2017",
            "path": "http://example/HrAnalytics/dataPackage"
    }],
    "privacyLogs": [{
            "script_name": "",
            "description": ""
    }]}
```

Listing 1.3. A data package example

In our data service architecture, the data package acts two roles as below:

Data Package as a Resource. As introduced in Sect. 4.1, the *packager* can package data into a non-inline resource by a path pointing to the remote storage. Apart from the link to the data, the scripts inside the package also record the user's exploration process. Data package can be created through POST and retrieved through GET. The included data, scripts, and metadata can be acquired, updated and deleted by the HTTP methods (GET, PUT and DELETE).

Data Package as a Context Service. Data package provides provenance information, the upstream lineage, and the data constraints like privacy compliance policy. For example, data publisher can use a random value perturbation techniques to hide sensitive data by randomly modifying the data values using additive noise while preserving the underlying probabilistic properties of the dataset so that a predictive analysis can be performed. The metadata in the data package describes this manipulation and other privacy constraints so that data consumers are more informed on the assumptions of data for later analysis.

By using the packager resource and created packages, data providers can package and share the processed data with the scripts applied to the data. Due to the data package, data consumers can be more informed what happened to the data, and take more effective actions to do further analysis without preparing data from scratch.

5   Evaluation

We conducted a case study to do a comparative evaluation of the proposed data service design against the OData REST design. OData is an OASIS standard protocol that defines how to build the RESTful APIs for open data. Our evaluation focused on three metrics including REST maturity, interoperability, and discoverability.

5.1   Case Study

To exercise our design and validate its feasibility, we selected one dataset and related kernels (data processing scripts) from Kaggle[12], which is a public platform for data analytics community to explore and produce predictive models on

---

[12] https://www.kaggle.com/datasets.

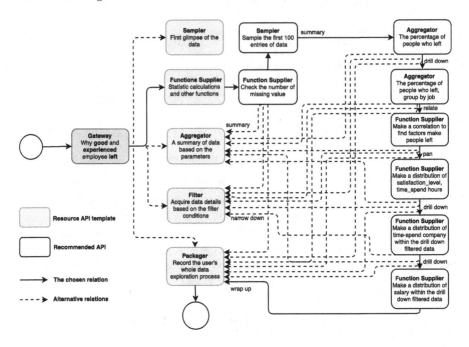

Fig. 4. HR analytics data exploration roadmap

the open datasets. The selected dataset is a Human Resource (HR) analytics dataset with 15000 rows.

Our RESTful APIs are implemented using Apache CXF JAX-RS in java. All the data returned are in JSON value. We simulated data exploration processes based on 8 published kernels on this HR dataset using our data service APIs.

Figure 4 shows the roadmap of one data retrieval process with the alternative relations and the resources. Based on the data exploration process, data analysts starts from *gateway* which responds with a list of resources to be selected. He starts his work from checking the data quality by the resource function supplier, which returns the numbers of missing values for the selected attributes, as well as links pointing to the *packager*, the *function supplier*, and the *aggregator*. Then the analyst sends a GET request to the *sampler* to retrieve a sample data, the returned response contains a defined size of data sample as well as links to other resources. Next, the analyst chooses *aggregator* to retrieve the summary information of the data.

In every step of the response, apart from a link pointing to the main resource API template, a specific API with predicted parameters will be recommended with an indicative **href** property. When the analyst makes a request of the percentage of left people, the response includes a *drill down* link pointing to a predicted *aggregator* API to group left people by their job. Afterward, the analyst can *pan* in the *function supplier* to gain other features of retrieved data until he is satisfied. Finally, the analyst moves to *filter* to retrieve the data of the best and most experienced employee who have left. Alternatively, he can send a POST request to *packager* which can wrap up the data with his previous operations. The data package created can be shared on any data sharing platform for the purpose of reusing result and process of the data exploration.

5.2 Analysis

Maturity. We applied the Richardson Maturity Model[13] to evaluate how well our data service APIs adhere to REST principles. This Model categorizes a RESTful Web service into three levels of maturity according to the degree of its adherence to REST principle. Level 1 and level 2 specify resources and the HTTP methods respectively. The highest level uses HATEOAS to discover the next possible actions towards the clients.

Compared with OData service APIs which fails at level 3 because there is no guidance for services to include links or self-documentation in response. Our approach follows HATEOAS to provide links in the message body to trigger state transition in the client application. For instance, a GET operation on the gateway resource returns a response body with a list of all resources that can be of interest to start interacting with. Based on the navigation model, data service can navigate the users through resources and perform the user-desired operations using hyperlinks. Thus, our data service APIs achieve the highest level of maturity of REST.

Interoperability. Interoperability refers to the ability not only to exchange information (syntactic interoperability) between two systems via interface but also to correctly interpret data being exchanged (semantic interoperability). The important aspects of interoperability involve discoverability of services and handling of response from service requestor [13]. The Levels of Conceptual Interoperability Model (LCIM) defines five levels of interoperability maturity. The lowest level signifies systems that do not share data at all. The highest level indicates systems that work together seamlessly without mistakes interpreting each other communication [14].

Most OData REST APIs achieve syntactic interoperability inherently because they provide uniform, standard, and stateless interface on top of HTTP. However, their semantic interoperability is not guaranteed due to their simple message format without containing any context information. Table 1 compares the OData service design and our Data Service from three aspects, including analytical operation, analytics process, and context information shared in the analytics pipeline at semantic level.

Our proposed data service API design enables semantic interoperability of REST-based application and so partially reaches the highest level of LCIM for data analytics in following two points:

---

[13] https://martinfowler.com/articles/richardsonMaturityModel.html.

Table 1. Comparison of information sharing at semantic level

	OData service	Our design
Analytics operation	• Mapping to the under-lying data schema	• Conforming to data analytic operations
Analytics process	• User driven • Manually constructing	• Define analytical relations in HATEOAS • Intelligent recommendation
Context information	• Manually collected by data users	• Package chain • Record data exploration process

Interpretation of Analytics Domain Operation. With the help of the navigation mechanism, which semantically interprets the underlying interactions in analytics process, a resource pointed by another known resource can be discovered by the users. Further, the navigation model provides the request with predictive parameters targeting users'requirement. As described in Sect. 5.1, an aggregator API to group the percentage of left employee by job can be recommended for client who requested the percentage of left employee.

Sharing of Data Context Information. The data package has a rich, extensive, and self-descriptive structure. A data package containing all the context information of analytics pipeline ensures the data consumers and data publishers have a common view of the requested services and data. The data package clearly shows the provenance information about when and what has been done by whom on the provided data and privacy information determining how, when and to what extent information about the provided data will be released to data users.

Discoverability. Discoverability means that when a service consumer requests a resource, it receives URLs pointing to the resources associated with the current resource in the response message. HATEOAS enables the discoverability of web services. However, it is difficult to discover a service automatically without specifying the semantics of operations in the response. Discovering services in services using conventional REST design is time-consuming and error-prone.

Our data service proposes a roadmap of data exploration that defines different relations in links property so that a service can be reached from different resources. In addition, we use HTTP OPTIONS to inform users what operations and parameters can be performed on the resource. The proposed data service design partially fill the semantic gap of HATEOAS. Our HATEOAS with semantics enables auto-discovery for applications and presents the services as a graph illustrated in Fig. 2.

The Discoverability makes it possible to automate service interactions. Compared with the general-purpose search API like Twitter REST API, our data service APIs automatically provide developers with a list of available endpoints along with information on how to interact with the endpoints.

Reusability. Reusability is the degree to which a component can be used in multiple business process or applications, without much overhead on configuration and modification. Data package, as a media type, can support reusable data and processing scripts. For example, when we GET and run the scripts that the data package created from HR data exploration process, we can reproduce the previous data operations. Given the same dataset and deterministic query, the result is identical to the old one. This proves that the data package can be reused and shared among analysts with the same data exploration purpose on the same dataset. In addition, since the data package is a light-weight data container that packages links to diverse data source and metadata, it will not cause big performance burden for client environment. The flexible and extensive data structure of data package allows users to customize their package based on their specific requirement, which further improves the reusability of the data package.

5.3 Discussion

The case study demonstrates that our data service satisfies the first requirement in Sect. 3 by supporting the data exploration processes from Kaggle using Python or R library. Second, the case study shows that our data service satisfies the second requirement and achieves better interoperability and discoverability compared with the existing solution. Last, the case study shows that using data package is an effective way to reuse and share the derived data and processing scripts among analysts, so the third requirement is satisfied.

6 Conclusion and Future Work

This paper proposes a REST-based data service API design, which specifies data retrieval interface targeting data analytics. Our approach takes advantage of REST properties and its related hypermedia-driven features to make resource APIs generate and navigate each other automatically based on analytical needs. In addition, we introduce a mechanism to package data source, primitive operations, and data context together for users to customize and reuse the data exploration process. Our evaluation shows that this approach can enhance the interoperability and discoverability of data services and the reusage of data exploration processes. Our future plans include an extension of the approach to accommodate multiple data sources, enhance service discovery. We also plan to conduct more user studies.

References

1. Jagadish, H., Gehrke, J., Labrinidis, A., Papakonstantinou, Y., Patel, J.M., Ramakrishnan, R., Shahabi, C.: Big data and its technical challenges. Commun. ACM **57**(7), 86–94 (2014)
2. Khan, H.A., Sharaf, M.A., Albarrak, A.: Divide: efficient diversification for interactive data exploration. In: Proceedings of the 26th International Conference on Scientific and Statistical Database Management. ACM (2014)

3. Idreos, S., Papaemmanouil, O., Chaudhuri, S.: Overview of data exploration techniques. In: Proceedings of the 2015 ACM SIGMOD International Conference on Management of Data, pp. 277–281. ACM (2015)
4. Borkar, V., Carey, M., Mangtani, N., McKinney, D., et al.: Xml data services. Int. J. Web Serv. Res. **3**(1), 85 (2006)
5. Dillon, S., Stahl, F., Vossen, G.: Towards the web in your pocket: curated data as a service. In: Nguyen, N., Trawiński, B., Katarzyniak, R., Jo, G.S. (eds.) Advanced Methods for Computational Collective Intelligence. Studies in Computational Intelligence, vol. 457, pp. 25–34. Springer, Heidelberg (2013). https://doi.org/10.1007/978-3-642-34300-1_3
6. Fielding, R.T.: Architectural styles and the design of network-based software architectures. University of California, Irvine Doctoral Dissertation (2000)
7. Wilde, E., Pautasso, C.: REST: From Research to Practice. Springer, New York (2011). https://doi.org/10.1007/978-1-4419-8303-9
8. Page, K.R., De Roure, D.C., Martinez, K.: Rest and linked data: a match made for domain driven development. In: Proceedings of the Second International Workshop on RESTful Design, pp. 22–25. ACM (2011)
9. Robinson, I.: RESTful Domain Application Protocols, pp. 61–91. Springer, New York (2011). https://doi.org/10.1007/978-1-4419-8303-9_3
10. Richardson, L., Amundsen, M., Ruby, S.: RESTful Web APIs: Services for a Changing World. O'Reilly Media, Inc. (2013)
11. Hernández, A.G., García, M.N.M.: Metadata Architecture in RESTful Design, pp. 459–471. Springer, New York (2011). https://doi.org/10.1007/978-1-4419-8303-9_21
12. Hellerstein, J.M., Sreekanti, V., Gonzalez, J.E., Dalton, J., Dey, A., Nag, S., Ramachandran, K., Arora, S., Bhattacharyya, A., Das, S., et al.: Ground: A data context service. In: CIDR (2017)
13. Clements, P.C.: Software architecture in practice. Diss. Software Engineering Institute (2002)
14. Tolk, A., Muguira, J.A.: The levels of conceptual interoperability model. In: Proceedings of the 2003 Fall Simulation Interoperability Workshop, vol. 7, pp. 1–11. Citeseer (2003)

Virtual Machine Profiling for Analyzing Resource Usage of Applications

Xuesong Peng, Barbara Pernici, and Monica Vitali[✉]

Politecnico di Milano, Piazza Leonardo da Vinci 32, 20133 Milano, Italy
monica.vitali@polimi.it

Abstract. From the cloud provider perspective, applications are usually black boxes hosted on Virtual Machines. Managing these black boxes without knowing anything about the features of the workload can generate inefficiencies in the performance. In fact, this information can be relevant to take deployment decisions which consist both in considering the interferences between applications with similar resources demands and predicting future peak demands avoiding performance degradation. Monitoring applications in cloud facilities and data centers is the only approach to manage and ensure the performance level of the hosted applications. This paper considers applications as black boxes and, using monitoring data analysis of the VMs on which applications are running, provides a methodology for building an application profile reflecting relevant behavioral features of a VM. This information is precious to lead deployment and adaptive decisions in data center management. The approach is validated on a real monitoring data set of an Italian data center.

Keywords: VM profile · Intensiveness · Periodicity
Applications resource usage · Data center

1 Introduction

Cloud computing helps achieving high-performance levels in enterprise applications for a potentially lower cost than traditional ways. Application deployed using the Infrastructure as a Service (IaaS) paradigm can take advantage of the scalability and agility of the cloud to meet variable workload demands and to improve overall availability. Most of the applications running in a cloud infrastructure are black boxes for the cloud provider, which is not aware of what the application does and doesn't have any clue on the expected behavior and resource demand. The only knowledge on the application is obtained by the configuration and monitoring of the Virtual Machines (VMs) hosting it. Taking decisions on application deployment and migration is not easy in this blind situation. In fact, deployment should take into consideration the resources required by the application and possible interferences with other applications hosted on the same physical machine. The lack of knowledge about the application behavior

© Springer International Publishing AG, part of Springer Nature 2018
J. E. Ferreira et al. (Eds.): SCC 2018, LNCS 10969, pp. 103–118, 2018.
https://doi.org/10.1007/978-3-319-94376-3_7

usually results in a waste of computational power: servers are usually under-loaded to avoid performance issues in case of a peak load. Currently, the cloud service model has been flanked by the edge paradigm, in which applications are executed as near as possible to the final customer or to where the data that they have to analyze are collected. This is possible as far as enough computational resources are available in such limited devices. In this context, knowing the expected behavior of an application is even more crucial than in the cloud scenario. In fact, a wrong decision can affect the experienced quality of service.

In this paper, we propose a methodology for building an application profile from the data collected by the monitoring system during the application execution on a VM. The aim of the profile is to capture the dynamic behavior and resources intensity of an application hosted on a monitored VM. Having this information can be helpful to attain several objectives: supporting deployment decisions, detecting anomalies, and classifying homogeneous VMs in terms of resource usage and patterns of usage in time. The profile proposed in this paper takes into consideration two main aspects: (i) *intensiveness* in resource usage of the VM and (ii) *periodicity* of the VM behavior. We base the analysis on monitoring data of typical indicators for data centers, extracting VMs profiles and developing techniques to analyze them.

The paper is structured as follows. In Sect. 2, we discuss related work on monitoring and profiling applications and virtual machines in data centers and on analyzing periodic behaviors in general. In Sect. 3, we outline the method for analyzing VM profiles, then detailing its steps in Sects. 4 and 5. Finally, in Sect. 6, we analyze in detail the characteristics of VMs in a real data center, exploiting the proposed VM profiles.

2   Related Work

The management of data centers is a complex task that is getting more and more challenging with the increase of the heterogeneity of both the infrastructure employed in most of the data centers (old and new generation servers) and of the applications hosted by the infrastructure. In order to provide a reliable management, the monitoring system plays a key role since it collects all the information needed to detect issues and to ensure the required performance levels. However, the big amount of data collected and its complexity can make this fundamental task difficult. In [1] the authors analyze the issue of cloud monitoring, focusing both on its challenges and its properties, stating the important role that monitoring systems have nowadays in such an environment. In [4], different cloud monitoring solutions are compared. Monitoring is often associated with data analytics since it enables the extraction of relevant information from the collected data. As described in [21], this task can be expensive and time-consuming and a trade-off between benefits and costs has to be analyzed. The issue of managing the big amount of monitoring data in a scalable way is faced in [7], where the authors propose an innovative data warehousing system for performance-related information. Monitoring information can be also addressed to improve the energy efficiency and the sustainability of clouds and data centers [16]. In projects like the European FP7 project $ECO_2Clouds$[1], the issue of sustainability has been managed with an adaptive approach basing decisions about application deployment on the data retrieved with the monitoring system [3,20]. Finally, in [5] the authors propose a method to optimize application deployment based on the maximization of the quality and completeness of information gathered by the monitoring system in a multi-cloud environment.

Many researches exploited the monitoring data to model the application, the VMs, and the physical machine behavior profile. In those profiles, multiple monitoring dimensions are involved, including mostly CPU, memory usage, IO, and network usage, and sometimes also power and temperature are considered for energy efficiency and thermal awareness [9,22]. Various metrics are carried out to measure specific properties. For instance, [15] measures average disk writes per second, [10] measures the percentage of CPU time occupied by the process of user state. Some work [8,14] use the profiles directly to estimate resources demands and support decision making, but other work try to go a step further. In [12], authors analyze sensitivity of VMs to cloud resources (CPU, Memory, and Storage) in order to profile the application behavior under intensive workloads. In [11], authors map the VM profile to an execution state space and use this to interpret state transitions of co-located VMs. A penalty-based profile matching algorithm (PPMA) is developed in [14] to obtain an assignment solution, which gives near-optimal allocations whilst satisfying energy-efficiency, resource utilization efficiency and application completion time constraints. The methodology is based on the strong assumption of a stable workload. Most research takes the profile as an instant screen shot of the system, rather than an aspect of self-repeatable and stable normality of the system. The authors of [23] exploit recurring patterns to estimate future resource consumption for VM consolidation. But their method assumes the behaviors of all VMs in all dimensions are 100% periodic, which is generally not true. Another focus of the VM behavior profile is to analyze the performance bottlenecks. For instance, the memory used in system buffers can help measuring memory intensiveness [2], the number of interrupts per second can help measuring CPU intensiveness [10], throughput can be used to evaluate the performance of applications [13]. These approaches analyze only simple benchmark applications under pre-defined workloads.

In this paper we claim that periodicity of VMs is a relevant information for data center management. The two most common used functions to measure periodicity of a signal are Periodogram and ACF (auto-correlation function). Periodogram function analyzes the signal in frequency domain using the Discrete Fourier Transforms (DFT). However, considering the increasing size of DFT, the resolution of Periodogram becomes very coarse for longer periods. Due to this reason, detecting large periods with Periodogram can be very inaccurate, sometimes false alarms are raised because of the absences of power in the DFT bin. ACF examines how similar a sequence x is to its shifted (lagged) copies for different t lags, calculating the auto-correlation with the sequence itself. In the

---

[1] http://eco2clouds.eu.

auto-correlation graphs, multiples of the same basic period also appear as peaks. Therefore, the method introduces many false alarms that need to be eliminated in a post-processing phase. As both functions have some deficiencies in detecting periodic behaviors of VM indicators in isolation, in the following of the paper we base our work on a fusion method of the two above-mentioned functions, which has been proposed by [17].

3   Profiling Methodology

In this section, we illustrate the proposed method for deriving and analyzing VM profiles in data centers. The methodology is illustrated in Fig. 1, which describes the process through which the monitoring data are transformed into VM profiles for single VMs and how the profiles are used to detect similarities between VMs. The figure shows the main data items and the connecting edges are labeled with the transformation steps. We assume to have a monitoring system able to collect information on the VMs behavior and store them in a monitoring database. To build the profile, we extract the raw data from this database for each of the VMs that we want to analyze.

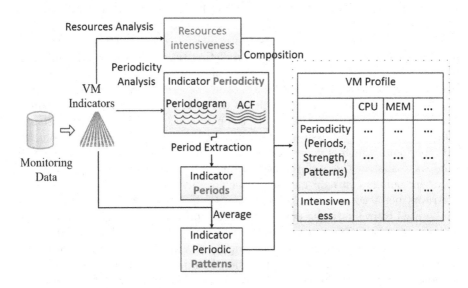

Fig. 1. Method for profiling VMs

Two parallel analyses are performed to build the profile: (i) *Resource intensiveness analysis* - the data collected through the monitoring system are analyzed in order to assess the intensiveness of the VM according to the resource consumption; (ii) *Indicator Periodicity* - collected data are used to assess if a periodic behavior in the resource usage of the VM can be detected. Combining together the characteristics analyzed above, we build a *VM profile* which describes resources characteristics *Intensiveness* and *Periodicity* of the VMs, for all relevant indicators. In the following, we illustrate the two steps for building the VM profile, analyzing the intensity of resources in Sect. 4, then defining periodicity in Sect. 5.

We study VMs through the performance indicators recorded by the monitoring system, and in particular, we focus on four indicators: (i) CPU, (ii) MEM, (iii) BW, and (iv) IO. These indicators are available in most monitoring systems and are generally used to analyze VMs in data centers [20]. We illustrate two examples of profile for two VMs, denoted as $A12$ and $C3$, in Fig. 2, which shows intensiveness and periodicity (with associated periods and strength) for the considered indicators. The periodicity contains also the patterns for the periodic indicators, as shown in Fig. 3 for the CPU weekly pattern of VM $C3$.

VM name		CPU	MEM	BW	IO
A12	PERIODS/STRENGTH(ACF)	1 day/0.66	1 day/0.31	-	0.3day/0.19
		-	-	-	7 days/0.28
	INTENSIVENESS	medium-intensive	non-intensive	non-intensive	medium-intensive
C3	PERIODS/STRENGTH(ACF)	1 day/0.64	1 day/0.15	1 day/0.73	1 day/0.73
		7 days/0.63	3.5 days/0.2	-	-
		-	7 days/0.7	-	-
	INTENSIVENESS	medium-intensive	non-intensive	medium-intensive	non-intensive

Fig. 2. Example profiles of two VMs

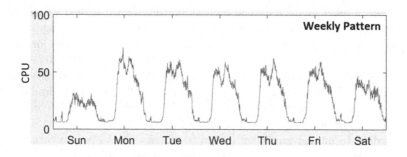

Fig. 3. CPU weekly pattern of VM C3

4 Profiling Intensity of Application Usage of Resources

In this section we discuss the methodology used to detect the intensiveness of applications according to their resource usage. The VM profile includes resources usage characteristics of VMs, in order to be able to identify the specific resources that can limit VM performances. The aim is to find relevant resources for the applications running on the VM, enabling us to prevent shortages of these resources and improve performance. Existing methods for detecting intensiveness are based on the knowledge of the applications running on the VMs. As an example, in [12] the authors provide a methodology to extract the profile systematically. The authors stress the different system components and, as a result, associate tags to the applications: CPU-intensive, MEM-intensive, disk-intensive, and so on.

If information about applications is not available, which is the case for our scenario, we can only mine the historical resource usage from monitoring data on VMs to derive the resource intensiveness. For each resource of a specific VM we propose three candidate metrics as follows:

- avg: the average resource usage of all the samples in the dataset;
- $p_{warning}$: the percentage of samples of a specific resource which exceed a given threshold $th_{warning}$;
- $p_{critical}$: the percentage of samples of a specific resource which exceed a given threshold $th_{critical}$.

The avg metric takes all samples into consideration while the $p_{warning}$ and $p_{critical}$ only consider stressful situations of the resource. Therefore, $p_{warning}$ and $p_{critical}$ focus on the crucial moments when a resource becomes a bottleneck for the VM performance. This is important for CPU and memory since the shortage of these resources might cause inefficiency and QoS failures in a very short time. To get appropriate thresholds for $th_{warning}$ and $th_{critical}$, we refer to the literature of data center management practice. The Data Center Maturity Model (DCMM) [6] is a reference to evaluate the maturity of individual data centers. It suggests best practice according to the level of maturity that the data center aims at achieving. The highest maturity level (called "Visionary"), which should be reached in the next five years, requires the average monthly CPU utilization above 60%. Another reference for setting thresholds for the VM CPU and memory usage is the VMware Knowledge Base [18, 19]. According to this source, the CPU is considered in a warning condition if its usage is above 75% and in an alarm condition if its usage is above 90% for 5 min. Similarly, the memory warning condition sets a threshold of 85%, while an alarm condition is detected if the resource usage is above 95% for 10 min.

According to intensiveness, we intend to classify the VMs into three groups (*intensive*, *medium-intensive*, and *non-intensive*), and also to define the conditions to place a VM in these groups. Since thresholds can change according to the specific scenario, we can choose thresholds for each resource starting from the thresholds values mentioned above. For the network bandwidth BW and IO, unlike for CPU and MEM, the immediacy of handling stress peaks is usually not emphasized in the literature, if only the VM can finish its work smoothly. Therefore, the intensiveness of BW and IO are mainly relying on the total resource demands, but not only on the stressful demands peaks. We will therefore base the intensiveness analysis on the average consumptions of VMs, grouping them in three groups with homogeneous characteristics, to define intensive, medium-intensive, and non-intensive characteristics. A detailed example of intensiveness analysis in a real data center can be found in the case study discussed in Sect. 6.1.

5 Profiling Application Periodicity

5.1 Identifying Periods

The goal of this step is to identify periods for the indicators. In real data centers, noises makes detecting the periodic behaviors of VMs a hard job. We exploit the mechanism described in [17] to filter insignificant periods of the VMs indicators, ensuring that we are analyzing VMs excluding noises. As discussed in Sect. 2, both ACF and Periodogram functions can examine periodic signals, but the detected period accuracy and the false positive rate could be a problem if we adopt these techniques separately, so, following their proposal, this work exploits both functions sequentially to identify the true and precise periods. Figure 4 illustrates the methodology which is proposed by [17]: first, the Periodogram is used to extract period candidates, and then ACF is applied to validate those candidates. More specifically, if the candidate period from the Periodogram lies on a hill of ACF, it can be inferred that a peak of ACF is nearby which confirms the validity of the period (*valid period*), otherwise, if the Periodogram falls in a valley of ACF it is discarded as a false alarm. Finally, the ACF peak nearer to the Periodogram position is taken as the true period, refining the candidate period.

In this step, we analyze the data gathered by the monitoring system for each VM in order to build the periodicity part of its profile. For each of the selected indicators, the periodicity is detected using the described approach. Figure 5 gives an example. The original data shows CPU usage of a VM in almost 100 days. We can observe obvious daily peaks and a weak weekly pattern. Thus we expect the periodicity to be 1 day and 7 days. In periodicity analysis, we focus on peaks of Periodogram which indicate their periodic strength, and select k candidate frequencies by filtering with their power and distances between them. For simplicity of the graph, we take $k = 3$ in this example. Then we map candidate frequencies to periods (namely, 0.3 days, 1 day and 7.2 days), and by verification of ACF, we take 1 day and 7.2 days as valid periods, but discard the 0.3 days as a false alarm because it is a valley in ACF diagram, according to the methodology of [17]. Following the procedure described above, we refine the 7.2 day period to the corresponding hill peak of ACF, namely, 7 days.

It is useful to analyze and compare behaviors characteristics of different indicators. Referring to Fig. 2, we see that for VM A12 most of the indicators are periodic, except for bandwidth. However, the periods are different: CPU and memory have daily periods, while IO has a weekly period.

5.2 Establishing Periodic Patterns

Detecting periodicity of a VM is not enough to represent its behavior. For having a deeper knowledge it is also important to represent how the VM behaves

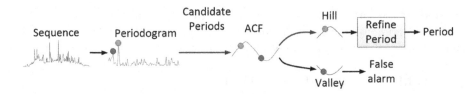

Fig. 4. Period Detection methodology [17]

in this periods according to resources demands. Each valid period, identified in the previous step, corresponds to a periodic behavior of a VM indicator, namely, a *pattern*, which repeats itself through the considered time interval for the analyzed VM. For instance, as a result of human activities characteristics, most applications on the cloud have daily, weekly, or yearly workloads patterns (although other periods can be significant in some cases), so that we can find these patterns on most VM indicators. The pattern is essential to understand VM behavior and it provides the possibility to predict and optimize VM resources demands in data centers.

Once the relevant periods for each indicator of a VM have been detected, we can move to the analysis of the periodic behavior by considering the raw data. The goal is to build a typical shape for the considered signal. In order to do so, the continuous indicators are first cut into several segments, where each segment is as long as the refined period, representing an instance of the repeating behavior. Then for every time stamp in this period, we take the average of all instances to construct a pattern describing usual behavior in this period. Taking the VM in Fig. 5 as an example, we build the weekly pattern and observe clear differences between workdays and weekends, as Fig. 3 depicts.

6   Profiling of Virtual Machines in a Real Data Center

In the previous sections, we illustrated the method to derive application profiles, and in this section, we derive and analyze the profiles to understand behaviors of VMs in a data center using a private cloud. The considered dataset, from a real data center of a telecommunication company in Italy, consists of the monitoring data of 304 VMs, and all indicators were sampled simultaneously with a sampling interval of 5 min. The indicators include the usage of multiple resources of VMs and hosts, covering CPU, memory, bandwidth and I/O, and so on. On the other hand, the dataset contains no information about the applications so that we do not know what kind of applications are running on the VMs and what is the performance of the applications. The data used in this paper cover the period of 3 months. All the steps of the profiling method discussed in Sects. 4 and 5 are validated with this dataset.

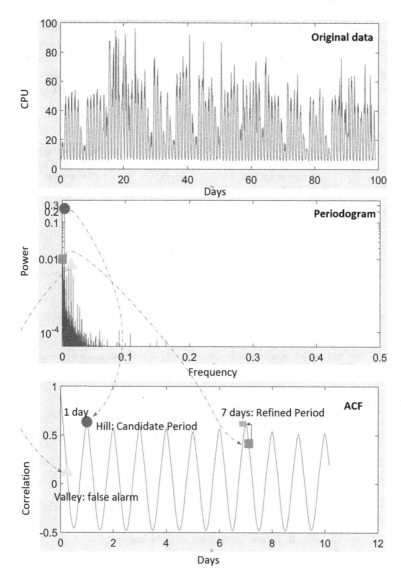

Fig. 5. Detecting periods of CPU for VM C3

6.1 Intensiveness Validation

Using the available historical monitoring data of the real data center, we have analyzed the intensiveness of resource usage for each VM considering the four main resources: CPU, memory, bandwidth, and IO. The results of the analysis are shown in Fig. 6 in which on the x-axis we represented each VM in the test bed (with the VMs arranged in a descending order) and on the y-axis we draw the normalized value of the metrics of the VM. As already discussed in Sect. 4, the average value is the only information used for evaluating the intensiveness of the VMs for the bandwidth and IO metric, while the $p_{critical}$ and $p_{warning}$ metrics are used for CPU and memory. To analyze our dataset, we applied the thresholds for CPU and memory intensiveness indicated by VMware [18,19] as a starting point. Thresholds are set as follows: (i) $th_{warning}(\text{CPU}) = 75\%$; (ii) $th_{critical}(\text{CPU}) = 90\%$; (iii) $th_{warning}$ (MEM) $= 85\%$; (iv) $th_{critical}(\text{MEM}) = 95\%$.

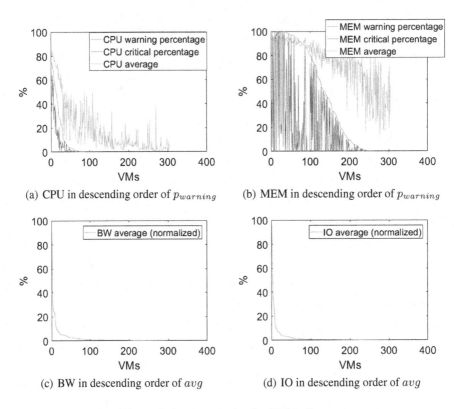

(a) CPU in descending order of $p_{warning}$ (b) MEM in descending order of $p_{warning}$

(c) BW in descending order of avg (d) IO in descending order of avg

Fig. 6. Intensive metrics for VM indicators

Looking at the results shown in Fig. 6, we classified the VMs into three groups, namely, intensive VMs, medium-intensive VMs, and non-intensive VMs. According to the values of the four metrics, we identify the conditions of groups for each of them. Considering the CPU usage, only the VMs for which $p_{warning}(CPU) > 10\%$ are classified as CPU-intensive, because the average CPU usage of this group of VMs is significantly higher (e.g., the $avg(CPU)$ is mostly larger than 50% for this group). VMs are considered non-intensive in relation to CPU if they never exceed the warning threshold ($p_{warning}(CPU) = 0\%$). This group contains the most of the VMs analyzed and they are characterized by a low average CPU consumption (most of these VMs have $avg(CPU) < 30\%$).

Finally, other VMs with $0\% < p_{warning}(CPU) \leq 10\%$ are classified as medium-intensive in CPU usage. Thus, we have defined the conditions of CPU intensiveness over the metric $p_{warning}$. As an alternative to exploiting only $p_{warning}$ to classify the groups, we also considered to use the values for $p_{critical}$ and avg to build alternative conditions (e.g., a VM is intensive if $p_{critical}(CPU) > 10\%$ and $avg(CPU) > 60\%$). We choose $p_{warning}$ because it is a mixture of the other two metrics, and its behavior is more suitable to classify VMs into the 3 intensiveness groups. Similarly, observing Fig. 6(b) we selected as threshold for memory intensiveness $p_{warning}(MEM) > 90\%$. As a result of this threshold, we classified 75 VMs as memory intensive, since they exceed this threshold for most of their lifetime. We also classified as non-intensive memory group the VMs with $p_{warning}(MEM) \leq 10\%$, since their average consumption of MEM is generally below 80% and they seldom exceed the warning threshold. As a result, medium-intensive VMs for memory are the VMs with $10\% < p_{warning}(MEM) \leq 90\%$. As discussed in Sect. 4, we use only avg to evaluate intensiveness for IO and bandwidth. As shown in Fig. 6(c) and (d), most VMs use the network and IO rarely, only a small number of VMs use the network or IO occasionally, and some of them use the network or IO extremely frequently. Based on the shape of avg we define the thresholds for CPU, MEM, IO, and BW as in Table 1.

Table 1. Conditions of resource intensiveness groups

	CPU	MEM	BW	IO
Intensive	$p_{warning} > 10\%$	$p_{warning} > 90\%$	$avg > 2\%$	$avg > 2\%$
Medium-intensive	$0\% < p_{warning} \leq 10\%$	$10\% < p_{warning} \leq 90\%$	$0.6\% < avg \leq 2\%$	$0.4\% < avg \leq 2\%$
Non-intensive	$p_{warning} = 0\%$	$p_{warning} \leq 10\%$	$avg \leq 0.6\%$	$avg \leq 0.4\%$

Using the discovered thresholds, it is possible to detect the intensiveness of each VM in the dataset. As an example, for the two VMs considered in Fig. 2, we evaluated the intensiveness metrics and derived intensiveness as shown in Table 2

Table 2. Intensiveness of two VMs

VM id	A12				C3			
Metric	Intens.	p_warning	p_critical	avg	Intens.	p_warning	p_critical	avg
CPU	not-int	0.04%	0.03%	28.77%	medium	4.07%	1.58%	26.38%
MEM	non-int	4.40%	1.83%	74.05%	non-int	9.28%	0.00%	78.71%
BW	non-int	–	–	0.48%	medium	–	–	0.96%
IO	medium	–	–	0.83%	non-int	–	–	0.38%

6.2   Analysis of Application Periodicity

The second step for building the profile of a VM consists in evaluating the VM periodicity. We computed the periodicity profiles of VMs in the data center as illustrated in Sect. 4. As a result, we detected that: (i) 275 VMs have some CPU-periodic behavior; (ii) 278 VMs have some memory-periodic behavior; (iii) 223 VMs have some BW-periodic behavior; (iv) 227 VMs have some IO-periodic behavior. Using the periodicity profiles, we can also extract a general overview of the VMs periodicity of the data center, summarizing the occurrence of periods for each indicator and showing the distribution of periods for each indicator as shown in Fig. 7. For an easier comparison of the different cases, the number of occurrences is given in terms of percentages in the figure.

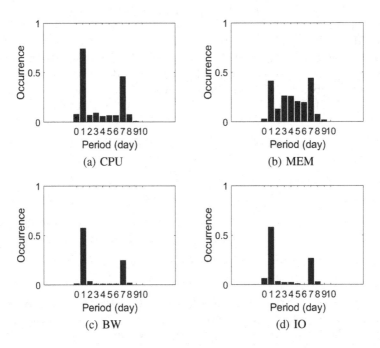

Fig. 7. Period occurrences (normalized) over four indicators

The two most common periods for all indicators are the daily period and weekly period, this conforms to the reality as most application workloads are daily or weekly periodic. It can also be noticed that periodicity varies for different indicators. From the IO perspective, more than half of VMs have a daily period, and more than 25% of VMs are weekly periodic. This characteristic may relate to the daily/weekly dumps of some applications (in this case we see peaks of high values for BW/IO weekly, for a short time, and mainly in the weekend and at night). The BW of the data center is very similar to the IO behavior: This similarity can be explained because most IO activities generate or are generated by network transmissions. The CPU periodicity is also strong, with almost 70%

of the VMs with a daily and 50% with a weekly periods. However, the MEM behaves differently: the daily/weekly periods are no longer stand-out compared to others. The possible reason might be that the memory demands of most applications are generally very static and the periodicities are not significant.

6.3 Relating VMs Behavior to VM Profiles

We analyze the behavior of the profiles of the 304 VMs of the analyzed data center, and we compare periodicity characteristics with the intensity of resources. We have also analyzed the correlation between the resource intensiveness and the VMs migrations observed in the data center[2].

Periodicity and Resource Usage Relation. In this section, we analyze the characteristics of resources consumption on both periodicity and intensiveness, and try to find if there is a relation between them. We calculate the percentage of VMs that are daily-periodic and the percentage of VMs that are intensive for certain resources, as Fig. 8 depicts. The percentage of VMs having a daily periodicity is very high in this data center, especially for CPU, where more than 70% of VMs are daily periodic. The overall resource intensiveness in the data center is limited (below 30% for all the resources). The most intensive resource is memory. As can be observed, there isn't a strong relation between intensiveness and periodicity for a given resource. A possible reason could be that the periodic behaviors are easier to predict thus the administrator can prevent the intensive situations better compared to the non-periodic behaviors.

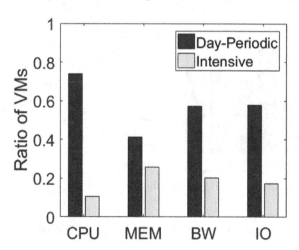

Fig. 8. Resources usage characteristics of the data center

We have also analyzed the combined characteristics of multiple resources, for both periodicity and intensiveness. For the sake of brevity, we focused on CPU

---

[2] Information on migrations is available in the monitoring data of the data center.

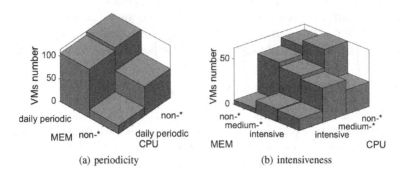

(a) periodicity   (b) intensiveness

Fig. 9. Periodicity and intensiveness situations over CPU and MEM

and memory. Figure 9 depicts the relation between CPU and memory periodicity and intensiveness. As can be observed in Fig. 9(b), most VMs are either non-intensive to CPU or non-intensive to MEM, only 13 VMs are intensive for both CPU and MEM. This may help us to understand the critical situations in the data center, and the administrator needs to be careful with those 13 VMs.

Impact of Resource Intensiveness on VM Migration. In data centers, moving VMs between different physical servers is common practice, which can improve the total efficiency of resources utilization and decrease power consumption. Usually, a VM is moved to a new host in two situations: (i) the server hosting the VM is overused; (ii) the server hosting the VM is underused.

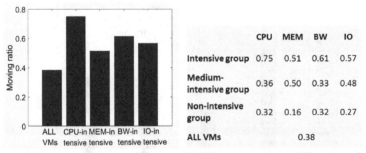

	CPU	MEM	BW	IO
Intensive group	0.75	0.51	0.61	0.57
Medium-intensive group	0.36	0.50	0.33	0.48
Non-intensive group	0.32	0.16	0.32	0.27
ALL VMs		0.38		

(a) VMs movements for intensive groups   (b) VMs movements for different intensiveness groups

Fig. 10. Impact of resource intensiveness on VM migration

In order to validate our intensiveness metric, we extracted the events of VM movements from the dataset, and analyze the relations between the VM migrations and its resource intensiveness. Figure 10(a) depicts the percentage of VMs migrated grouped for intensive resource. As can be seen in the first column, most VMs (more than 60%) have never been migrated during the analyzed period of 3 months. However, the intensive VMs have a higher probability to be migrated, regardless of which is the intensive resource. The CPU intensiveness is the most important factor for VM movements: 75% of CPU-intensive VMs have been migrated at least once in this period. A more detailed analysis is summarized in Fig. 10(b).

7   Conclusions and Future Work

This paper introduced a systematic method to build profiles of VMs in data centers, focusing on their resource intensiveness characteristics and on their periodic behavior. In the paper, we have defined a VM profile as composed of two main part: (i) the resource intensiveness in which for each resource (CPU, memory, bandwidth, IO) the level of intensiveness has been evaluated, and (ii) the resource periodicity in which the periodic behavior of each resource is analyzed and described. Applying the methodology for building the profile of VMs to the monitoring data of a real data center, we have demonstrated that the intensity of resource usage and periodicity are important features in the identification of a VM profile. We have also discussed the relationships between intensity and periodicity and the relationship between intensity and VM migration decision in the studied date set, retrieving that intensive use of resources, especially CPU, can be a driver for migration.

In future work we envision to exploit the VM profile for further analysis tasks, such as resource planning, enabling better VM placements and migrations, anomaly detection, and to support the analysis of the periodicity of bursts.

Acknowledgments. The authors thank the company Eco4Cloud (http://www.eco4cloud.com.) for sharing monitoring data for the purpose of this analysis.

References

1. Aceto, G., Botta, A., De Donato, W., Pescapè, A.: Cloud monitoring: a survey. Comput. Netw. **57**(9), 2093–2115 (2013)
2. Awasthi, M., Suri, T., Guz, Z., Shayesteh, A., Ghosh, M., Balakrishnan, V.: System-level characterization of datacenter applications. In: Proceedings of the 6th ACM/SPEC International Conference on Performance Engineering, Austin, TX, USA, 31 January–4 February, 2015, pp. 27–38 (2015)
3. Cappiello, C., Ho, T.T.N., Pernici, B., Plebani, P., Vitali, M.: CO_2-aware adaptation strategies for cloud applicationDs. IEEE Trans. Cloud Comput. **4**(2), 152–165 (2016)
4. Da Cunha Rodrigues, G., Calheiros, R.N., Guimaraes, V.T., d. Santos, G.L., de Carvalho, M.B., Granville, L.Z., Tarouco, L.M.R., Buyya, R.: Monitoring of cloud computing environments: concepts, solutions, trends, and future directions. In: Proceedings of the 31st Annual ACM Symposium on Applied Computing, pp. 378–383. ACM (2016)
5. Fadda, E., Plebani, P., Vitali, M.: Optimizing monitorability of multi-cloud applications. In: Nurcan, S., Soffer, P., Bajec, M., Eder, J. (eds.) CAiSE 2016. LNCS, vol. 9694, pp. 411–426. Springer, Cham (2016). https://doi.org/10.1007/978-3-319-39696-5_25

6. Huusko, J., de Meer, H., Klingert, S., Somov, A. (eds.): E2DC 2012. LNCS, vol. 7396. Springer, Heidelberg (2012). https://doi.org/10.1007/978-3-642-33645-4

7. Loboz, C., Smyl, S., Nath, S.: Datagarage: warehousing massive performance data on commodity servers. Proc. VLDB Endow. **3**(1–2), 1447–1458 (2010)

8. Moreno, I.S., Yang, R., Xu, J., Wo, T.: Improved energy-efficiency in cloud data-centers with interference-aware virtual machine placement. In: 11th International Symposium on Autonomous Decentralized Systems, ISADS 2013, Mexico City, Mexico, 6–8 March 2013, pp. 1–8 (2013)

9. Nasim, R., Taheri, J., Kassler, A.J.: Optimizing virtual machine consolidation in virtualized datacenters using resource sensitivity. In: 2016 IEEE International Conference on Cloud Computing Technology and Science, CloudCom 2016, Luxembourg, 12–15 December 2016, pp. 168–175 (2016)

10. Peng, J., Chen, J., Zhi, X., Qiu, M., Xie, X.: Research on application classification method in cloud computing environment. J. Supercomput. **73**(8), 3488–3507 (2017)

11. Rameshan, N., Navarro, L., Monte, E., Vlassov, V.: Stay-Away, protecting sensitive applications from performance interference. In: Proceedings of the 15th International Middleware Conference, Bordeaux, France, 8–12 December 2014, pp. 301–312 (2014)

12. Taheri, J., Zomaya, A.Y., Kassler, A.: vmBBThrPred: a black-box throughput predictor for virtual machines in cloud environments. In: Aiello, M., Johnsen, E.B., Dustdar, S., Georgievski, I. (eds.) ESOCC 2016. LNCS, vol. 9846, pp. 18–33. Springer, Cham (2016). https://doi.org/10.1007/978-3-319-44482-6_2

13. Taheri, J., Zomaya, A.Y., Kassler, A.: vmBBProfiler: a black-box profiling approach to quantify sensitivity of virtual machines to shared cloud resources. Computing **99**(12), 1149–1177 (2017)

14. Vasudevan, M., Tian, Y., Tang, M., Kozan, E.: Profile-based application assignment for greener and more energy-efficient data centers. Future Gener. Comp. Syst. **67**, 94–108 (2017)

15. Verboven, S., Vanmechelen, K., Broeckhove, J.: Black box scheduling for resource intensive virtual machine workloads with interference models. Future Gener. Comp. Syst. **29**(8), 1871–1884 (2013)

16. Vitali, M., Pernici, B.: A survey on energy efficiency in information systems. Int. J. Coop. Inf. Syst. **23**(3), 1450001 (2014)

17. Vlachos, M., Philip, S.Y., Castelli, V.: On periodicity detection and structural periodic similarity. In: SDM, vol. 5, pp. 449–460. SIAM (2005)

18. VMware Knowledge Base. Virtual machine CPU usage alarm (2015)

19. VMware Knowledge Base. Virtual machine memory usage alarm (2015)

20. Wajid, U., Cappiello, C., Plebani, P., Pernici, B., Mehandjiev, N., Vitali, M., Gienger, M., Kavoussanakis, K., Margery, D., García-Pérez, D., Sampaio, P.: On achieving energy efficiency and reducing CO_2 footprint in cloud computing. IEEE Trans. Cloud Comput. **4**(2), 138–151 (2016)

21. Wang, C., Schwan, K., Talwar, V., Eisenhauer, G., Hu, L., Wolf, M.: A flexible architecture integrating monitoring and analytics for managing large-scale data centers. In: Proceedings of the 8th ACM International Conference on Autonomic Computing, ICAC 2011, pp. 141–150 (2011)

22. Wang, L., Khan, S.U., Dayal, J.: Thermal aware workload placement with task-temperature profiles in a data center. J. Supercomput. **61**(3), 780–803 (2012)

23. Wolke, A.: Energy efficient capacity management in virtualized data centers. Ph.D. thesis, Technical University Munich (2015)

Configurable IoT-Aware Allocation in Business Processes

Kunal Suri[1,2(✉)], Walid Gaaloul[2], and Arnaud Cuccuru[1]

[1] CEA, LIST, LIDEO, P.C. 174, Gif-sur-Yvette, France
{kunal.suri,arnaud.cuccuru}@cea.fr
[2] TELECOM Sudparis, SAMOVAR UMR 5157,
Université Paris-Saclay, Evry, France
walid.gaaloul@telecom-sudparis.eu

Abstract. Based on specific requirements, various Internet of Things (IoT) devices participate in multiple cross-organizational business processes. However, to achieve the desired business value, these IoT resources must be managed efficiently. Configurable Process Model (CPM) facilitates flexibility and reuse by sharing a family of process variants, which can be customized based on concrete business requirements. The classical approaches to develop CPMs focus mainly on the control-flow perspective, without providing concepts to tackle the complexity involved in the IoT domain. In this paper, we address this research gap by proposing configuration concepts for modeling IoT resource variability, which arises due to specific resource properties and behavior such as Replication and Shareability, at the CPM level. Furthermore, we validate our approach based on the results of our experimentation and demonstrate its feasibility through an implemented prototype.

Keywords: Internet of Things · Business Process Management
Configurable Process Model · Resource management
Retail management

1 Introduction

Recent years have witnessed a tremendous growth in the use of interconnected heterogeneous devices. These devices can be broadly classified into *Sensors*, *Actuators* and *Tags* (such as Radio Frequency Identification (RFID)). They enable sensing, actuating (or re-acting) and exchanging or collection of data through a communicating network such as the internet, thus creating the Internet of Things (IoT) [5]. Each of these devices perform a specific task to generate some value for an end user (or system). Further, they are considered as key technology enablers to bring the concept of "Smart Environments" such as smart cities, smart logistics, Industry 4.0, closer to reality. Moreover, in a real-world situation, one or more of such heterogeneous devices need to be orchestrated in a specific sequence to achieve a specific outcome. In fact, many organizations

© Springer International Publishing AG, part of Springer Nature 2018
J. E. Ferreira et al. (Eds.): SCC 2018, LNCS 10969, pp. 119–136, 2018.
https://doi.org/10.1007/978-3-319-94376-3_8

already use Process-Aware Information Systems (PAIS) [1], which efficiently manage and executes (orchestrates) various enterprise services and resources such as human-workforce and systems on the basis of process models, to provide the best return on investment [22]. Thus, it is natural to see these devices allocated to one or more business processes (BPs), which spreads across time, space (geographic location) and organizations, for being orchestrated in a specific order, to achieve some predefined business goals.

To optimally manage processes involving resources, i.e., both human and non-human (devices and systems), these PAIS need to become resource-aware [6] and evolve into *Process- and IoT-Aware Information Systems*. Thus, realizing the importance of IoT resource management in Business Process Management (BPM), there has been a growing trend on research towards integration of IoT and BPM domain [20,23]. Even though these works focus on integrating IoT concepts at an individual process variant level, they are relevant to facilitate optimal management of IoT resources involved in BPs.

In another side, the rapidly changing business requirements, customer needs or government regulations (in context of smart ecosystems) forces these PAIS to imbibe the traits of flexibility and reuse. In other words, these systems must facilitate the "Principle of Reuse" for modeling and/or (re-)designing the processes by taking into consideration the preexisting knowledge about similar processes and/or best practices existing in an organization, rather than forcing analysts to design processes "from scratch". In order to support the flexibility and reusability for modeling BPs, our work focuses on using Configurable Process Model (**CPM**) [21], which is an active area of research for managing process variability in BPM domain [17]. A CPM consolidates various process variants (multiple process solutions) into one customizable process model via variation points called *configurable elements* (activity or gateways) [11]. In other words, a consolidated customizable model captures a family of process variants. This helps to avoid redundancy and allows improvements efforts made on one variant to benefit other variants. Moreover, the classical approaches to develop a CPM focuses mainly on configuring the *control-flow perspective* [17], without giving much consideration to the resource perspective. Additionally, the limited proposals that do consider the extension of configuration to resources [13–15], are too generic to tackle the complexity and specificity involved in the IoT domain (i.e., IoT specific features (properties), constraints, and deployment strategies). Indeed, even though the concepts of configurable process modeling being highly complementary to IoT, to the best of our knowledge there has not been any uptake in this area.

In this paper, we address this research gap by proposing configuration concepts for modeling IoT resource variability, which arises due to specific resource features, i.e., properties and behavior such as Replication and Shareability, at the CPM level. Concretely, we define a novel approach for developing CPMs with *Configurable IoT Resource Allocation* operators. This allows inclusion of explicit knowledge (options/variability) about various alternatives and constraints that exists for a typical IoT resource based on its behavior. These IoT-aware CPM can be individualized into a process variant via transformations including both,

(i) the control-flow perspective, and (ii) IoT resource perspective, to meet a given set of business requirements. Further, we developed a proof of concept tool to illustrate the feasibility of our work and assist the development of conceptual models for configurable IoT-aware processes, intended for communication and analysis purposes. To demonstrate the effectiveness of our approach, we evaluate it on a CPM developed for the Retail industry.

The remainder of this paper is organized as follows: in Sect. 2, some basic concepts related to CPM and IoT are detailed. In Sect. 3, a use-case from Retail/Logistics domain is used to motivate our research. The Sect. 4, details the need for modeling IoT resource perspective in BPs. In Sect. 5, describes our approach to model configurable IoT-aware allocation. In Sect. 6, we detail our implemented proof of concept and evaluation results from the experimentation. In Sect. 7, we describe related work, and in Sect. 8, we conclude our work and provide a perspective on our future work.

2   Preliminaries

This section presents the preliminaries used in the remainder of this paper. In Sect. 2.1, we detail concepts related to configurable process modeling, and in Sect. 2.2, we detail key concepts from IoT domain.

2.1   Configurable Process Modeling

A Configurable Process Model (CPM) is an integrated representation of a family of processes in a given domain [21]. It uses variation points (configurable elements) to capture the differences among the process variants (similar to techniques from Software Product Line Engineering) [17]. It maintains a clear distinction between the *commonalities* (i.e., parts shared by all process variants) and *variability* (i.e., parts specific to certain process variants) in a process family. These modeling techniques allows sharing of knowledge and best-practices, which enables analysts to develop processes based on various guidance and rules (options) provided in these models (at design-time) [17,21]. In literature, various languages exist for modeling configurable processes such as configurable Event-driven Process Chains (C-EPCs), UML Activity Diagrams (ADs), configurable Business Process Model and Notation (**c-BPMN**) [17].

In our work we use c-BPMN as it is based on extending BPMN, which is the most popular modeling language in both academia and industry [3]. In c-BPMN, the configurable elements, i.e., activities and gateways are modeled with a thick line. These elements can be included, i.e., configured to *ON* or excluded, i.e., configured to *OFF*, depending on the specific business requirements. Likewise, a configurable gateway has a generic behavior that is restricted by its configuration. Depending on the type of the gateway, it can be configured by, (i) changing its type while preserving its behavior and/or, (ii) restricting its incoming and outgoing branches [21]. Moreover, after choosing the configurable elements, specific variants can be derived by removing the excluded nodes and edges based on algorithms such as presented in [3, 21]. For instance, Fig. 1 represents a CPM modeled using c-BPMN. In this CPM, the activity $a2$ and $a3$ are configurable, i.e., they can be configured either to ON (to keep it in the model) or to OFF (to exclude it) in the derived process variant. Similarly, the configurable OR (see ORc-2 in Fig. 1) can be configured to any type of gateway (i.e., OR, XOR, AND), while a configurable AND (AND^c) can be only configured to an AND gateway. Using this CPM, a retailer can proficiently diffuse their process expertise and knowledge with their conglomerates. Furthermore, this type of variability management technique tackles only the control-flow perspective, without dealing with the complexity and constraints involved in the resource perspective, especially from the IoT domain.

2.2   Internet of Things (IoT)

IoT comprises of connected devices such as Sensor, Actuators, Tags (e.g. RFID), which supports the creation of an smart (intelligent) environment. This intelligence when applied for making successful inferences offers a huge potential to change everyday life. Additionally, it allows decision makers to have superior transparency and value-added understanding of their complete product life-cycle. However, to efficiently consume and manage deployed IoT resources, there is an evident need to grasp the fundamental concepts in IoT such as topology of network, power usage, bandwidth, intermittent connectivity [5] along with the underlying infrastructure, i.e., Cloud, Fog or Edge computing [18], used for deployment and management of the IoT devices.

Some of these concepts are: (i) *Power Usage*: Devices consume considerable amount of power while transmitting data, particularly over long ranges. (ii) *Bandwidth*: The rate of data transmission depends on the capacity of the network, and parameters such as volume of data (raw or aggregated), number of devices, connectivity (constant stream or intermittent bursts of data), packet size of the networking protocol, to name a few. (iii) *Intermittent Connectivity*: To conserve power and bandwidth, devices connect and transmit data periodically (rather than continuously). However, other situations such as an unreliable network or issues with the quality of service (e.g., interference on a wireless network using a shared spectrum), hamper the connectivity.

Thus, the efficient use of IoT resources calls for inclusion of such information in the process models (at design-time). This will ensure proper usage, deployment and management of IoT resources during the deployment phase.

3   Motivating Example

We motivate our research through a CPM (see Fig. 1), which represents a process family from the Retail/Supply Chain Management domain. We considered this domain as various processes executing in the Retail industry effect the day-to-day life of a large number of people. Moreover, we developed this CPM using c-BPMN by adapting and merging (consolidating) a collection of model description from the "IoT in Practice:Examples" [9] based on algorithms presented in [4,16]. The process models in [9] focus on the application of IoT in various processes and were used in the European FP7 project, *Internet of Things Architecture* (IoT-A[1]). Overall, this CPM will assist retailers to share their process knowledge and policies (rules and constraints) in a reusable and customizable manner with their affiliates spread across the globe. The CPM in Fig. 1 represents a family of process variants (control-flow perspective) for monitoring items involved in the Retail industry that fall in two main categories: (i) *fast-moving consumer goods* (FMCG) such as vegetables, cheese, flowers, and (ii) *durable goods* such as electric appliances, cars, clothes. This process can start based on a timer event for enabling periodic monitoring of goods. After the process starts, there are two possibilities represented by two sub-processes interconnected via a configurable *XOR* gateway (*XORc-1*). The sub-process I should be employed to monitor an item from FMCG category, while the sub-process II should be used for durable goods.

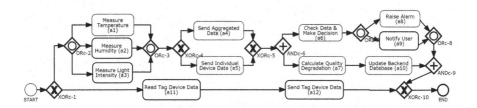

Fig. 1. Configurable process model from retail management domain

To demonstrate the need of including IoT-resource perspective at CPM level, we first describe a process variant (*Variant-1*) derived from the CPM based only on the control-flow perspective. Next, we show how including the IoT resource perspective increases the complexity of this process variant. Let us assume that a French retailer (such as Carrefour) at a location A, decides to individualize the CPM to include only a temperature monitoring step for a perishable item such as *Chinese Orchids* (adapted from [23]). Thus, at the design-time an expert will customize the CPM into a process variant, i.e., Variant-1 represented via Fig. 2. The Variant-1 is configured to include activities $a1$, $a5$, $a6$, $a7$, $a8$, $a10$. Moreover, the derivation (individualization) of a process variant based on the classical control-flow perspective is done by removing the unwanted nodes (detailed in Sect. 2.1). Nonetheless, for efficient resource management, there is a need to capture explicit knowledge about the IoT resources (i.e., IoT properties, behavior and deployment strategies) in the process models at the variant level (detailed in our previous work [23]). For instance, based on some business needs, the activity $a1$ needs a *digital temperature sensor* having high-accuracy, i.e., Accuracy of $\pm0.5\,°C$ (max) from $0\,°C$ to $+65\,°C$ (e.g., a TMP112[2] sensor

---

[1] IoT-A project: http://cordis.europa.eu/project/rcn/95713_en.html.

[2] TI's TMP112 - http://www.ti.com/lit/ds/symlink/tmp112.pdf.

from Texas Instruments (TI)). Additionally, during deployment this device will need a network resource, i.e., *Network-01*, which should be long range, consumes lower power and allows secure data transmission such as Low Power Wide Area Network (LPWAN) based LoRaWAN[3]. Further, this resource can be deployed on a public cloud infrastructure. All these parameters and information depict the IoT specific features, i.e., *Resource Properties*, which should be included in the process models.

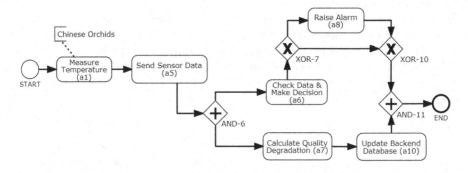

Fig. 2. Process variant 1 derived from Fig. 1 based on control-flow perspective

In Fig. 3, we use the Variant-1 and enrich it with information about the IoT resource features in form of text annotations. Likewise, IoT resource have specific *Resource Behavior* that should be included in the process models. For instance, a device and the network can be *Shareable*, i.e., it shall share its data using publish/subscribe (pub-sub) middleware, e.g., Eclipse Mosquitto[4]. Additionally, the activity $a1$ can be connected to more than one temperature sensor provided they exhibit similar capability, i.e., aggregation of a set of similar physical devices via a logical interface. This results in improvement of availability, fault-tolerance, and helps to achieve higher *Quality of Information (QoI)* [19] (detailed in Sect. 4). These Resource Behavior are also included as text annotation as observable in the Fig. 3.

Likewise, another Carrefour market (let say at a location B), decides to individualize the CPM (in Fig. 1) into another process variant, i.e., *Variant-2*, having same control-flow as the Variant-1, but different IoT specific requirements. For example, in Variant-2, activity $a1$ requires a low-accuracy digital temperature sensor with Accuracy of $\pm 2\,°C$ (max) from $-40\,°C$ to $+125\,°C$ (e.g., TI's TMP103) and a cellular network resource (*Network-02*). Similarly, there could be another variant, i.e., *Variant-3*, having same control-flow as Variant-1 but requiring a *low-power dust resistant* sensor (e.g., TI's HDC1080). Additionally, this resource can be deployed using both cellular network or LoRA network depending on availability at deployment time. Table 1 illustrates the complexity

---

[3] https://www.lora-alliance.org.
[4] https://mosquitto.org/.

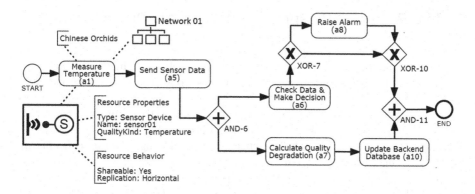

Fig. 3. Process variant 1 in Fig. 2 enriched with IoT resource features

involved in capturing the IoT resource variability while considering just a single activity (a1) from the CPM.

Table 1. IoT resource variability in process variants

Variant	Control-flow	Resources	Res. property	Res. behavior
Variant-1	Derived from CPM	Sensor, network	High-accuracy (HA)	Shareable
Variant-2	Same as Variant-1	Sensor, network	Low-accuracy (LA)	Shareable
Variant-3	Same as Variant-1	Sensor, network	HA & Low-power	Non-shareable

These example clearly illustrate that the process variants share commonalities not only at the *structural* and *behavioral* level (i.e., control-flow perspective) but even at the resource level. In practice, various variants have similar requirements for the allocated resources with slight changes such as choice of accuracy, network, capability, deployment strategies, or Shareability (i.e., Resource Behavior). However, not having a configuration support to model this resource variability at CPM level, causes several disadvantages: (i) the allocation parameters are hard-coded at each individual variant level in an ad-hoc manner, (ii) there is no knowledge coming from CPM level, i.e., no guidance (rules or constraints), (iii) variant creation is time-consuming and error-prone, (iv) the process enrichment (and best practices) takes place at the variant level, leading to redundancy and segregation of improvement efforts for each variant, without benefiting others. Thus, we advocate creation of configuration support for IoT resource variability at CPM level, i.e., shifting the IoT allocation parameters from the variant level to the CPM level.

4   IoT Resource Perspective in Business Processes

Even with a growing interest for integration of IoT and BPM domain for developing processes related to smart environments such as Industry 4.0 [24] and smart Retail/Logistics processes [9], overall research on IoT resource perspective in BPM has been scarce. In literature, some recent work have contributed towards modeling, allocation and management of IoT resources involved in BPs [19,20,23]. However, they focus on including the IoT features into individual process models (variant level) rather than developing reusable concepts at the CPM level. Besides, there are certain features associated with IoT resource perspective that are significant for incorporation at the CPM level. Broadly speaking, IoT consists of Sensor, Actuator and Tag devices, which can be battery operated or connected to main power supply. These devices need a network with a specific bandwidth, range and latency (detailed in Sect. 2.2). Thus, the two key features associated with IoT resources are: (i) *Replication* and (ii) *Shareability*. Further, this work assumes that IoT resources consists of a set of IoT devices and a set of network (e.g., Orange IoT networks[5]), where both can be mapped together in a process based on business needs.

Replication has been widely studied for distributed environment because it strongly impacts the following: (i) *Availability*, (ii) *Reliability*, and (iii) *Performance* [10]. Reliability and Availability have also been widely studied in context of data-centric services. For instance, Decandia et al. [8] detail their need for creating highly reliable systems, and discuss the tradeoffs between availability, consistency, cost-effectiveness and performance. Many organizations such as Amazon consider reliability as one of the most significant requirements. This is because a slightest outage can have substantial financial consequences and impacts customer trust [8]. Additionally, each IoT device has a specific *Access Cost* (*AC*) parameter, i.e., device energy consumption cost (*Processing Cost*), communication energy cost (cost for bandwidth, latency, radio range). The AC and Quality of Information (QoI) are interdependent as higher rate of sampling will increase the QoI but will also lead to higher AC [19]. Basically, in context of IoT (both centralized or distributed architecture), it is essential to explicitly detail and model these replication features (properties) to maintain optimal AC, and QoI along with high-availability, reliability and fault-tolerance, especially while dealing with time-critical systems (i.e., systems using real-time data for decision making). In this work, we consider Replication subsumes all four sub-properties, i.e., AC, QoI, Availability, and Reliability.

Likewise, Shareability subsumes two sub-properties, i.e., *Privacy* and *Security* of information, which is highly important in both IoT and BPM domain. These devices capture and transmit data that can contain sensitive or private information such as GPS location, video or audio data. Thus, the processes must be designed keeping data protection policy in mind (e.g. EU GDPR[6]). Based on such policies at both the process and resource level, the analysts can

---

[5] https://partner.orange.com/orange-iot-networks/.

[6] https://www.eugdpr.org/.

design variants having allocated resources that may or may not be shareable between multiple processes or multiple activities of the same process or even between the multiple instances of the same activity. Overall, this work focuses on modeling and including these IoT resource features at the CPM level based on the approach detailed in Sect. 5 without going into details about managing the sub-properties.

5   Approach: Configurable IoT-Aware Allocation

In this section, we detail our approach for including IoT resource variability at the CPM level by taking into account two main parameters: (i) resources and their properties, and (ii) resource behavior (i.e., Replication and Shareability). We introduce three main operators: (i) *Configurable IoT Assignment* operator (A^c) (adapted from our previous work [12]) in Sect. 5.1, (ii) *Configurable IoT Replication* operator (R^c) in Sect. 5.2, and (iii) *Configurable IoT Shareability* operator (S^c) in Sect. 5.3.

Figure 4 represents a process fragment taken from the CPM detailed in Fig. 1, wherein the activity *a1* is allocated with IoT resources using the above mentioned configurable resource allocation operators. This process fragment is used as a running example while detailing the operators in the following sections.

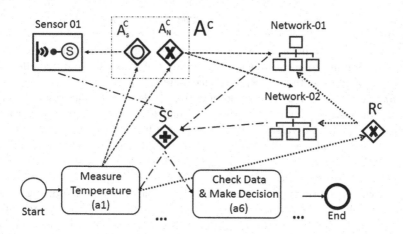

Fig. 4. Fragment from Fig. 1 illustrating configurable IoT allocation operators

5.1   Configurable IoT Assignment Operator

The configurable IoT assignment operator (A^c) allows modeling of various IoT resources allocated to a particular activity. It is the main operator for facilitating the modeling of IoT resource variability at the CPM level. It allows to define a pool of resources and set of guidelines (rules and constraints), which shall be used to derive sound process variants [25] with relevant resources allocated to the process activities. In this work, we consider the IoT resources to be divided in two main groups: (i) the choice of an IoT device (Sensor, Actuator or Tags), and (ii) the choice of a network (based on bandwidth, range, and latency). For instance, the process fragment in Fig. 4, illustrates an activity $a1$ allocated via A^c to one sensor (via OR^c represented by A_s^c) and two network resources (via XOR^c represented by A_n^c). It represents a resource variability such as, (i) a temperature sensor and a *LoRaWAN* based network resource, or (ii) a temperature sensor and *cellular* (2G or 4G) based network resource. Using A^c, CPM can be configured to a specific variant (based on business needs) with assistance from the parameters and guidelines injected in A^c. Further, the A^c operator consists of the following three parameters (summarized in Table 2).

Configurable Type: This parameter corresponds to one of the configurable gateways, i.e. OR^c, XOR^c, AND^c. The gateways in A^c behave similar to classical configurable gateway (control-flow perceptive) and are configured in the same manner(detailed in Sect. 2.1). For instance, AND^c is configured to an AND, implying that all devices should be allocated. XOR^c is configured to an XOR, implying that the resource has can be allocated exclusively or cannot be allocated. Whereas OR^c can be configured to AND, OR, or XOR, depicting allocation based on the required features of the IoT resource.

Range: This parameter corresponds to the minimum and maximum number of the resources that can be allocated to an activity, i.e., *rangeD* for IoT device and *rangeN* for network. Let us assume that the activity $a1$ in Fig. 4 has guidelines to include at least one IoT device and one network resources, i.e., $min(rangeD) = 1$ and $min(rangeN) = 1$. This will correspond to the allocation shown in process variant in Fig. 3. The default setting for minimum range equals 0, while maximum range equals the total number of a specific resource allocated to an activity, represented by $|R_D|$ (device) and $|R_N|$ (network).

Assignment Policies: This parameter corresponds to guidelines specific to IoT resources for assisting analysts to derive semantically correct process variants. It consists of certain default policies along with advanced policies. For instance, (i) an activity should be allocated with an IoT device belonging to only one category, i.e., same activity cannot be allocated to a sensor and to an actuator, (ii) an activity can be allocated to multiple resources (e.g., multiple sensors) of the same type or hybrid type, i.e., having at least one of the needed functionality.

For example, in Fig. 4, the activity $a1$ can be allocated with a temperature sensor or a hybrid temperature-humidity sensor. Figure 4 represents a process fragment (excerpt from Fig. 1) with an activity $a1$ allocated with one sensors and two network resource. Thus, an analyst can configure to keep one sensor and one network resource by transforming the OR^c to AND, and keeping either Network-01 or Network-02 (as represented in the derived process model in Fig. 3). The AND implies that both the sensor and network are needed. Moreover, such configuration should not violate the range defined for the resources above let us say, *rangeD* ($min = 1$, $max = 3$); *rangeN* ($min = 1$, $max = 2$).

Table 2. Parameters for configurable IoT assignment operator

Parameters	Behavior and constraints
Configurable type (AND^c, OR^c, XOR^c)	Same as classical configurable gateways
Range	$0 \leqslant range_D \leqslant |R_D|$
	$0 \leqslant range_N \leqslant |R_N|$
Assignment policies	Domain & geography specific constraints

5.2 Configurable IoT Replication Operator

For every IoT resource allocated in a process, there exists some specific requirements in terms of the QoI, AC, Availability and Reliability, i.e., Resource Behavior (detailed in Sect. 4). Each of these requirements will generate different process variants that behave in a different way. The Replication operator (R^c) will
express these resource behavior requirements in terms of Replication Type. They
are *Horizontal Replication* and *Vertical Replication* (inspired from *Elasticity* in
Cloud computing), which are defined as follows:

Horizontal Replication (HR): The possibility to allocate and aggregate multiple resources (both device and network) with a constraint that the resources
have the same AC and QoI features. Further, the total number of allocated
resources should fall in the allowed *Range* (see *Range* in A^c). HR permits the
system to have a higher reliability while keeping the AC lower (i.e, energy and
other costs). For example, a room having four temperature sensors (all having
similar AC and QoI) connected to an activity via a logical interface, allowing
one or more to be active at a given time.

Vertical Replication (VR): The possibility to allocate and aggregate multiple
resources (both device and network) having different AC and QoI (both higher
or lower), within the allocation *Range*. VR allows to maintain high availability
and high reliability, without any upper limit on AC (i.e, energy and other costs),
especially for critical systems. For example, a room having four temperature
sensors, with one simple sensor, one hybrid (temperature-humidity) sensor and
two hybrid (temperature-humidity) dust resistant sensor (all having variable AC
and QoI) mapped via a logical interface. For modeling such variability, R^c has
following three parameters (summarized in Table 3):

Configurable Type: depicting the set of resources that can be replicated. The
configurable type can be either an OR^c, XOR^c or AND^c (similar to A^c). For
instance, AND^c is configured to an AND, implying that all devices should be
replicated. XOR^c is configured to an XOR, implying that the resource has can
be replicated exclusively or cannot be replicated.

Configurable Replication Type: depicting the type of replication allowed. R^c
can model various resources that can be replicated based on replication type
that specifies the replication behavior (RB^c), which can be of two types, i.e.,
HR and VR. Thus, the RB^c can be configured to one of the HR or VR.

Replication Policies: depicting specific guidelines related to QoI and AC.
The replication policy parameter comprises of guidelines, rules and constrained

specified by domain expert for configuration of the replication type. These guidelines assist in deriving variants conforming to domain requirements and Service Level Agreements (SLAs). For instance, the Fig. 4 illustrates that both $Network01$ or $Network02$ can be replicated (lets say with HV), however as only one of them can be configured at a time, thus they are connected via XOR^c.

Table 3. Parameters for configurable IoT replication operator

Parameters	Behavior and constraints
Configurable type (AND^c, OR^c, XOR^c)	Same as classical configurable gateways
Replication type (RB^c)	HR, VR
Replication policies	Access cost & QoI related constraints

5.3   Configurable IoT Shareability Operator

Some BP activities may share various IoT resources (and their data). These BPs include stakeholders from within the same organization or different organizations. Thus, various constraints related to sharing of the resources and data (based on privacy and security concerns) should account for another layer of variability. For managing this type of variability, we define the configurable IoT Shareability operator, represented as S^c. It permits modeling the variability based on: (i) the way the activities share the IoT resources (and data) within the process, and (ii) the number of process instances or activities that can share the corresponding resource. This operator comprises of the following three parameters (summarized in Table 4).

Configurable Type: it is similar to other configurable IoT operators, i.e., OR^c, AND^c or XOR^c. It allows to model the Shareability feature. *Shareability Type*: the Shareability type ST^c comprises of two sub-types: (i) Shareable (S), and (ii) Non-Sharable (NS). Thus, the ST^c can be configure to one of the them. *Shareability Policies*: the policies contains guidelines and rules specific to a domain or geographic needs.

For instance, to derive a process such as variant-01 (see Fig. 3) having Shareability, the configurable IoT Shareability operator in Fig. 4 must be configured as follows: (i) S^c operator (having AND^c gateway) associated with $a1$, $a6$, along with the sensor and network resources, and (ii) ST^c is configured to a S, to depict data Shareability between multiple activities. Further, it is important to note that the Replication and Shareability operators are semantically dependent on assignment operator. This is because a device needs to be first assigned before it can exhibit Replication or Shareability behavior. This makes the formal verification for resource allocation an essential work, however it is out of the scope of this paper.

Table 4. Parameters for configurable IoT Shareability operator

Parameters	Behavior and constraints
Configurable type (AND^c, OR^c, XOR^c)	Same as classical configurable gateways
Configurable shareability Type (ST^c)	S, NS
Shareability policies	Privacy & Security constraints

6   Validation

In this section, we illustrate the feasibility of our approach by implementing a proof of concept as detailed in Sect. 6.1. In Sect. 6.2, we detail the experimentation performed on datasets developed using three different approaches on the same CPM. The experimentation result illustrates that our approach reduces the complexity involved in modeling IoT specific features at the CPM level.

6.1   Proof of Concept

We implemented a proof of concept by extending the Signavio[7] process editor (open-source version). Signavio provides a web-based graphical environment for developing process models in BPMN (serializable as BPMN.xml). This extension supports the development of configurable IoT-aware BPs, detailed in our university web-page[8]. As illustrated in Fig. 5, our prototype supports the following functionality for managing process variability at design-time:

IoT Resource Modeling: We extended the BPMN 2.0 semantics to include concepts from IoT domain, i.e, Sensor, Actuator, RFID and the Network, along with their properties (based on IoT-A framework). These specifications integrated within the Signavio extension allows users to drag and drop IoT resources during process modeling.

Configurable IoT Allocation Operators: These operators assist modeling and integrating the IoT resource perspective at the CPM level by allocating configurable operators to activities based on the approach presented in Sect. 5. These three configurable IoT resource operators, i.e., Assignment (A^c), Replication (R^c) and Shareability (S^c) are used to link the process activities to their allocated IoT resources (e.g., Fig. 4). These operators consist of various configurable parameters such as configurable type, configurable replication type, and policies, which will assist the users during development of process variants.

6.2   Experimentation

In this section, we illustrate the effectiveness of our approach by performing experiments on a CPM from the Retail domain (see Fig. 1). This CPM was

---

[7] https://code.google.com/archive/p/signavio-core-components/source.

[8] http://www-inf.it-sudparis.eu/SIMBAD/tools/ConfigurableIoTBPM.

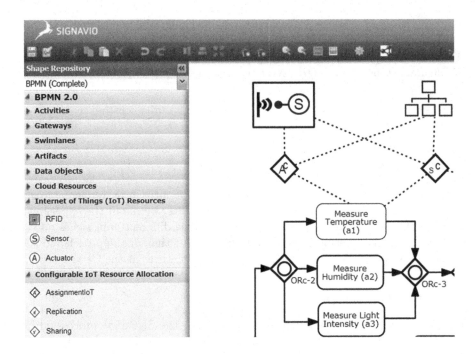

Fig. 5. Screenshot illustrating the implemented proof of concept

developed by integrating process variants[9] adapted from [9]. Our work consolidates both, the control-flow perspective and the IoT resource perspective, along with their allocation strategies for developing configurable IoT-aware process models. Thus, to compare our approach with the current state-of-the-art, we developed the same *IoT-aware* CPM using three different approaches, detailed as follows:

First, we develop an IoT-aware CPM using the classical control-flow perspective, which does not consider any variability at the resource level. To do so, an activity is duplicated in the model in a choice block to express the existence of different resource allocation possibilities. This CPM (see Process Fragment-1 in Fig. 6) represents the IoT resource variability, and can be individualized based on business requirements. However, it leads to an increase in process complexity. Second, we develop an IoT-aware CPM based on the approach from La Rosa et al. [15]. Their approach supports basic resource configuration without considering the complex IoT features such as resource behavior. Thus, the activities need to be duplicated to depict these features. For instance, an activity may have different Shareability requirements in different process variants, which is depicted by duplicating activities and including these features (see Process Fragment-2 in Fig. 6), leading to increase in model complexity. Third, we use our approach to develop the IoT-aware CPM, which represents the variability

---

[9] https://github.com/kunalsuri/process-models.

considering both the control-flow perspective and the IoT resource allocation
(see Process Fragment-03 in Fig. 6). Figure 6 represent three process fragments
taken from three separate IoT-aware CPM developed as explained above. For
simplicity reasons, the fragments in Fig. 6 represent an activity *a1*, assigned to
a *Sensor-01* and a *Network-01*, wherein both resources are *Shareable*.

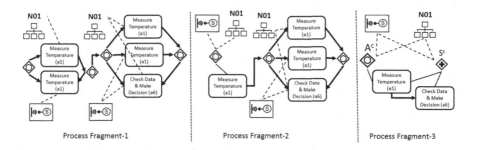

Fig. 6. Process fragments illustrating three different approaches

In the classical approach represented via Process Fragment-01, activity *a1*
has been duplicated multiple time to represent the configurable resource assignment concept. One *a1* is linked to the network resource *N01* and another *a1* to
Sensor01, both *a1* are connected via a configurable *OR*. Likewise, to represent
the concept of configurable resource shareability between *a1* and *a6*, the activities *a1* is duplicated and linked to the IoT resources and connected to *a6* via a
configurable *OR*. Likewise, following the approach in [15] (see Process Fragment-
2), the allocation of two IoT resources is done using a OR^c. However, to represent
the concept of configurable resource shareability, *a1* is duplicated and connected
with *a6*. Further, based on our approach (see Process Fragment-3), the concept
of configurable resource allocation is depicted by linking the IoT resources with
activity *a1* via a configurable IoT assignment operator (A^c). While the resources
Shareability is represented by linking the resources to activities *a1* and *a6* via a
configurable IoT shareability operator (S^c).

To evaluate the quality of these three IoT-aware CPMs, we calculate and compare a well-known complexity metric, i.e., Control-Flow Complexity (CFC) [7].
The CFC_c evaluates the process complexity in terms of the classical gateways
and is used to better understand and examine process models before their actual
implementation [7]. As the resource allocation operators are based on the control-
flow gateways, we also apply this metric to them. However, we distinguish it by
calling it CFC_r. Further, we developed three datasets, i.e., one for each approach,
wherein each dataset has five IoT-aware CPM (using the same CPM from Fig. 1),
developed by allocating IoT resource features (with varying complexity). The
results are summarized in Table 5. The results illustrate that our approach has
lower aggregated CFC values than other two approaches. As compared to [15],
our resource-flow complexity is higher since we need to duplicate the control-
flows (subsuming the resource-flow operators (see Sect. 5.3)) for assignment and

Table 5. Complexity metrics comparing different approaches

Complexity Metric	DataSet 1 Classical Approach	DataSet 2 La Rosa Approach	DataSet 3 Our Approach
Average CFC_c	37	30	**15**
Average CFC_r	N.A	6	16
Total CFC	37	36	**31**

behavior, both falling under CFC_r, to model the resource behavior such as Shareability.

7 Related Work

In literature, various existing work on CPM focus mostly on the control-flow perspective [17,21] . Though, some works such as [13–15] extended the configuration to include the resource perspective [17], but then again they are not sufficient to handle the complexity of IoT domain. La Rosa et al. [15] proposed the configurable integrated EPC (C-iEPC), which included features for capturing resource, data and physical objects via configurable connectors (based on control-flow perspective) to model the variable allocation of resources. However, they focus on human resources and generic non-human resources without any support for IoT specific features. Kumar et al. [14] proposed an approach based on templates and rules for creating configurable processes allowing some integration of both resources and data. However, their approach does not cover flexible resources selection and is not suitable for IoT resources. Hallerbach et al. [13] extend the process variants by options (Provop framework) to model and manage large collections of process variants without going in depth for considering concepts related to resource selection and allocation. Overall, these works consider the resources perspective in a generic way without considering the intricacy of the IoT domain, which leads to creation of multiple IoT-specific process variants. Recently, in literature there has been a growing focus on including resource perspective to PAIS, i.e., developing Process- and Resource-Aware Information Systems (PRAIS) [6]. Thus, some researchers have contributed on including Cloud computing concepts at CPM level [12] and its simulation for finding optimal variants [2]. However, there has been no uptake on integrating IoT resource perspective to CPMs.

8 Conclusion and Future Work

In this paper, we propose configuration concepts for handling IoT resource variability to be integrated at a Configurable Process Model (CPM) level. Concretely, we defined a set of configurable IoT-aware allocation operators, which will enable the inclusion of explicit information (options/variability) about various alternatives and constraints for IoT resources based on their features (properties) and behavior such as Replication and Shareability. These IoT-aware CPMs can be individualized into a specific process variant via transformations that includes both, (i) the control-flow perspective, and (ii) IoT resource perspective, to meet a given set of business requirements. Our research is motivated and illustrated through a CPM from the Retail management domain. Furthermore, we implement a proof of concept using Signavio process editor, and validate our proposal through our experimentation results.

As a perspective, we plan to work with a larger dataset for further evaluation of our approach. We intend to formalize the operators (and its constraints). We also plan to do implementation of the configuration step and the formal verification to obtain a sound variant.

References

1. Van der Aalst, W.M.: Process-Aware information systems: lessons to be learned from process mining. In: Jensen, K., van der Aalst, W.M.P. (eds.) Transactions on Petri Nets and Other Models of Concurrency II. LNCS, vol. 5460, pp. 1–26. Springer, Heidelberg (2009). https://doi.org/10.1007/978-3-642-00899-3_1
2. Ahmed-Nacer, M., Suri, K., Sellami, M., Gaaloul, W.: Simulation of configurable resource allocation for cloud-based business processes. In: 2017 IEEE International Conference on Services Computing (SCC), pp. 305–313. IEEE (2017)
3. Assy, N., Chan, N.N., Gaaloul, W.: An automated approach for assisting the design of configurable process models. IEEE Trans. Serv. Comput. 8(6), 874–888 (2015)
4. Assy, N., Gaaloul, W., Defude, B.: Mining configurable process fragments for business process design. In: Tremblay, M.C., VanderMeer, D., Rothenberger, M., Gupta, A., Yoon, V. (eds.) DESRIST 2014. LNCS, vol. 8463, pp. 209–224. Springer, Cham (2014). https://doi.org/10.1007/978-3-319-06701-8_14
5. Atzori, L., Iera, A., Morabito, G.: The internet of things: a survey. Comput. Netw. 54(15), 2787–2805 (2010)
6. Cabanillas, C.: Process-and resource-aware information systems. In: 2016 IEEE 20th International Enterprise Distributed Object Computing Conference (EDOC), pp. 1–10. IEEE (2016)
7. Cardoso, J.: Evaluating the process control-flow complexity measure. In: 2005 Proceedings of the IEEE International Conference on Web Services, ICWS 2005. IEEE (2005)
8. DeCandia, G., Hastorun, D., et al.: Dynamo: Amazon's highly available key-value store. In: ACM SIGOPS Operating Systems Review, vol. 41, pp. 205–220. ACM (2007)
9. Fiedler, M., Meissner, S.: IoT in practice: examples: IoT in logistics and health. In: Bassi, A., et al. (eds.) Enabling Things to Talk, pp. 27–36. Springer, Heidelberg (2013). https://doi.org/10.1007/978-3-642-40403-0_4
10. Goel, S., Buyya, R.: Data replication strategies in wide-area distributed systems. In: Enterprise Service Computing: From Concept to Deployment, pp. 211–241. IGI Global (2007)

11. Gottschalk, F., Van der Aalst, W.M., Jansen-Vullers, M.H.: Configurable process models-a foundational approach. In: Becker, J., Delfmann, P. (eds.) Reference Modeling, pp. 59–77. Springer, Heidelberg (2007). https://doi.org/10.1007/978-3-7908-1966-3_3

12. Hachicha, E., Assy, N., Gaaloul, W., Mendling, J.: A configurable resource allocation for multi-tenant process development in the cloud. In: Nurcan, S., Soffer, P., Bajec, M., Eder, J. (eds.) CAiSE 2016. LNCS, vol. 9694, pp. 558–574. Springer, Cham (2016). https://doi.org/10.1007/978-3-319-39696-5_34

13. Hallerbach, A., Bauer, T., Reichert, M.: Capturing variability in business process models: the Provop approach. J. Soft. Evol. Process **22**(6–7), 519–546 (2010)

14. Kumar, A., Yao, W.: Design and management of flexible process variants using templates and rules. Comput. Ind. **63**(2), 112–130 (2012)

15. La Rosa, M., Dumas, M., Ter Hofstede, A.H., Mendling, J.: Configurable multi-perspective business process models. Inf. Syst. **36**(2), 313–340 (2011)

16. La Rosa, M., Dumas, M., Uba, R., Dijkman, R.: Business process model merging: an approach to business process consolidation. ACM Trans. Soft. Eng. Methodol. (TOSEM) **22**(2), 11 (2013)

17. La Rosa, M., Van Der Aalst, W.M., Dumas, M., Milani, F.P.: Business process variability modeling: a survey. ACM Comput. Surv. **50**(1), 2 (2017)

18. Mahmud, R., Kotagiri, R., Buyya, R.: Fog computing: a taxonomy, survey and future directions. In: Di Martino, B., Li, K.-C., Yang, L.T., Esposito, A. (eds.) Internet of Everything. IT, pp. 103–130. Springer, Singapore (2018). https://doi.org/10.1007/978-981-10-5861-5_5

19. Martinho, R., Domingos, D.: Quality of information and access cost of IoT resources in BPMN processes. Procedia Technol. **16**, 737–744 (2014)

20. Meyer, S., Ruppen, A., Hilty, L.: The things of the internet of things in BPMN. In: Persson, A., Stirna, J. (eds.) CAiSE 2015. LNBIP, vol. 215, pp. 285–297. Springer, Cham (2015). https://doi.org/10.1007/978-3-319-19243-7_27

21. Rosemann, M., Van der Aalst, W.M.: A configurable reference modelling language. Inf. Syst. **32**(1), 1–23 (2007)

22. Schrepfer, M., Kunze, M., Obst, G., Siegeris, J.: Why Are process variants important in process monitoring? the case of Zalando SE. In: vom Brocke, J., Mendling, J. (eds.) Business Process Management Cases. MP, pp. 431–448. Springer, Cham (2018). https://doi.org/10.1007/978-3-319-58307-5_23

23. Suri, K., Gaaloul, W., Cuccuru, A., Gerard, S.: Semantic framework for internet of things-aware business process development. In: 2017 IEEE 26th International Conference on Enabling Technologies: Infrastructure for Collaborative Enterprises (WETICE), pp. 214–219. IEEE (2017)

24. Suri, K., Cadavid, J., et al.: Modeling business motivation and underlying processes for RAMI 4.0-aligned cyber-physical production systems. In: 2017 22nd IEEE International Conference on Emerging Technologies and Factory Automation (ETFA). IEEE (2017)

25. Van Der Aalst, W.M., Van Hee, K.M., Ter Hofstede, A.H., Sidorova, N., Verbeek, H., Voorhoeve, M., Wynn, M.T.: Soundness of workflow nets: classification, decidability, and analysis. Form. Asp. Comput. **23**(3), 333–363 (2011)

A Multi-stage Dynamic Game-Theoretic Approach for Multi-Workflow Scheduling on Heterogeneous Virtual Machines from Multiple Infrastructure-as-a-Service Clouds

Yuandou Wang⬡, Jiajia Jiang, Yunni Xia^(✉), Quanwang Wu^(✉), Xin Luo^(✉), and Qingsheng Zhu

College of Computer Science, Chongqing University, Chongqing 400030, China
xiayunni@hotmail.com, wqw@cqu.edu.cn, luoxin21@gmail.com

Abstract. Distributed computing systems such as clouds continue to evolve to support various types of scientific applications, especially scientific workflows, with dependable, consistent, pervasive, and inexpensive access to geographically-distributed computational capabilities. Scheduling multiple workflows on distributed computing systems like Infrastructure-as-a-Service (IaaS) clouds is well recognized as a fundamental NP-complete problem that is critical to meeting various types of Quality-of-Service (QoS) requirements. In this paper, we propose a multi-objective optimization workflow scheduling approach based on dynamic game-theoretic model aiming at reducing workflow make-spans, reducing total cost, and maximizing system fairness in terms of workload distribution among heterogeneous cloud virtual machines (VMs). We conduct extensive case studies as well based on various well-known scientific workflow templates and real-world third-party commercial IaaS clouds. Experimental results clearly suggest that our proposed approach outperform traditional ones by achieving lower workflow make-spans, lower cost, and better system fairness.

Keywords: Dynamic game · Workflow scheduling
Multi-clouds system · Multi-objective optimization · QoS

This work is supported in part by the International Joint Project funded jointly by the Royal Society of the UK and the National Natural Science Foundation of China under grant 61611130209, National Science Foundations of China under grants Nos. 61472051/61702060, the Science Foundation of Chongqing under No. cstc2017jcyjA1276, China Postdoctoral Science Foundation No. 2015M570770, Chongqing Postdoctoral Science special Foundation No. Xm2015078, and Universities Sci-tech Achievements Transformation Project of Chongqing No. KJZH17104, Chongqing grand R&D projects Nos. cstc2017zdcy-zdyf0120 and cstc2017rgzn-zdyf0118.

J. E. Ferreira et al. (Eds.): SCC 2018, LNCS 10969, pp. 137–152, 2018.
https://doi.org/10.1007/978-3-319-94376-3_9

1   Introduction

Recently, various scientific fields employ workflows to analyze large amounts of data and to perform complex simulations and experiments efficiently. A process in such scientific applications can be modeled as a workflow by dividing it into smaller and simpler tasks. These tasks can then be distributed to multiple computing resources [1]. They usually present graphical interfaces to combine different technologies along with efficient methods for using them, and thus increase the efficiency of scientists. They are usually represented as directed graphs with their nodes representing discrete computational components and the edges representing connections along which data and results can communicate among components. They have different types and usually their execution needs computing platforms with different QoS requirements, e.g. most completion time, load balancing, economics.

Recently, cloud computing is recognized as a promising solution and paradigm for providing a flexible, on-demand computing infrastructure over the Internet for large-scale scientific-workflow-based applications. The services that can be provided from the cloud include Software-as-a-Service (SaaS), Platform-as-a-Service (PaaS), and Infrastructure-as-a-Service (IaaS) [2]. SaaS clouds offer web applications/software over the Internet, running on cloud infrastructure. PaaS and SaaS clouds are thus less suitable for scientific workflows than IaaS ones because they mainly offer an environment to design, develop and test web based applications. Instead, IaaS clouds offer an easily accessible, flexible, and scalable infrastructure suitable for the deployment of large-scale scientific workflows based on on-demand and pay-per-use patterns [3].

One of the most challenging NP-complete problems that researchers try to address is how to schedule large-scale scientific applications to distributed and heterogeneous computational nodes, e.g., IaaS clouds, such that quantitative objective functions such as process make-span are optimized, and certain execution constraints such as communication cost and storage requirements are considered and fulfilled. From the end-users perspective, a low make-span is always preferred, whereas from the systems perspective system-level efficiency and fairness are often considered as a good motivation such that the scientific applications and tasks are supposed to be fairly distributed among computational resources in order to avoid hot spots and performance bottle-necks. However, a careful investigation into related work shows that only a few schemes are able to deal with both perspectives, such as optimizing user objectives (e.g., make-span) while fulfilling other constraints, and providing a good fair workload distribution among physical computational resources of clouds.

The primary aim of the paper is therefore to propose a multi-objective scheduling method to address the real-time workflow scheduling problem on multiple IaaS cloud. Specifically, we consider a multi-objective optimization workflow scheduling approach based on dynamic game-theoretic model. It aims at reducing workflow make-spans, reducing cost, and maximizing system fairness in terms of workload distribution among heterogeneous VMs. We conduct extensive case studies as well based on various well-known scientific workflow templates and

Table 1. Notations and description summary

Notations	Description
N	The total number of workflows
n_i	The total number of tasks in workflow
K	The total number of tasks
M	The total number of cloud service providers (CSPs)
m_p	The total number of virtual machines in CSP p
T_{ij}	The jth task of the workflow i
T^l_{option}	The set of the optional task (s) at stage l
VM_{pk}	The kth virtual machine of CSP p
VM	The set of virtual machines ($VM = \{VM_{11}, VM_{12}, \ldots, VM_{pk}\}$)
VM^l_{idle}	The set of the idle virtual machines at stage l
C_{ijpk}	The completion time of T_{ij} on VM_{pk}
t_{ijpks}	The setup time of T_{ij} executed at VM_{pk}
t_{ijpk}	The cutting time of T_{ij} executed at VM_{pk}
ET_{ijpk}	The execution time of T_{ij} executed at VM_{pk}
x_{ijpk}	A Boolean variable indicating whether VM_{pk} is selected for T_{ij}
u_{pk}	The unit-price-per-time of VM_{pk}
w^l_i	The weight matrix of ith player at l^{th} stage
S^l	The strategies set of players in the lth stage of the game tree
S^l_i	The strategy set of ith player in the lth stage of the game tree
$u^l_i(S^l_i)$	The utility function of ith player at l^{th} stage
L	The maximum stage number of a game tree
a^0	The actions combination at l^{th} stage
a^l	The actions combination at l^{th} stage
h^0	The origin history information of game tree ($h^0 = \emptyset$)
h^l	The lth stage history information set of game ($h^l = (a^0, a^1, \ldots, a^{l-1})$)
H^l	The total history information set in l stages ($H^l = \{h^l\}$)
$A_i(H^l)$	The optional action set of ith player in l stages of the game tree

heterogeneous VMs created on real-world third-party commercial IaaS clouds, i.e., Amazon, Tencent, and Ali clouds. Experimental results clearly suggest that our proposed approach outperforms traditional ones by achieving lower work-flow make-spans, lower cost, and better system fairness. Table 1 summarized the notations and description.

The paper is structured as follows. In Sect. 2, we review related work. In Sect. 3, we present the formulation for the heterogeneous-VM-based multi-workflow scheduling problem. In Sect. 4, we present the real-time multi-objective scheduling algorithm based on the dynamic game-theoretic model. In Sect. 5, we conduct extensive case studies to validate our proposed approach. This paper concludes in Sect. 6 with a summery.

2   Related Work

Along with rapidly growing data and computational requirements of large-scale workflow applications, scheduling multiple workflows in distributed systems has become a important and challenging research topic. In this section, we briefly cover a part of the important or relevant related work.

2.1   Multi-objective Workflow Scheduling

The optimization model for workflow (single or multiple) scheduling aim at finding tradeoffs among multiple quantitative objectives, e.g., make-span, cost, reliability, energy consumption, security, or load balancing. Extensive efforts, e.g., [4–11] are paid in this direction. Durillo et al. [12] proposed tradeoff solutions generated using a multi-objective-heterogeneous-earliest-finish-time (MOHET) algorithm for multi-objective workflow scheduling problem. Yassa et al. [13] proposed an approach based on dynamic voltage and frequency scaling (DVFS) technique for multi-objective workflow scheduling in clouds to minimize energy consumption, and introduced a hybrid particle swarm optimization (PSO) algorithm to optimize the scheduling performance.

Many multi-objective evolutionary algorithms have been extended to deal with the multi-objective problems. Khajemohammadi et al. [14] proposed a genetic fast workflow scheduling over grid infrastructures. Zhu et al. [15] proposed an evolutionary multi-objective optimization (EMO)-based workflow scheduling algorithm with novel schemes for problem-specific encoding and population initialization, fitness evaluation and genetic operators. Chen et al. [16] proposed an ant colony optimization (ACO) algorithm to schedule large-scale workflows with make-span and cost. Padmaveni et al. [17] introduced a hybrid algorithm called particle swarm memetic (PSM) algorithm make-span and deadline as the optimization objectives.

Recently, the Pareto-optimal methods are frequently employed. It aims at pursuing a set of compromise solutions that represent good approximations to the Pareto-optimal fronts (PFs). For instance, Zheng et al. [18] proposed a Pareto-based fruit fly optimization algorithm (PFOA) to solve the task scheduling and resource allocating (TSRA) problem in cloud computing environment. Hou et al. [19] studied the Pareto optimization to schedule crude oil operations in a refinery via genetic algorithm. Ebadifard et al. [20] introduced a recent heuristic algorithm called black-hole-optimization (BHO) framework for workflow scheduling based on Pareto optimizer algorithm. It allows users to select the best from the proper solution set of candidate scheduling plans.

2.2   Game-Theoretic-Based Scheduling

Game theory models and methodologies are widely applied to the multi-constraint process scheduling on cloud social, economic and resource scheduling problems. Fard *et al.* [21] suggested a novel pricing model and truthful scheduling mechanism to find the best resource using the game-theoretic concepts. Duan *et al.* [22] modeled workflow scheduling the problem as a sequential cooperative game and proposed a communication and storage-aware multi-objective algorithm with network bandwidth and storage requirements as the constraints. Sujana *et al.* [23] applied the game multi objective algorithm for minimizing the execution time and cost of single workflow applications.

3   Model and Formulation

In this section, we first present the problem description and formulation of multi-objective workflow scheduling over heterogeneous cloud VMs. Then, we propose a finite multi-stage game model, i.e., Fig. 1, to reconcile multiple objectives and introduce a dynamic game-theoretic-based algorithm to reduce make-span, optimize system fairness and reduce the total cost.

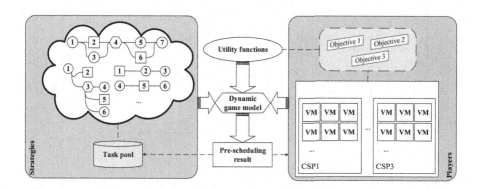

Fig. 1. The abstract model for multi-workflow scheduling problem

3.1   Problem Formulation

In this study, we consider that scientific computational processes can be described by multiple workflows which are supposed to be scheduled into heterogeneous VMs created over multiple IaaS CSPs. Each workflow can be represented by a directed acyclic graph (DAG), $W = (V, E)$, where V is a set of n tasks, i.e., $\{t_1, t_2, \ldots, t_n\}$. E is a set of precedence dependencies. Each task t_i represents an individual application with a certain task execution time v_i on a VM. A precedence dependency $e_{ij} = (t_i, t_j)$ indicates that t_j starts only after the data from t_i are received. The source and destination of a dependency e_{ij} are called the parent and the child task, respectively. Each workflow has an input and output task, which are added to the beginning and the end, respectively. When multiple workflows are ready for execution, we first partition their tasks into multiple phases based on their hops from the input task as shown in Fig. 2. After the partition, tasks are scheduled to VMs according to our proposed method and tasks at earlier phases are scheduled earlier than those at later ones. Three quantitative objectives are considered: make-span, fairness, and total cost. Note that reducing make-span, i.e., the time required to execute all workflows, usually contradicts with cost reduction and thus we consider game-theoretic approaches to reconcile such conflicting optimization aims. The fairness maximization objective aims at achieving fair distribution of workloads among all VMs and avoiding hot-spots and performance bottle-necks.

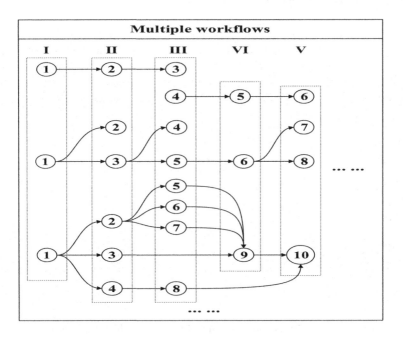

Fig. 2. The partition procedure of multiple workflows

The following hypotheses are stipulated to facilitate the development of the game-theoretic-based method: (1) VMs are created on multiple CSPs. (2) Each task can be executed by only one VM. (3) The task execution duration is the interval between the task setup time and the task cutting time. (4) The dynamic game is finite because the number of workflows and tasks are finite. The game is thus able to end within finitely many moves and every player has finitely available choices at every moment.

Based on the above hypotheses, we can formulate the problem into a multi-stage dynamic game-theoretic model:

$$Min \ f_1 = make - span = Max \ C_{ijpk} \tag{1}$$

$$Max \ f_2 = fairness \ index = \frac{(\sum_{i=1}^{K} ET_{ijpk})^2}{K \cdot \sum_{i=1}^{K} ET_{ijpk}^2} \tag{2}$$

$$Min \ f_3 = cost = \sum_{p=1}^{m} \sum_{k=1}^{m_p} \sum_{i=1}^{n} \sum_{j=1}^{n_i} (t_{ijpk} - t_{ijpks}) \cdot u_{pk} \cdot x_{ijpk} \tag{3}$$

subject to:

$$i \in [1,n], j \in [1,n_i], p \in [1,m], k \in [1,m_p] \tag{4}$$

$$C_{ijpk} \leq C_{i,j+1,p,k} - t_{i,j+1,p,k} - t_{i,j+1,p,k,s}, C_{ijpk} \geq 0 \tag{5}$$

$$\sum_{k \in VM(T_{ij})} x_{ijpk} = 1 \tag{6}$$

$$VM(T_{ij}) \subset VM \tag{7}$$

3.2   The Proposed Dynamic Game Model

In this paper, the multi-stage dynamic game theory is applied to deal with the conflicts and competition among multiple optimization objectives for the multi-workflow scheduling problem. The optimization objectives can be seen as players in the multi-stage dynamic game model, and the players are usually assumed to be fully rational. The game equilibrium solutions can be obtained as the optimal results. It is assumed that players take actions sequentially and the choice of the former player has an effect on the selection of the latter because the latter can observe the action of the former. The condition upon which the later makes a choice is denoted as h^l. The utility functions of the first/second/third player correspond to make-span ($u_1 = f_1$), the utility function of the second player is the second objective function which corresponds to, fairness ($u_2 = f_2$), and the total cost ($u_3 = f_3$), respectively. Consequently, the multi-stage dynamic game formulation for the problem can be described as follows:

$$G(h^l) = \{p_1, p_2, p_3; \{S_1^l\}_{l=0}^{L}, \{S_2^l\}_{l=0}^{L}, \{S_3^l\}_{l=0}^{L}; u_1, u_2, u_3\} \tag{8}$$

Let $H^l = \{h^l\}$ be the history set of all possible l stage. The pure strategies for player i are defined as a contingency for every possible history h^l. Formally, the lth stage history information of the game is denoted as $h^l = (a^0, a^1, \ldots, a^{l-1})$. The mapping $\varphi_i : s_i \rightarrow \{S_i^l\}_{l=0}^{L}$ indicates the pure strategy for player i, which is a collection of mappings from all possible histories into available actions.

S_i^l is a mapping φ_i: $H^l \rightarrow A_i(H^l)$, i.e., for all h^l, S_i^l meets $S_i^l(h^l) \in A_i(h^l)$. The mapping φ_i: $f_i \rightarrow u_i$ indicates the utility functions of the game. At each stage l, the player i calculates its pure Nash equilibrium solution based on the history information in the last stage, i.e. h^{l-1}.

4   The Algorithm to Obtain Approximate Equilibrium

According to earlier discussions, each sequential game is represented by a game tree with game length of $L + 1$, shown as Fig. 3. To determine the optimal behaviors of players, we employ the sub-game perfectness in the finite multi-stage game with perfect information. A multi-stage dynamic game with perfect information may have multiple Nash equilibriums some of which are with non-credible threats or promises. The sub-game perfect Nash equilibrium (SPNE) is those able to pass credibility tests. The SPNE solution can be found through a standard procedure [24] by the backward induction method. However, the standard procedure requires a traverse through the game tree and unfortunately such tree for the multi-VM multi-workflow problem is extremely large. We therefore consider approximate equilibrium solutions with reduced complexity. The approximate equilibriums can be defined as follows:

$$\sum_{l=0}^{L} u^l(S_1^l, S_2^l, S_3^l, h^{l-1}) \geq \sum_{l=0}^{L} u^l(S_1^*, S_2^*, S_3^*, h^{l-1}) \tag{9}$$

The approximate equilibrium $S^* = (S_1^*, S_2^*, S_3^*)$ is a set of strategies based on the game in Eqs. (8)–(9), where S^* is combination of the pure strategies Nash equilibriums at L stages. The decision strategies space S equals variables space X.

We introduce a multi-stage dynamic game-theoretic (MDGT) algorithm, **Algorithm 1**, to obtain the approximate equilibrium solutions. In this algorithm, during each stage l of the implementation of the workflow planning, a dynamic-game theory-based real-time scheduling method is triggered so that the tasks can be assigned to the most suitable VMs based on the real-time cloud environment. The aim of the scheduling layer is to map optional tasks to the most appropriate VMs. The algorithm repeatedly handles each stage until all tasks are scheduled and the major steps within each stage are as follows:

Step 1: create a real-time scheduling task pool with multi-phase tasks from multiple workflows to put T_{option}^l into it. T_{option}^l is supposed to meet topological dependence of its corresponding workflow, i.e., a task is executed only after all its preceding ones are executed.

Step 2: assign VM_{idle}^l to three objectives in turns. Each virtual machine of VM_{idle}^l which is allocated to f_i could choose the corresponding task from the real-time scheduling task pool. The mapping of tasks to idle virtual machines is called the strategies of the players.

Step 3: calculate the utility functions based on Eqs. (1)–(3) using the pure strategy Nash equilibrium based on historical information h^{l-1}. Each T^l_{option} will best match with VM^l_{idle} at stage l.

Step 4: construct a finite dynamic game model and obtain the equilibrium solutions.

Algorithm 1. The MDGT scheduling algorithm

Input: $task\_pool$: a priority queue of workflows; T^l_{option} ; VMs ; w^l_i

Output: opt_stra : the real-time scheduling strategies

1: $opt\_stra = \emptyset$

2: **for** l =1 **to** L **do**

3:     **if** $task\_pool \neq \emptyset$ is true **then**

4:         dequeue from $task\_pool$ as T^l_{option}

5:         calculate $u^l_1(S^l_1)$ by using Eq.(1) and w^l_1;

6:         save the startegy branch of payoff to opt_stra;

7:     **else**

8:         break

9:     **end if**

10:     **if** $task\_pool \neq \emptyset$ is true **then**

11:         dequeue from $task\_pool$ as T^l_{option}

12:         calculate $u^l_2(S^l_2)$ by using Eq.(2) and w^l_2;

13:         save the startegy branch of payoff to opt_stra;

14:     **else**

15:         break

16:     **end if**

17:     **if** $task\_pool \neq \emptyset$ is true **then**

18:         dequeue from $task\_pool$ as T^l_{option}

19:         calculate $u^l_3(S^l_3)$ by using Eq.(3) and w^l_3 ;

20:         save the startegy branch of payoff to opt_stra;

21:     **else**

22:         break

23:     **end if**

24: **end for**

25: **return** opt_stra

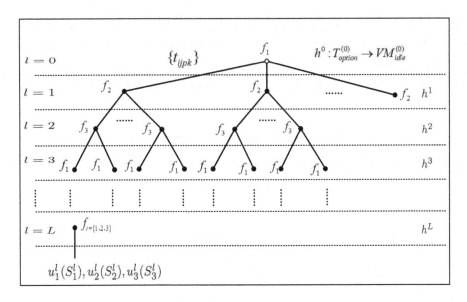

Fig. 3. The game tree template of multiple players

Table 2. The unit price of heterogeneous VMs from three IaaS providers

CSP	vType	vCPU	Memory	Unit price/hour
Amazon EC2	t2.nano	1	0.5	$0.0058/h$
	t2.small	1	2	$0.023/h$
	t2.medium	2	4	$0.0464/h$
	t2.large	2	8	$0.0928/h$
Tecent Cloud	s2.standard	1	1	$0.0185/h$
	s2.standard	1	2	$0.0246/h$
	s2.standard	2	4	$0.0493/h$
	s2.standard	2	8	$0.0739/h$
Ali Cloud	ecs.c5.large	2	4	$0.1053/h$
	ecs.g5.large	2	4	$0.1244/h$
	ecs.sn1.medium	2	8	$0.1373/h$
	ecs.c5.xlarge	2	8	$0.2502/h$

5   Case Study

In this section, we conduct extensive case study based on 5 well-known scientific workflow templates as shown in Fig. 4 and real-world third-party commercial clouds, i.e., Amazon EC2, Tencent, and Ali Clouds. Every task in all workflows

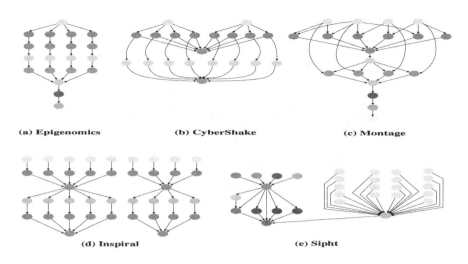

(a) Epigenomics   (b) CyberShake   (c) Montage

(d) Inspiral   (e) Sipht

Fig. 4. The case templates of five workflows

implements a GaussCLegendre calculation procedure with 8M of digits through executing the Super-Pi program on VMs. We create heterogeneous VMs on these clouds and expose them to the scheduling algorithms.

Table 2 shows the price-per-unit-time of such VMs with different resource configurations. A resulting scheduling scheme generated by our proposed method is shown in Fig. 5.

We compare our proposed method with a traditional non-game-theoretic algorithm proposed in [25]. Note that: (1) we notice several other game-theoretic scheduling algorithms, e.g., [22, 23, 26], but find out that they are intended for different problems and based on different architectural configurations and resource constraints. We are therefore unable to compare them with our proposed method, (2) other non-game-theoretic methods can be found in, e.g., [5, 27]. However, our tests show that their performance is actually very close to that of the baseline one, (3) we are pretty aware of the fact that meta-heuristic algorithms, e.g., PSO and GA-based ones, could well be promising options. However, we do not implement them and compare them with our proposed method because we consider scientific applications to be time-critical and meta-heuristic algorithms are with high time complexity.

Tables 3 and 4 present the comparisons of make-span and cost, respectively. As the total number of tasks from five workflows increases, the number of game stage increases. And our proposed MDGT method performs better than the baseline method.

In Fig. 6, we show the comparisons of fairness indexes with different IaaS cloud service providers. The curves represents that our method outperforms the baseline method. Similarly, the results in Fig. 7 show that the MDGT method performs better than baseline method on the average fairness.

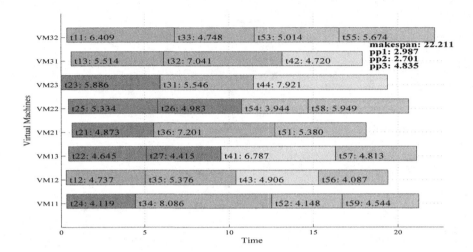

Fig. 5. An example of multi-objectives scheduling scheme for five workflows by using our proposed method

Table 3. The comparisons of make-span

No. of tasks	Game stage	Make-span	
		MDGT method	Baseline method
29	4	22.607	25.296
79	10	57.686	61.343
99	12	70.313	75.586
129	16	92.018	98.199
149	19	106.066	112.267
179	22	127.505	134.302
199	25	140.638	148.571
229	29	163.029	170.737
249	31	175.052	185.57
279	35	197.558	207.182
299	37	210.133	222.017
329	41	231.856	243.573
349	44	245.639	258.34
379	47	266.626	280.722
399	50	280.888	293.773

Table 4. The comparisons of the total cost

No. of tasks	Game stage	Cost	
		MDGT method	Baseline method
29	4	1.309	1.388
79	10	3.534	3.679
99	12	4.418	4.643
129	16	5.723	6.06
149	19	6.647	6.989
179	22	7.974	8.375
199	25	8.843	9.314
229	29	10.151	10.729
249	31	11.061	11.658
279	35	12.419	13.075
299	37	13.247	13.98
329	41	14.616	15.358
349	44	15.489	16.296
379	47	16.796	17.699
399	50	17.78	18.644

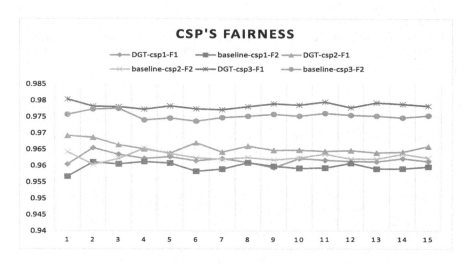

Fig. 6. The comparisons of different CSPs fairness

Fig. 7. The comparisons of average fairness

6 Conclusion

In this paper, we studied multi-objective multi-workflow scheduling problem over heterogeneous VMs created on multi-Clouds platforms and introduce a multi-stage dynamic game-theoretic (MDGT) scheduling approach. The proposed method is featured by approximation algorithm for identifying equilibrium solutions aiming at optimizing both workflow make-span, system fairness and the total cost. In addition, we conduct extensive experiments based on various well-kwon scientific workflow templates and real-world third-party commercial IaaS clouds. Experimental results demonstrate that our approach outperforms traditional baseline ones.

References

1. Rodriguez, M.A., Buyya, R.: A taxonomy and survey on scheduling algorithms for scientific workflows in IaaS cloud computing environments. Concurr. Comput. Pract. Exp. **29**(8), e4041 (2017)
2. Ye, X., Liang, J., Liu, S., Li, J.: A survey on scheduling workflows in cloud environment. In: Proceedings of the 2015 International Conference on Network and Information Systems for Computers. ICNISC 2015, pp. 344–348 (2015)
3. Buyya, R.: Market-oriented cloud computing: vision, hype, and reality of delivering computing as the 5th utility. In: 2009 9th IEEE/ACM International Symposium on Cluster Computing and the Grid. CCGRID 2009, vol. 25, no. 6, p. 1 (2009)
4. Chirkin, A.M., Belloum, A.S.Z., Kovalchuk, S.V., Makkes, M.X.: Execution time estimation for workflow scheduling. In: 2014 9th Workshop on Workflows in Support of Large-Scale Science, pp. 1–10 (2014)
5. Shi, L., Zhang, Z., Robertazzi, T.: Energy-aware scheduling of embarrassingly parallel jobs and resource allocation in cloud. IEEE Trans. Parallel Distrib. Syst. **28**(6), 1607–1620 (2017)

6. Chirkin, A.M., et al.: Execution time estimation for workflow scheduling. Futur. Gener. Comput. Syst. Int. J. eScience **75**, 376–387 (2017)
7. Wu, Q., Ishikawa, F., Zhu, Q., Xia, Y., Wen, J.: Deadline-constrained cost optimization approaches for workflow scheduling in clouds. IEEE Trans. Parallel Distrib. Syst. **28**(12), 3401–3412 (2017)
8. Yao, G., Ding, Y., Hao, K.: Using imbalance characteristic for fault-tolerant workflow scheduling in cloud systems. IEEE Trans. Parallel Distrib. Syst. **28**(12), 3671–3683 (2017)
9. Chen, H., Zhu, X., Qiu, D., Liu, L., Du, Z.: Scheduling for workflows with security-sensitive intermediate data by selective tasks duplication in clouds. IEEE Trans. Parallel Distrib. Syst. **28**(9), 2674–2688 (2017)
10. Liu, J., Pacitti, E., Valduriez, P., de Oliveira, D., Mattoso, M.: Multi-objective scheduling of scientific workflows in multisite clouds. Futur. Gener. Comput. Syst. **63**, 76–95 (2016)
11. Shukla, S.: An evolutionary study of multi-objective workflow scheduling in cloud computing. Int. J. Comput. Appl. **133**(14), 14–18 (2016)
12. Durillo, J.J., Nae, V., Prodan, R.: Multi-objective workflow scheduling: an analysis of the energy efficiency and makespan tradeoff. In: Proceedings - 13th IEEE/ACM International Symposium on Cluster, Cloud, and Grid Computing. CCGrid 2013, pp. 203–210 (2013)
13. Yassa, S., Chelouah, R., Kadima, H., Granado, B.: Multi-objective approach for energy-aware workflow scheduling in cloud computing environments. Sci. World J. **2013**, 13 (2013)
14. Khajemohammadi, H., Fanian, A., Gulliver, T.A.: Fast workflow scheduling for grid computing based on a multi-objective Genetic Algorithm. In: Proceedings of the IEEE Pacific RIM Conference on Communications, Computers, and Signal Processing, pp. 96–101 (2013)
15. Zhu, Z., Zhang, G., Li, M., Liu, X.: Evolutionary multi-objective workflow scheduling in cloud. IEEE Trans. Parallel Distrib. Syst. **27**(5), 1344–1357 (2016)
16. Chen, W.-N., Zhang, J.: An ant colony optimization approach to a grid workflow scheduling problem with various QoS requirements. IEEE Trans. Syst. Man, Cybern. Part C: Applications Rev. **39**(1), 29–43 (2009)
17. Padmaveni, K., Aravindhar, D.J.: Hybrid memetic and particle swarm optimization for multi objective scientific workflows in cloud. In: 2016 IEEE International Conference on Cloud Computing in Emerging Markets (CCEM), pp. 66–72 (2016)
18. Zheng, X., Wang, L.: A Pareto based fruit fly optimization algorithm for task scheduling and resource allocation in cloud computing environment. In: 2016 IEEE Congress on Evolutionary Computation (CEC), pp. 3393–3400 (2016)
19. Hou, Y., Wu, N., Zhou, M., Li, Z.: Pareto-optimization for scheduling of crude oil operations in refinery via genetic algorithm. IEEE Trans. Syst. Man, Cybern. Syst. **47**(3), 517–530 (2017)
20. Ebadifard, F., Babamir, S.M.: Optimizing multi objective based workflow scheduling in cloud computing using black hole algorithm. In: 2017 3rd International Conference on Web Research. ICWR 2017, pp. 102–108, April 2017
21. Fard, H.M., Prodan, R., Fahringer, T.: A truthful dynamic workflow scheduling mechanism for commercial multicloud environments. IEEE Trans. Parallel Distrib. Syst. **24**(6), 1203–1212 (2013)
22. Duan, R., Prodan, R., Li, X.: Multi-objective game theoretic schedulingof bag-of-tasks workflows on hybrid clouds. IEEE Trans. Cloud Comput. **2**(1), 29–42 (2014)

23. Sujana, J.A.J., Revathi, T., Karthiga, G., Raj, R.V.: Game multi objective scheduling algorithm for scientific workflows in cloud computing. In: IEEE International Conference on Circuit, Power and Computing Technologies. ICCPCT 2015, pp. 1–6 (2015)

24. Pettit, P., Sugden, R.: The backward induction paradox. J. Philos. **86**(4), 169–182 (1989)

25. Topcuoglu, H., Hariri, S., Wu, M.: Performance-effective and low-complexity task scheduling for heterogeneous computing. Parallel Distrib. Syst. **13**(3), 260–274 (2002)

26. Zhang, L., Zhou, J.: Task scheduling and resource allocation algorithm in cloud computing system based on non-cooperative game. In: 2017 IEEE 2nd International Conference on Cloud Computing and Big Data Analysis (ICCCBDA), pp. 254–259 (2017)

27. Balouek-Thomert, D., Bhattacharya, A.K., Caron, E., Gadireddy, K., Lefevre, L.: Parallel differential evolution approach for cloud workflow placements under simultaneous optimization of multiple objectives. In: 2016 IEEE Congress on Evolutionary Computation (CEC), pp. 822–829 (2016)

A Quality-Based Web API Selection for Mashup Development Using Affinity Propagation

Kenneth K. Fletcher[✉]

University of Massachusetts Boston, Boston, MA 02125, USA
kenneth.fletcher@umb.edu

Abstract. The rising interest in web APIs and mashups have led to a myriad of web APIs with similar functionality. Due to this reason, it is challenging to select relevant and quality web APIs for mashup developers, to compose quality and valuable mashups. On the other hand, clustering has proven to be one of the effective ways to select web APIs. However, methods, models and approaches that attempt to cluster web APIs for selection, by providing distinction between similar web APIs, focus either on their functionality or popularity and seldom consider quality of these web APIs. It is for this reason that this work proposes a method, based on topic modeling and clustering, to select quality web APIs for mashup development. First, we use Hierarchical Dirichlet Process (HDP) to identify a set of Web APIs that match a mashup developer's requirement, using the semantic distances between web API and developer's requirement topic distributions. Next, we use a black-box approach to analyze the quality of the subset of web APIs that match the mashup developer's requirement and employ Affinity Propagation (AP) clustering algorithm to cluster web APIs based on their quality. We perform experiments using dataset crawled from programmableweb.com and compare our results to other clustering-based selection methods.

Keywords: Mashup · Services · Mashup selection
Mashup recommendation · Web API
Hierarchical Dirichlet Process · Affinity propagation

1 Introduction

The extensive reach of the Internet has instituted it as the platform of choice for service provision and marketing over the past decade. The abundance of web services and web application programming interfaces (APIs) has introduced diversity and flexibility in web application development. For instance, Netflix.com has over 17,000 movies in its selection, Amazon.com has over 410,000 titles in its Kindle store alone [1] and the number of (APIs) on programmableweb.com passed the 19,000 mark in January 2018 [2].

© Springer International Publishing AG, part of Springer Nature 2018
J. E. Ferreira et al. (Eds.): SCC 2018, LNCS 10969, pp. 153–165, 2018.
https://doi.org/10.1007/978-3-319-94376-3_10

Atomic services, web APIs and data could be combined (mashup) to provide new services with value-added functionalities to serve user needs. The current demand for service mashups, coupled with over abundant web APIs with similar functionality, poses a challenge for Mashup developers to select relevant and quality web APIs for their mashup development. Existing methods for web API selection or recommendation focuses on selecting web APIs based on their functionality [3–5]. In a number of these works, topic modeling such as Latent Dirichlet Allocation (LDA) [6] are used to find the semantic distances between web API description documents and user requirements [3]. However, LDA suffers from low efficiency, excessive long training time and low accuracy, especially in applications where the input document is relatively short.

In spite of this, since there are so many web APIs with similar functionality, there is the need for a method that can provide a differentiation between these functionally-similar web APIs. Some works that attempt to do so focus on selecting or recommending web APIs using the usage history and popularity of web APIs [4,7]. These works skew the selection of web APIs towards popularity which sometimes cause mashup developers to miss out on potentially good web APIs that are not popular. To resolve this issue, Cao et al. [3] proposed an integrated content and network-based web API recommendation method for mashup development. However, their work focused so much on making unpopular web APIs popular with no consideration of the quality of these unpopular web APIs.

Cluster analysis is an important component of scientific and industrial data analysis, and many clustering methods have been proposed [8]. Web API clustering is an enabling technique used to facilitate the selection of web APIs, from an immense number of web APIs, for mashup development. Clustering web APIs, based on their functionality, has shown to be an effective way for web API discovery [5]. Most clustering-based web API/service selection methods employ either the K-means or hierarchical clustering [3,5,9–11] methods because they may be fast, easy to implement and result in tighter clusters. These methods however, have some limitations which make them unsuitable clustering methods for web API selection. For instance, predicting the number of clusters, K, in K-means clustering is a challenging task and is very sensitive to outliers.

To address these limitations and provide accurate, relevant and quality web APIs for mashup development, this work proposes a method that employs Hierarchical Dirichlet Process (HDP) [12] and Affinity Propagation (AP) clustering algorithm [13] to cluster and select web APIs, based on quality, for mashup developers. We adopt a quality model by Cappiello et al. [14] to evaluate the quality of over 12,000 web APIs on programmableweb.com and subsequently cluster the web APIs, based on their quality, for selection. The contributions of this work are summarized as follows:

1. We employ HDP to extract the topic distributions from both user requirements and each web API description document, and use the Jensen-Shannon divergence [15] to compute the similarity between the two distributions. In doing so, we obtain a list of web APIs that closely match users requirement.

2. To select services based on quality, we adopt and extend a quality model for mashup components [14] to evaluate the quality of 12,879 web APIs from programmableweb.com. This quality model is based on black-box approach because with web APIs, their internal details and complexity are usually hidden.
3. We also adopt AP clustering algorithm to cluster similar web APIs using quality measure. Our choice of clustering method is based on the advantages AP has over other clustering types for web API clustering.
4. Finally, we conduct experiments to evaluate our proposed method. For our experiments we considered web API dataset previously crawled from programmableweb.com[1]. However, the available fields in the dataset were insufficient to conduct our experiments. Due to this, we also crawled programmableweb.com to collect additional information for our experiments. Our new dataset has records of 12,879 web APIs.

The rest of the paper is outlined as follows. In Sect. 2 we discuss some of the notable and significant web APIs/service selection works based on clustering. We present our proposed quality-based web API selection method in detail in Sect. 3 followed by our experiments, evaluations and results analysis in Sect. 4. Finally, we conclude our paper and discuss some of the open ended challenges as a part of our future work in Sect. 5.

2   Related Work

Web service/API discovery and selection is heavily based on identifying ranking services according to some user's requirement [16,17]. Web service/API clustering has been employed to not only increase the performance of service discovery/selection methods, but to also improve the efficiency of these selection processes. It would improve the ability of service users to discover and select relevant and quality services quickly, based on their requirements (functional/non-functional), by tremendously reducing the number of similarity computations, during the discovery/selection process. Most existing web service clustering methods cluster web services based on either their functionality or non-functional attributes (quality of service).

Elgazzar et al. [18] proposed a semantic clustering method based on functional properties such as service name, operations and messages. Dong et al. [19] proposed a clustering-based search approach for Web services, focused on functional descriptions of services. In their work, they extract a set of semantic concepts using natural language descriptions from WSDL document. In their work, Chen et al. [20] also focused on clustering web services based on functionality, by introducing WordNet lexical database. They used this database together with the Vector Space Model (VSM), by analyzing and processing service WSDL document, to represent feature vectors of web services patterns. They then used Self

---

[1] http://49.123.0.60:8080/MashupNetwork2.0/dataset.jsp.

Organizing Map (SOM) neural network to cluster the web services. Their representation of web services patterns improved the clustering results. In another web service functionality-based clustering work proposed by Xie et al. [21], Web services ontology was employed for service matching using an accurate semantic concept of the domain ontology.

Web service clustering methods based on non-functional attributes typically focus on quality of services (QoS). Karthiban [10] proposed a web service clustering method based on QoS factors. In his work, he considered QoS factors such as response time, throughput, availability, successability and reliability, to eliminate irrelevant services to cluster the web services. Kumara [22] proposed a QoS clustering approach using negative QoS attributes to compute affinity values from which QoS similarity are obtained and web service clusters are subsequently generated. Xia et al. [23] proposed an algorithm, based on clustering methods, to organize a large number of atomic web services into K clusters according to their QoS factors. Their method takes QoS factors such as cost, execution time and reliability into account.

Most of the web services clustering methods discussed above, compute the similarity between web services based on some similarity function, such are the euclidean or cosine similarity. Basically, these functions count the number of occurrences among terms in WSDL documents to compute similarity between web services. The limitation of using such similarity functions for web services, is they fail to capture the semantic correlation between them. It is due to this limitation that we employ HDP in our proposed work to implicitly capture the semantic correlation between web services/APIs description documents.

3   Proposed Method

This section first discusses an overview of our proposed method and subsequently describes the main modules that drives our method. Figure 1 shows an overview of our proposed method.

We crawled programmableweb.com and retrieved several information on web APIs, including those necessary information for analyzing the quality of web APIs. This information was stored in a *Web API* repository. Using the descriptions of web APIs in the repository, we apply *HDP* to extract all topic distributions from each web API document description. Similarly, When a mashup developer submits a request for web API (requirement), we apply *HDP* to obtain the topic distribution from the mashup developer's requirement. We then obtain the similarity between the mashup developer's requirement topic distribution and each web API topic distribution by computing the *Jensen-Shannon divergence*, and choosing web APIs, whose topic distribution closely match the mashup developer's requirement topic distribution. We subsequently compute the quality of all web APIs meeting mashup developer's requirement using our *Quality Model* and cluster the web APIs using *Affinity Propagation Clustering*. Cluster with the highest quality are then selected to the mashup developer. Details of our proposed method's main components are described in the sections that follow.

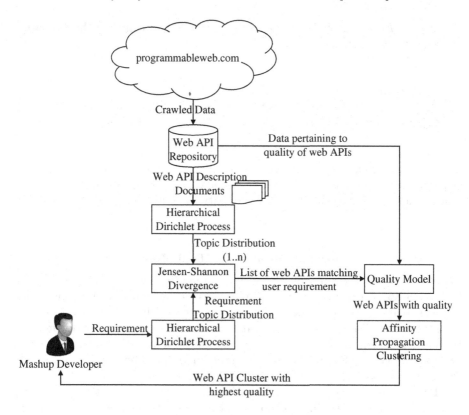

Fig. 1. Overview of the proposed quality-based Web API selection method

3.1 Problem Definition

Formally, let R be a mashup developer's requirement and let $W = \{w_1, w_2, .., w_n\}$ be the set of web APIs crawled from programmableweb.com. For each web API, W_i, there is a set of properties, $P_{W_i}<D, L, S, A, F, O>$, associated to W_i.

Where:

- D: Web API description
- L: Supported languages
- S: SSL support
- A: Authentication model
- F: Data formats supported
- O: Other properties like number of SDKs, sample source code, etc.

Given $P_{W_i}.D$, we can obtain Γ_{W_i} and Γ_R as the topic distribution of W_i and R respectively, by employing HDP as:

$$HDP(P_{W_i}.D) :\rightarrow \Gamma_{W_i}$$
$$HDP(R) :\rightarrow \Gamma_R \tag{1}$$

Given Γ_{W_i}, Γ_R and a similarity measure, Sim, we can compute the similarity between the two distributions as:

$$Sim(\Gamma_{W_i}, \Gamma_R) = JS(\Gamma_{W_i}, \Gamma_R) \qquad (2)$$

where JS is the Jensen-Shannon Divergence [15].

Let $C = \{c \mid c \in W\}$ be a set of candidate web APIs that match a mashup developer's requirement R such that each $c \in C$. A candidate web API, $c \in C$, if

$$Sim(\Gamma_c, \Gamma_R) > \delta \qquad (3)$$

where δ is the similarity cut-off threshold. Given C, and a quality model, Φ, we can generate a web API quality set $Q = \{q_1, q_2, ..., q_m\}$, where $|Q| = |C|$, such that for each $c \in C$ we can compute the quality using its properties P_c as follows:

$$Q(P_c) :\rightarrow q_c \qquad (4)$$

3.2   Hierarchical Dirichlet Process for Topic Recognition

Recently, probabilistic topic models such as latent dirichlet allocation (LDA) [6], have been applied to extract and represent users preference in different application scenarios [24]. LDA has been applied successfully to identify topics in documents and discover implicit semantic correlation among those documents. However, it suffers from low efficiency, excessively long training time and low accuracy, especially in applications where the input document is relatively short. Due to these reasons, we employ HDP for our topic modeling.

HDP, an extension of LDA, is a multi-layer form of the Dirichlet process (DP), designed to address cases in topic document modeling where the number of topic terms is not known in advance. For each document, a mixture of topics are drawn from a Dirichlet distribution, and then each word in the document is treated as an independent draw from that mixture [12]. Figure 2 shows a graphical model formalism of HDP. The global measure, G_0 is distributed as a Dirichlet process with concentration parameter γ and base probability measure H:

$$G_0 \mid \gamma, H \sim DP(\gamma, H) \qquad (5)$$

and the random measures G_j are conditionally independent given G_0, with distributions given by a Dirichlet process with base probability measure G_0:

$$G_j \mid \alpha_0, G_0 \sim DP(\alpha_0, G_0) \qquad (6)$$

The hyperparameters of the hierarchical Dirichlet process consist of the baseline probability measure H, and the concentration parameters γ and α_0. The baseline H provides the prior distribution for the topic of the ith word in the jth WSDL document, θ_{ji}. For each j let $\theta_{j1}, \theta_{j2}, ...$ be independent and identically distributed random topics distributed as G_j. Each θ_{ji} is a topic corresponding to a single observation x_{ji}. The likelihood is given by:

$$\begin{aligned} \theta_{ji} \mid G_j &\sim G_j \\ x_{ji} \mid \theta_{ji} &\sim F(\theta_{ji}) \end{aligned} \qquad (7)$$

which is the hierarchical Dirichlet Process mixture model [12].

3.3   Affinity Propagation Algorithm

Affinity Propagation (AP) has been receiving a lot of attention for use in many applications recently. It has been successfully used in many applications in various disciplines such as initial training set selection in active learning, key-phrase extraction, image clustering, representative image extraction, and supervised dimensionality reduction [8]. AP is a novel clustering algorithm proposed by Dueck [13]. It transmits real-valued messages between all pairs of data points recursively until message values converge. AP determines a set of clusters and "exemplars" (i.e. their representative data points), based on the converged message values. AP has a number of noteworthy advantages:

1. it achieves much lower clustering error than existing clustering methods such as k-means clustering,
2. it can support similarities that are not symmetric or do not satisfy the triangle inequality, and
3. it is deterministic, i.e., its clustering results do not depend on initialization, unlike most clustering methods such as k-means [8].

It is based on these advantages that we employ AP as the clustering method to cluster web APIs.

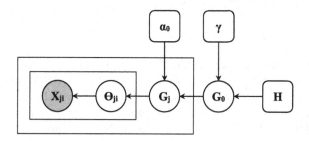

Fig. 2. A hierarchical Dirichlet process mixture model. In the graphical model formalism, each node in the graph is associated with a random variable, where shading denotes an observed variable. Rectangles denote replication of the model within the rectangle [12].

Formally, given a similarity matrix $s[i,j](i,j = 1, 2, ..., N)$, where $s[i,j]$ is the pair-wise similarity between each pair of data points (e.g. negative Euclidean distance for real valued data, Jaccard coefficient for non-metric data, or a pre-computed similarity), AP attempts to find the exemplars that maximize the overall sum of similarities between all exemplars and their member data points. The process of Affinity Propagation can be viewed as a message passing process with two kinds of messages exchanged among data points: *responsibility* and *availability* [13]. Responsibility, $r[i,j]$, is a message from data point i to j that reflects the accumulated evidence for how well-suited data point j is to serve as the exemplar for data point i. Availability, $a[i,j]$, is a message from data point

j to i that reflects the accumulated evidence for how appropriate it would be for data point i to choose data point j as its exemplar [8]. All responsibilities and availabilities are set to 0 initially, and their values are iteratively updated as follows to compute convergence values:

$$r[i,j] = (1 - \lambda)\rho[i,j] + \lambda r[i,j]$$
$$a[i,j] = (1 - \lambda)\alpha[i,j] + \lambda a[i,j] \tag{8}$$

where λ is a damping factor introduced to avoid numerical oscillations, and

$$\rho[i,j] = \begin{cases} s[i,j] - max_{k \neq j}\{a[i,k] + s[i,k]\} & (i = j) \\ s[i,j] - max_{k \neq j}\{s[i,k]\} & (i = j) \end{cases} \tag{9}$$

$$\alpha[i,j] = \begin{cases} s[i,j] - min\{0, r[j,j] + \Sigma_{k \neq i,j} max\{0, r[k,j]\}\} & (i = j) \\ \Sigma_{k \neq i,j} max\{0, r[k,j]\} & (i = j) \end{cases} \tag{10}$$

are propagating responsibility and propagating availability, respectively. That is, messages between data points are computed from the corresponding propagating messages. The exemplar of data point i is finally defined as:

$$argmax r[i,j] + a[i,j] : j = 1, 2, ..., N \tag{11}$$

3.4 Quality Model for Web APIs

We adopt the quality model proposed by Cappiello et al. [14] to define our quality model for web APIs. Typically, web APIs hide their internal complexity and details and therefore external quality factors drive the evaluation of its suitability for integration into a mashup application [14]. For this reason, our quality model is based on a black-box approach. Figure 3 gives an overview of the quality attributes of a web API, which we organize along three main dimensions, namely *Functionality*, *Reliability* and *Usability*. Formally, the quality of a web API can be computed as the normalized sum of these three dimensions.

$$Quality_{WebAPI} = \frac{1}{3}[F + R + U] \tag{12}$$

where F, R, and U are functionality, reliability and usability of the web API respectively.

The functionality, F, of a web API can be refined by considering the interoperability, the compliance, and the security level of that web API [14]. Interoperability of a web API depends on its capability to be used in different and heterogeneous environments. Compliance is the ability of the web API to at last support one of the standard data formats. This in turn increases the interoperability level. The security of a web API is related to the protection mechanism that is used to rule the access to the offered functionalities. Two main aspects are considered: SSL support and authentication mechanisms.

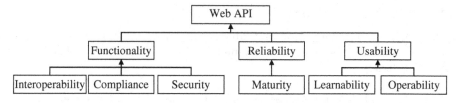

Fig. 3. Quality model based on Cappeillo et al. [14]

Formally, the functionality dimension of a web API can be computed as follows:

$$F = \frac{1}{3}[(1 + \frac{|lang|}{k} + \frac{|dformat|}{l}) + 3comp + \frac{3}{5}sec] \qquad (13)$$

where *lang* and *dformat* are the languages and data formats supported by the web API, and *comp* and *sec* are compliance and security levels of the web API respectively.

Reliability of a web API is measured with respect to its maturity. This is because the black-box approach does not allow one to evaluate the level of performance of a component under stated conditions for a stated period of time [14]. Reliability can be evaluated in terms of maturity, by considering the available statistics of usage of the component together with the frequency of its changes and updates. Formally, it can be computed as:

$$Maturity = max(1 - \frac{cdate - ludate}{\frac{cdate-crdate}{|ver|}}, 0) \qquad (14)$$

where *cdate*, *ludate*, and *crdate* are the current date, last use date and creation date of the web API respectively, and *ver* is the set of version available for that web API.

The final dimension a web API quality is usability. A web API's usability is evaluated in terms of understandability. Given the black box approach, understandability can be evaluated by considering the web API documentation. Particularly relevant in the mashup scenario is the support offered to mashup composers by means of examples, API groups, blogs, or forums, and any other kind of documentation [14]. The availability of each type of support contributes to increase these quality attributes.

4   Experiments and Results

This section describes the experiments we conducted to evaluate and validate our proposed quality-based web API selection for mashup development. We also discuss our results.

4.1   Dataset Description

To conduct our experiments, we initially considered a web API dataset crawled from programmableweb.com[2] in November 2016. The available fields in this dataset include:

Table 1. Top 10 Web API categories from programmableweb.com

Category	Number of Web APIs
Tools	787
Financial	583
Enterprise	486
eCommerce	434
Social	402
Messaging	388
Payments	374
Government	306
Mapping	295
Science	287

- *APIname*: web API name,
- *APIhref*: web url to the web API on programmableweb.com,
- *tags*: different tags associated to the web API,
- *APIDesc*: description of the web API,
- *primary_category_url*: web url of the web API's primary category,
- *primary_category*: web API primary category,
- *scName*: sub categories of the web API, and
- *submitDate*: date web API was submitted to the programmableweb.com web site.

However, because the fields contained in this dataset were not sufficient for our experiments, we also crawled the programmableweb.com website to obtain the additional field information. The additional field information includes:

- *ssl_support*: indicates if the web API supports SSL,
- *authentication_model*: type of authentication the web API supports,
- *data_formats*: data formats supported by the web API,
- *version*: version number of the web API,
- *sdks*: number of SDKs available for the web API,
- *how_tos*: number of how tos and tutorial contents available for the web API, and
- *sample_codes*: number of sample codes available for the web API.

In all, our new web API dataset from programmableweb.com contains 12,879 web APIs, with 383 categories. Table 1 shows a list of the top 10 categories in the dataset.

---

[2] http://49.123.0.60:8080/MashupNetwork2.0/dataset.jsp.

4.2   Evaluation Metrics

To quantitatively evaluate the clustering results, precision, recall, and F-measure were computed. These metrics were used over pairs of web APIs. For each pair of web APIs, the metrics attempts to estimate whether the prediction of the pair, as being in the same cluster, was correct with respect to the underlying true categories in the data. By definition:

$$Precision(W_i) = \frac{tPositive(W_i)}{tPositive(W_i) + fPositive(W_i)}$$

$$Recall(W_i) = \frac{tPositive(W_i)}{tPositive(W_i) + fNegative(W_i)}$$

$$F - Measure = 2 \times \frac{Precision \times Recall}{Precision + Recall}$$

where $tPositive$, $fPositive$ and $fNegative$ are true positive, false positive and false negative respectively. Higher precision, recall and F-measure values indicates better performance.

4.3   Results

Using our web API dataset, we used our proposed method to cluster web APIs and compared our results to a few other clustering methods:

- LDA-K-Means: A K-means clustering algorithm that utilizes LDA for topic modeling of web API descriptions.
- HDP-K-Means: A K-means clustering algorithm that utilizes HDP for topic modeling of web API descriptions.
- LDA-Affinity: An Affinity Propagation clustering algorithm that utilizes LDA for topic modeling of web API descriptions.
- HDP-Affinity: An Affinity Propagation clustering algorithm that utilizes HDP for topic modeling of web API descriptions. This is our proposed method.

Table 2. Evaluation comparison

Clustering method	Precision	Recall	F-measure
LDA-K-Means	0.5192	0.3449	0.4174
HDP-K-Means	0.6022	0.4178	0.4986
LDA-Affinity	0.6215	0.3854	0.4611
HDP-Affinity	**0.6670**	**0.5438**	**0.6056**

Table 2 shows the evaluation comparison. From the table, it can be seen that the precision, recall and F-measure of our proposed method were the highest, compared to the other methods. This can be attributed to the use of HDP for topic modeling, which is able to better model topics in documents than its counterparts. In addition, the use of affinity propagation algorithm for clustering allows our method to achieve a much lower clustering error than other clustering methods.

5 Conclusion

The challenge of selecting relevant and quality web APIs for mashup development still exist due to the rising interest in web APIs and mashups, which have led to a myriad of web APIs with similar functionality. This work have presented a quality-based affinity propagation clustering method to select quality and relevant web APIs for mashup developers. In our proposed method, first, we use Hierarchical Dirichlet Process (HDP) to identify a set of Web APIs that match a mashup developer's requirement, using the semantic distances between each web API and developer's requirement topic distributions. Next, we use a black-box approach to analyze the quality of the subset of web APIs that match the mashup developer's requirement and employ Affinity Propagation (AP) clustering algorithm to cluster web APIs based on their quality. We have performed experiments using dataset crawled from programmableweb.com and compare our results to other clustering-based selection methods. Our results show that our proposed method is able to give the best clustering results to aid web API selection.

References

1. Fletcher, K.K., Liu, X.F.: A collaborative filtering method for personalized preference-based service recommendation. In: Proceedings of the 2015 IEEE International Conference on Web Services, pp. 400–407, June 2015
2. Santos, W.: Research shows interest in providing APIs still high (2018). https://www.programmableweb.com/news/research-shows-interest-providing-apis-still-high/research/2018/02/23. Accessed 15 Mar 2018
3. Cao, B., Liu, X., Rahman, M.M., Li, B., Liu, J., Tang, M.: Integrated content and network-based service clustering and Web APIs recommendation for mashup development. IEEE Trans. Serv. Comput. **PP**(99), 1 (2017)
4. Cao, B., Liu, J., Tang, M., Zheng, Z., Wang, G.: Mashup service recommendation based on user interest and social network. In: 2013 IEEE 20th International Conference on Web Services, pp. 99–106, June 2013
5. Xia, B., Fan, Y., Tan, W., Huang, K., Zhang, J., Wu, C.: Category-aware API clustering and distributed recommendation for automatic mashup creation. IEEE Trans. Serv. Comput. **8**(5), 674–687 (2015)
6. Blei, D.M., Ng, A.Y., Jordan, M.I.: Latent Dirichlet allocation. J. Mach. Learn. Res. **3**, 993–1022 (2003)
7. Samanta, P., Liu, X., Golisano, T.: Recommendation of APIs for mashup creation (2016)

8. Fujiwara, Y., Irie, G., Kitahara, T.: Fast algorithm for affinity propagation. In: Proceedings of the Twenty-Second International Joint Conference on Artificial Intelligence, IJCAI 2011, vol. 3, pp. 2238–2243. AAAI Press (2011)
9. Kumar, S., Purohit, L.: Exploring k-means clustering and skyline for web service selection. In: 2016 11th International Conference on Industrial and Information Systems (ICIIS), pp. 603–607, December 2016
10. Karthiban, R.: A QoS-aware web service selection based on clustering. Int. J. Sci. Res. Publ. (IJSRP) **4**(2) (2014)
11. Zhang, X., Wang, Z., Lv, X., Qi, R.: A clustering-based QoS prediction approach for web service selection. In: 2013 International Conference on Information Science and Cloud Computing Companion, pp. 201–206, December 2013
12. Teh, Y.W., Jordan, M.I., Beal, M.J., Blei, D.M.: Hierarchical Dirichlet processes. J. Am. Stat. Assoc. **101** (2004)
13. Dueck, D.: Affinity propagation: clustering data by passing messages. Ph.D. dissertation, University of Toronto (2009)
14. Cappiello, C., Daniel, F., Matera, M.: A quality model for mashup components. In: Gaedke, M., Grossniklaus, M., Díaz, O. (eds.) Web Engineering, pp. 236–250. Springer, Berlin (2009)
15. Fuglede, B., Topsoe, F.: Jensen-Shannon divergence and Hilbert space embedding. In: Proceedings of the International Symposium on Information Theory, ISIT 2004, p. 31, June 2004
16. Fletcher, K.K., Liu, X.F., Tang, M.: Elastic personalized nonfunctional attribute preference and trade-off based service selection. ACM Trans. Web **9**(1), 1:1–1:26 (2015)
17. Liu, X., Fletcher, K.K., Tang, M.: Service selection based on personalized preference and trade-offs among QoS factors and price. In: 2012 IEEE First International Conference on Services Economics, pp. 32–39, June 2012
18. Elgazzar, K., Hassan, A.E., Martin, P.: Clustering WSDL documents to bootstrap the discovery of web services. In: 2010 IEEE International Conference on Web Services, pp. 147–154, July 2010
19. Dong, X., Halevy, A., Madhavan, J., Nemes, E., Zhang, J.: Similarity search for web services. In: Proceedings of the Thirtieth International Conference on Very Large Data Bases, VLDB 2004, VLDB Endowment, vol. 30, pp. 372–383 (2004)
20. Chen, L., Yang, G., Zhang, Y., Chen, Z.: Web services clustering using SOM based on kernel cosine similarity measure. In: The 2nd International Conference on Information Science and Engineering, pp. 846–850, December 2010
21. Xie, L., Chen, F., Kou, J.: Ontology-based semantic web services clustering. In: 2011 IEEE 18th International Conference on Industrial Engineering and Engineering Management, vol. Part 3, pp. 2075–2079, September 2011
22. Kumara, B.T.G.S., Paik, I., Siriweera, T.H.A.S., Koswatte, K.R.C.: QoS aware service clustering to bootstrap the web service selection. In: 2017 IEEE International Conference on Services Computing (SCC), pp. 233–240, June 2017
23. Xia, Y., Chen, P., Bao, L., Wang, M., Yang, J.: A QoS-aware web service selection algorithm based on clustering. In: 2011 IEEE International Conference on Web Services, pp. 428–435, July 2011
24. Liu, X.: Modeling users' dynamic preference for personalized recommendation. In: Proceedings of the 24th International Conference on Artificial Intelligence, IJCAI 2015, pp. 1785–1791. AAAI Press (2015)

Perfomance Evaluation of Java, JavaScript and PHP Serialization Libraries for XML, JSON and Binary Formats

Jan Vanura and Pavel Kriz[✉]

Department of Informatics and Quantitative Methods, Faculty of Informatics and Management, University of Hradec Kralove, Hradec Kralove, Czech Republic
Pavel.Kriz@uhk.cz

Abstract. The aim of this paper is to compare the formats and libraries used for serialization and deserialization of data, typically with RESTful web services, in terms of the processing time and size of the output data. The formats tested include XML, JSON, MessagePack, Avro, Protocol Buffers, and native serialization of each of the tested programming languages. Serialization and deserialization is tested in PHP, Java and JavaScript using 49 different official and third party libraries. The benchmark is fully open-sourced and automated, thus easily repeatable and extensible. The testing environment is designed to be isolated from the rest of the operating system using Docker containers having zero performance penalty in contrast to virtualization. The results show huge differences in processing time among libraries. Considering the output data size, binary formats with predefined schema, such as Avro and Protocol Buffers, provide the best efficiency.

Keywords: Benchmark · Web services · Serialization · Marshalling
XML · JSON · MessagePack · Avro · Protocol buffers · Java · PHP
JavaScript · Docker

1 Introduction

With the development of information technology, there is a growing need for information exchange. Today, we usually develop thin-client applications, especially web-based ones. They require only minimal resources on the client side, which is often a web browser. Mobile applications are another example. In recent years, we have seen their unprecedented growth. Essentially, thin applications are just displaying data and enabling manipulation with these data through a graphical user interface (GUI). Data operations are then executed and the data are stored on the server.

In order to exchange the data between the client and the server (a Web service), it is necessary for the data to be transmitted in a format that is understood

© Springer International Publishing AG, part of Springer Nature 2018
J. E. Ferreira et al. (Eds.): SCC 2018, LNCS 10969, pp. 166–175, 2018.
https://doi.org/10.1007/978-3-319-94376-3_11

by both sides. The process of converting data structures from a program code into these formats is called serialization or marshalling. In general, it transforms the data into a stream of bytes, so a complex object can be saved into a file or sent via a network. The reverse process is called deserialization or unmarshalling. This is the process of converting a stream of bytes back into the programming language data structures.

The aim of this paper is to compare the performance of various serialization and deserialization libraries – both native and third party – in Java, PHP and JavaScript. The serialization output data size will also be compared among individual data formats.

The rest of this paper is organized as follows. Section 2 describes the existing work on benchmarks of different serialization formats and libraries. Section 3 describes the methodology – measures, inputs etc. Different formats tested in the benchmark are briefly described in Sect. 4. We present the results of the benchmark in Sect. 5. Section 6 concludes the paper.

2 Related Work

There are many papers dealing with the evaluation and benchmarking of serialization libraries. Most of them focus on the comparison of Extensible Markup Language (XML) and JavaScript Object Notation (JSON) formats [1–3]. Comparison with other formats is not so common. A large majority of benchmarks aimed at comparing different formats is written in Java, probably due to a high popularity of the language. Significantly less benchmarks are written in PHP or JavaScript, despite the fact that these formats are also widely used.

Renaud [4] compares 18 different libraries for JSON serialization in Java. The results are clearly presented in the form of graphs and tables. The versions of all libraries and the hardware and software of the computer where the benchmark was launched are described clearly. In contrast to Renaud, Smith [5] compares more data formats in Java. Again, the results are presented in graphs and tables, but versions of the libraries and the input data description are missing. Maeda [6] and Aihkisalo [7] did similar benchmarks in Java, but versions of the libraries are also missing in both papers. Sumaray [8] focuses on XML, JSON, ProtoBuf and Thrift on the Android platform. We have also concerns regarding the missing versions of the Android platform, where the benchmark was run.

Suarez [9] compares three native PHP functions. The results are presented only numerically, without graphs. However, a PHP version, hardware specification and an input data description are omitted. Sági-Kazár [10] compares three formats in PHP: JSON, a native format and MessagePack. The results and concerns are the same as with Suarez.

Regarding the JavaScript language, Monsch [11] compares 5 formats in NodeJS: Avro, MessagePack, JSON, Protocol Buffers, PSON. The results are shown in graphs. Host computer hardware is described. However, only the version of Avro implementation is mentioned in the benchmark, not the versions of other libraries.

Some works focus strictly on one type of measurement. For example, Popić [12] measures the size of the output data for ProtoBuf, BSON and JSON considering their application in then Internet-of-Things field.

Other benchmarks for these languages can also be found. However, most of them are no longer up to date or do not contain enough relevant information to evaluate the results. None of the benchmarks found compares results across multiple programming languages, although real-world applications work across platforms (eg. a Java-based mobile application and PHP on the server). Existing work often lacks the versions of libraries, the hardware specification of the computer on which the test was run, or the description and size of the test data (a common problem for the above mentioned). Most benchmarks also contain only a small number of formats or a small number of libraries. Therefore, we have created a new benchmark across multiple programming languages that is well documented, extensible and easily deployable thanks to Docker Containers technology.

3   Methodology

In the benchmark, we can do several types of measurements (tests). First, we can measure the time to complete (de)serialization. It is also possible to measure the number of operations per second. Regarding the serialized (output) data, we can also measure its size. We pick a subset of these measures in order to interpret benchmark's results properly.

3.1   Performance Measures

We have chosen to measure the time of serialization and deserialization in milliseconds (ms). This is easily interpretable and comprehensible: the smaller the number, the faster the library (format). We also measure the size of the serialized data in kilobytes (kB); the smaller the size, the better the library (and format). The chosen measures are the same as in [5,11] and many others.

One pass of the (de)serialization takes only a few microseconds for the reasonably large input data. The measurement of such short intervals could result in a large error and variance. For this reason, we perform multiple measurements. The same data is repetitively (de)serialized many times and the total time is measured. The whole process is also repeated in order to acquire multiple samples. Both loops are implemented for example in Java according to the following code.

```
for (int j = 0; j < OUTER_REPETITIONS; j++){
    start = System.nanoTime();
    for (int i = 0; i < INNER_REPETITIONS; i++) {
        // (de)serialization performed here
    }
    t[j] = System.nanoTime() - start;    // time is stored
}
```

The values presented in our results represent an average time $\bar{t}$ of multiple runs of the whole inner loop according to the Eq. 1, where N is number of outer repetitions (OUTER_REPETITIONS in the Java code) and t_j is a time of the inner loop (t[j] in the Java code).

$$\bar{t} = \frac{\sum_{j=1}^{N} t_j}{N} \tag{1}$$

3.2 Input Data

Test data are integral to the benchmark. It should be large enough and diverse sufficiently in terms of data types used; integer numbers, decimal numbers, logical values, strings, objects and arrays/collections. Randomly generated data from http://www.json-generator.com/ were selected for the benchmark. They describe fictional users. The data meet the diversity requirement, contain numbers, arrays, strings of different lengths, collections of objects, etc. Ten user records are used in the benchmark. The resulting data in JSON format are approximately 12 kB in size. These data are the same for all three programming languages. Similar data structures are used by Renaud [4] and Smith [5].

4 Formats

This chapter describes today's most widely used formats that will be tested within our benchmark.

XML (eXtensible Markup Language) is one of the oldest widely used data formats. It was defined by W3C (World Wide Web Consortium) and is based on an older SGML (Standard Generalized Markup Language) format. In XML, data are structured using *elements* and *attributes*. XML's advantages are its wide spread across platforms, simplicity (human readable and writable), schema validation, and a variety of support technologies. On the other hand, one of its disadvantages is a high number of redundant elements [13]. The names of the elements (a start and end tag), which are often repeated, may be a major part of the output data size.

JSON (JavaScript Object Notation) is another widespread format. It is the lightweight format based on the JavaScript syntax, which often replaces XML due to XML's verbosity and size inefficiency [14]. In contrast to XML, where element contains other elements and/or text, JSON defines several basic data types: object, array, string, number, boolean, and null (undefined value). The overall benefits of JSON include its simplicity and human-readable format. The *object* and *array* structures indicate data types of variables into which the document should be deserialized in a particular programming language. One drawback may be that JSON does not support *attributes* that may be used for metadata in XML.

Avro is, in contrast to previous formats, a binary data format. Therefore, it is neither human-writable nor human-readable. Another difference is that Avro requires a *schema definition*. This schema must be defined before the data serialization can be performed. The advantage of Avro comes from the schema usage; the data structures are clearly described in terms of field names, data types, etc. The disadvantage of the Avro schema is the JSON format that is used to describe the schema itself. A complex schema in JSON is difficult for humans to write and read.

Protocol Buffers, Protobuf in short, is a serialization format developed by Google. Like Avro, it is a binary format that requires a pre-defined schema. The schema is defined using so-called *proto message* platform-independent format. Like Avro, one of the advantages of the Protobuf format is its schema, which ensures unambiguous definition of the data structure. The custom format for the schema definition is simply writable even for structures that are more complex. It is based on the object-oriented programming concepts.

MessagePack, MsgPack in short, is also a binary format. In contrast to Avro and Protobuf, it does not require any schema. It was designed as a binary alternative to JSON. The advantage of MessagePack is its size efficiency. The absence of a schema can be considered a disadvantage, but it depends on the use-case.

Each of the languages tested also supports a **native serialization**. PHP provides `serialize()` and `unserialize()` functions. In Java, there are `ObjectOutputStream` and `ObjectInputStream` classes. JavaScript provides `JSON.stringify()` and `JSON.parse()` functions. These solutions are supported without any 3rd-party libraries. The disadvantage is usually (with the exception of JSON) the lack of interoperability with other languages.

5   Results

The benchmark we have created is programmed in three programming languages, Java, PHP and JavaScript. Individual applications are developed as console programs (without GUI). They can run on almost any operating system such as GNU/Linux, Windows or MacOS. All tests have been performed on an Intel Core I7-2600k 3.4 GHz CPU with 8 GB DDR3 RAM and Debian Linux 8. The versions of PHP 7.1, JDK 8 and NodeJS 7.7 have been used.

In order to run the whole benchmark simply without installing correct versions of PHP, Java and NodeJS (including the right configuration), all applications are ready to run in Docker containers. Thanks to the Docker, it is possible to run the benchmark in an isolated and clearly defined environment without performance being reduced (which is common in classic virtualization). The complete solution is available in the GitHub repository https://github.com/Daaarkling/benchmark.

5.1   Size of Serialized Data

First, we tested the size of the resulting data across libraries and formats. Theoretically, the formats that require a schema should achieve a smaller output data size, since they store the metadata (structure description) in the schema, not in the serialized data.

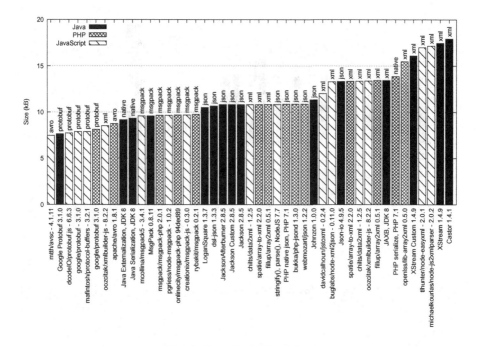

Fig. 1. Size of serialized data

Figure 1 shows the graph of the serialized data size in kilobytes for all libraries tested. The results show that Avro and Protobuf formats are the best followed by MessagePack, JSON and XML. This is confirmed by Monsch [11]. Purely deserialization libraries were omitted from the graph.

5.2 Serialization Performance

In the second test, we measure the time required to serialize the data. The test is performed using the same input data as the previous test. The same data are serialized a thousand times for one library, and this process is repeated a hundred times. Therefore, the total number of iterations is 100,000.

Figure 2 shows the graph of the serialization time. The smaller the resulting value, the better. Since the difference between the best time and the worst time is huge, the Y axis has a logarithmic scale for better clarity. Purely deserialization libraries were omitted from the graph.

Protobuf format serialization implemented in Java has achieved the best result of 7.4 ms. However, the same format's serialization implemented in PHP took 2.6 s, which is almost the worst result of the benchmark. Both Java and

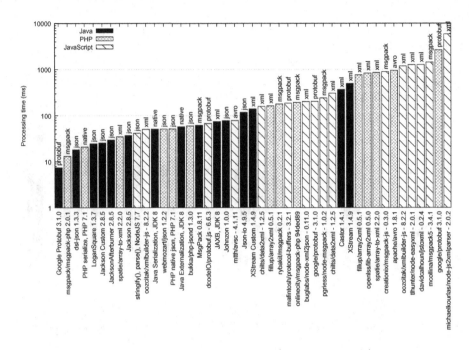

Fig. 2. Serialization performance (logarithmic scale)

PHP implementations have been provided official by Google. *Msgpack/msgpack-php*, the Message Pack library for PHP has a very good result of 13.1 ms. It is an official native extension. Even the implementation in Java performed well, serialization took 62 ms. Libraries for JavaScript (NodeJS) are much worse, especially the *pgriess/node-msgpack* library having 242 ms. Java has a good overall performance. Especially JSON libraries for Java that overcome JSON.stringify(), the native JavaScript function.

The results of JSON libraries in Java are on a par with Renaud's benchmark [4], where the JSON libraries are on the first three positions. The results have also confirmed that JSON is generally faster than XML. [1,2] also confirms these results. In contrast to our results, Protobuf format is always worse than the *dsl-json* library and the Message Pack format in [5].

5.3   Deserialization Performance

In the third test, we measure the time required to deserialize the data. The test is performed using the same data and the same number of repetitions as in the previous test. The results are shown in Fig. 3. Purely serialization libraries were omitted from the graph.

Again, Protobuf format deserialization implemented in Java achieved the best result of 21.8 ms. On the second position, there is the *dsl-json* library with its 25.9 ms, that overcome the *msgpack/msgpack-php* library which was the second in serialization test.

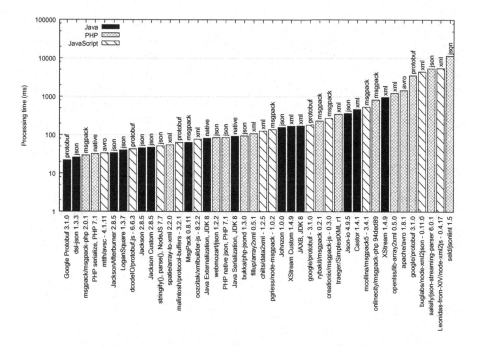

Fig. 3. Deserialization performance (logarithmic scale)

The JSON libraries in Java performed very well again. Their results are on a par with [4], where the first positions are occupied by *dsl-json, Jackson* and *LoganSquare*. Smith's results [5] diverted from ours in the same way as in the serialization test, see above.

The results show that the time required to deserialize the data is always slightly longer than the time required to serialize the data. This fact is confirmed by other benchmarks [9,10].

6 Conclusion

We have created a new benchmark that compares (de)serialization libraries across Java, PHP and JavaScript. It consists of several scripts and source-code files. They are available as open source, making our results easy to verify. Our experiments are repeatable and the benchmark is extensible with new versions of libraries, data formats, or entire platforms/languages. The testing environment is designed to be isolated from the rest of the operating system using Docker containers having zero performance penalty in contrast to virtualization.

Our results show that Avro and Protobuf formats achieve the best result in the first test. These binary formats require a schema definition. Therefore, part of the information does not need to be serialized because it is part of the schema. It implies a smaller size of the output data. The worst results are generally achieved by XML libraries.

Regarding the speed of serialization and deserialization, there are significant differences among languages and libraries, and it is not possible to determine the best format across platforms. The highest speed of serialization and deserialization has been achieved by Google's ProtoBuf library (version 3.1.0) implemented in Java. Generally speaking, JSON format performed well among languages in contrast to XML, which is one of the slowest formats. For other formats, the results vary greatly depending on the language and particular library.

In future research, the number of libraries and formats tested could be expanded and an additional platform could be tested, eg. C#, which is quite popular on the Windows platform.

Acknowledgements. The authors of this paper would like to thank Tereza Krizova for proofreading. This work and the contribution were also supported by a project of Students Grant Agency—FIM, University of Hradec Kralove, Czech Republic. Jan Vanura is a student member of the research team. The author would like to thank Jan Budina, a Ph.D. student at the University of Hradec Kralove, for testing and technical support.

References

1. Nurseitov, N., Paulson, M., Reynolds, R., Izurieta, C.: Comparison of JSON and XML data interchange formats: a case study. CAINE **9**, 157–162 (2009)
2. Pragmateek: JSON vs XML: some hard numbers about verbosity (2013). http://pragmateek.com/json-vs-xml-some-hard-numbers-about-verbosity/
3. Wang, G.: Improving data transmission in web applications via the translation between XML and JSON. In: 2011 Third International Conference on Communications and Mobile Computing, pp. 182–185, April 2011
4. Renaud, F.: Benchmark of Java JSON libraries (2017). https://github.com/fabienrenaud/java-json-benchmark
5. Smith, E., et al.: Benchmark comparing serialization libraries on the JVM (2017). https://github.com/eishay/jvm-serializers
6. Maeda, K.: Performance evaluation of object serialization libraries in XML, JSON and binary formats. In: 2012 Second International Conference on Digital Information and Communication Technology and it's Applications (DICTAP), pp. 177–182, May 2012
7. Aihkisalo, T., Paaso, T.: A performance comparison of web service object marshalling and unmarshalling solutions. In: 2011 IEEE World Congress on Services, pp. 122–129, July 2011
8. Sumaray, A., Makki, S.K.: A comparison of data serialization formats for optimal efficiency on a mobile platform. In: Proceedings of the 6th International Conference on Ubiquitous Information Management and Communication, ICUIMC 2012, pp. 48:1–48:6. ACM, New York (2012)
9. Suarez, T.N.: Benchmarking BSON, JSON, and native serializing in PHP (2016). https://coderwall.com/p/ccdryg/benchmarking-bson-json-and-native-serializing-in-php
10. Sági-Kazár, M.: PHP serialization benchmarks (2017). https://github.com/sagikazarmark/php-serialization-bench
11. Monsch, M.: Benchmarks (2017). https://github.com/mtth/avsc/wiki/Benchmarks

12. Popić, S., Pezer, D., Mrazovac, B., Teslić, N.: Performance evaluation of using protocol buffers in the Internet of Things communication. In: 2016 International Conference on Smart Systems and Technologies (SST), pp. 261–265, October 2016
13. Maeda, K.: Comparative survey of object serialization techniques and the programming supports. J. Commun. Comput. **9**(8), 920–928 (2012)
14. Richardson, L., Ruby, S.: Restful Web Services, 1st edn. O'Reilly, Sebastopol (2007)

Queue-Waiting-Time Based Load Balancing Algorithm for Fine-Grain Microservices

XiaoDong Liu[1,2(✉)], Yan Jin[2], YongHao Song[1,2],
and XiaoFang Zhao[2]

[1] University of Chinese Academy of Sciences, Beijing 100049, China
[2] Institute of Computing Technology, Chinese Academy of Sciences,
Beijing 100190, China
liuxiaodong@ict.ac.cn

Abstract. For fine-grain microservices, queue-waiting-time is defined as load index of a server for the first time. However, as internet traffic is bursty, queue-waiting-time is not merely calculated by adding up the normal service time of queued requests due to resource contention. Moreover, normal service time changes over time especially for database-driven web applications. Therefore, an adaptive load balancing algorithm is required. This paper focuses on load balancing algorithms under differentiated requests and heterogeneous servers. In order to solve the tuning problem in load balancing, an online learning algorithm of time-weight (OLTW) is designed, which can learn the time-weight of request adaptively. Based on OLTW, a shortest queue-waiting-time load balancing algorithm (SQLB) is then proposed, in this algorithm, an incoming request is dispatched to the server with shortest queue-waiting-time. The experimental results show that 80% prediction values of OLTW have relative error of less than 25%, and SQLB outperforms the classical load balancing algorithms in terms of throughput, mean response time and deadline drop rate.

Keywords: Load balancing algorithm · Queue-waiting-time
Fine-grain microservices · Machine learning

1 Introduction

Microservices architecture (MSA) [1] is a fine-grain service-oriented architecture (SOA) for building large-scale enterprise applications such as in Google, IBM, Tencent, Netflix et al. [1–3]. A MSA-based application is composed of a suite of small services, and each service communicates with other services through their exposing APIs. With the increase of applications and corresponding data, multiple-instances are adopted to handle an increasing number of requests so as to satisfy service level agreement (SLA) [7].

Actually, for fine-grain microservices, the service time of a request is instantaneous, usually within seconds. For example, in Ask Jeeves [4], 99% of web search requests are expected to be completed within a second and the mean response time is within a few hundreds of milliseconds. In Teoma [5] traces, a translation service contains two translation requests, one request provides the translation between query words and their internal representations has a mean service time of 22 ms, the other one supports a similar translation for web page descriptions with 209 ms. For fine-grain services, the main SLA requirements are throughput and response time [6]. Load balancing mechanism is one of the factors that directly influences the throughput and response time, and plays a critical role in making effective use of cluster resource [7, 12].

A lot of researches on load balancing algorithms have been investigated for web server farms [7]. Generally, these algorithms are classified into two categories: static algorithms and dynamic algorithms. Static algorithms are relatively simple, while very efficient in some specific scenarios, e.g., random (RAN) and round robin (RR) in homogeneous cluster. Weighted round robin (WRR) is proposed in the context of heterogeneous cluster, which places more requests to the server with more processing power. However, a challenging problem of WRR is how to accurately measure the weight of a server. In [11], the weight of a server is calculated as a linear combination of CPU, memory and other computing resources, but the weight is difficult to be derived because different requests have various resource demands, which is also called tuning problem [9, 10]. Static algorithms usually perform poorly because they ignore the factor of actual load of servers. In order to overcome the shortcoming, dynamic load balancing algorithms use real-time load states to distribute requests e.g., WRR_num, WRR_time [10], WSQ [13] and queue length (QL) [8].

As known to all, different types of requests have different service time and resource demand [9]. Considering the diversity of requests, a content-based load balancing algorithm (QSC) is proposed in [11]. Each request is endowed with a specific weight value calculated as: $weight = \alpha * CPU + \beta * Mem + (1 - \alpha - \beta) * Disk$, where the weight is the linear combination of CPU process time, memory use and disk access time, and α and β are relative weight-value coefficients. The load of a server is the sum of weight values of all queued requests. However, the issue on how to set the coefficients accurately is less investigated, which faces to the similar tuning problem. In [10], the author concludes that dynamic load balancing algorithms have serious tuning problems.

Actually, most of web service applications are database driven, and the database size dynamically changes during the runtime, which incurs the change of request weight. Request weight reflects the impact of the request on the workload. Therefore, the request weight should be adjusted to deal with the change of database; otherwise it will cause a load imbalance problem.

Motivated by the aforementioned observations, a scheme that focuses on intelligent and adaptive load balancing algorithm for fine-grain microservices under differentiated requests and heterogeneous cluster is proposed.

Our main contributions are shown as follows:

- Defining queue-waiting-time as load index for the first time, which is more accurate than queue length.
- Studying deeply three factors that influence queue-waiting-time, which are request type, queue length and request order of arrival, through theoretical derivation and experimental simulations.
- Proposing an online learning algorithm of time-weight OLTW, which can learn the time-weight of request adaptively.

- Proposing a shortest queue-waiting-time load balancing algorithm SQLB, in which, an incoming request is dispatched to the server with shortest queue-waiting-time.

The remainder of this paper is organized as follows: in Sect. 2, we present the preliminary on MSA and the implementation of microservice with multi-threaded programming model. Then we study three factors that influence queue-waiting-time in Sect. 3. Section 4 describes OLTW and SQLB. Section 5 evaluates the prediction accuracy of OLTW and the load balancing performance of SQLB. In Sect. 6, we draw the conclusion.

2   Preliminary

In this section, we present MSA and the implementation of microservice with multi-threaded programming model.

2.1   MSA

MSA is a design methodology inspired by service-oriented computing. Inside MSA, a microservice can function as both of service provider and consumer. As a service provider, it provides services by exposing APIs. Figure 1 illustrates an open-source microservices application of Acme Air [14], which simulates the website of a fictitious airline company and is widely used as case study in microservices research literature [15, 16]. In this figure, the Gateway service receives requests from Browser, accesses one or more microservices through API calls, and then returns results to the Browser. The Auth service performs user authentication. The Flight-booking service handles the flight search and flight booking requests. The Customer service manages booked flight information and user information. These four microservices cooperate with each other and provide services as a whole. Each of the microservices has multiple instances to handle increasing service requests. Note that we focus on load balancing inside MSA. That is, how to dispatch requests among the multiple instances.

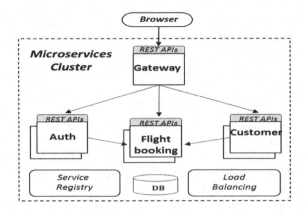

Fig. 1. Microservices architecture

2.2 Multi-threaded Programming Model of Microservice

In order to improve throughput and maximize resource utilization, multi-threaded programming is widely used for concurrently handling incoming requests in microservices. For example, Microservices based on Tars [23] are developed with multi-thread programming model, Tars is an open-source microservices development framework which is used by hundreds of business systems in Tencent. And a java-based microservices application in [15] exploits multiple CPU cores with multi-thread programming model. A microservice implemented with multi-threaded programming model maintains a shared FIFO request queue and a worker thread pool as shown in Fig. 2.

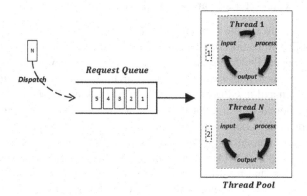

Fig. 2. Multi-threaded programming model

Any request will be queued until one idle thread is assigned to process it. Queue-waiting-time refers to how long an incoming request will wait at the queue before seved. The length of Request Queue is considered as unlimited. The thread pool size is set to a reasonable value according to concrete business logic, but typically has a limit to control resource contentions in a heavy loaded situation [6]. How to set the thread pool size is beyond the scope of our study.

3 Influence Factors of Queue-Waiting-Time

In this section, we study three main factors, namely, request type, queue length and request order of arrival, that influence queue-waiting-time through theoretical derivation and numerical experiment simulations. The key notations are shown in Table 1.

Table 1. Notations

Symbol	Basic definitions
N	Number of request types (APIs) within a microservice
R	Set of request types' names, i.e., $R = (r_1, ..., r_N)$
X	Number of requests corresponding to N types, i.e., $X = (x_1, ..., x_N)$

(continued)

Table 1. (*continued*)

Symbol	Basic definitions
ψ	Queue-waiting-time
μ	CPU utilization demand
λ	Queue length
ρ	Thread pool size
σ	Number of cores in a server
τ	Normal service time, refers to service time under an idle machine

3.1   Workload Characteristic and Test Microservice

Given the CPU resource is the main bottleneck of web server with dynamic workloads [12, 17, 18], CPU utilization demand is used to indicate workload characteristic of requests in this paper. For fine-grain services such as Ask Jeeves [4], Teoma [5] and Acme Air [14], service requests can be divided into three types according to the value of CPU utilization demand μ: CPU-bound (μ is almost 1), non-CPU-bound (μ is nearly 0) and mixed-CPU-bound ($0 < \mu < 1$). For example, the authentication request in Acme Air is one of typical CPU-bound requests, majority of service time is spent on crunching the hash, doing large amount of bitwise XORs and shifting for the input string assuming the encryption algorithm is SHA-1. On the contrary, the customer request is one of non-CPU-bound requests, and most of service time is waiting for query results from database. The web search request belongs to mixed-CPU-bound, at loading stage μ is low, and high at data processing stage. In our experiments, we generate different request types by combinations of the three request types.

For research purpose, we implement a fine-grain microservice as test microservice named *fM*, which provides four types of requests. The four types have different CPU utilization demand [0%, 30%, 60%, 100%], which is measured at a server with 1 CPU core 2.4 GHz and 2 GB memory. In order to simplify the analysis, the normal service time of the four types is all 100 ms. This simplification does not affect simulation conclusions. The thread pool size is 4 and it can lead to different degrees of CPU contentions ($\rho*\mu$) varies from 0% to 400%.

3.2   Request Type

As we know different request types have different CPU utilization demand and service time, the impact of request type on queue-waiting-time comes from the two aspects. Assuming there is no CPU contention, queue-waiting-time ψ is calculated as:

$$\psi = \frac{\sum_{i=0}^{i=\lambda} \tau_i}{\rho} \tag{1}$$

Where τ_i is the normal service time of the *i-th* request in the request queue.

In order to study the relationship between queue-waiting-time and request type, we conduct the following experiments.

Let queue length λ belongs to [8, 16, 24, 32], the number of all allocation strategies is [165, 969, 2925, 6545]. Any one allocation strategy meets the following formula:

$$\lambda = \sum_{i=0}^{i=N} x_i \tag{2}$$

For each queue length, we enumerate all allocation strategies. And for each allocation strategy, we initiate λ requests in a very short time to simulate the workload of the request queue at a certain moment. After λ requests are severed, we can get a queue-waiting-time. The cumulative distribution function (CDF) of allocation strategies with queue-waiting-time is shown in Fig. 3(a). In addition, statistics of queue-waiting-time and the sum of CPU utilization demand (*sum*$^\mu$) are shown in Fig. 3(b). $sum^u = \sum_{i=0}^{i=\lambda} \mu_i$, where μ_i is CPU utilization demand of the *i-th* request in the request queue.

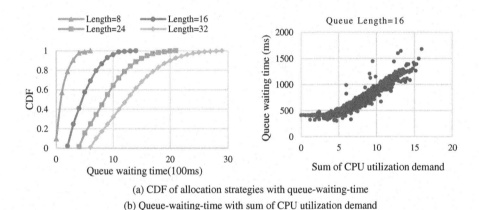

(a) CDF of allocation strategies with queue-waiting-time

(b) Queue-waiting-time with sum of CPU utilization demand

Fig. 3. Queue-waiting-time with request type

From Fig. 3(a), we can see:

1. Each interval of queue-waiting-time has a certain percentage of allocation strategies.
2. For the same queue length, even if all requests have the same normal service time (100 ms, in experiments), the span of queue-waiting-time (*span*$^\psi$) is about 4, which is calculated as:

$$\text{span}^\psi = \frac{\psi^{max} - \psi^{min}}{\psi^{min}} \tag{3}$$

From Fig. 3(b), we can conclude:

1. The larger sum^μ, the longer queue-waiting-time.
2. When $sum^\mu < 4$, ψ is about 400 ms. This is because there is no CPU contention under $\rho = 4$ and $\lambda = 16$. ψ can be calculated through Formula 1.

3. When $sum^\mu > 4$, CPU contention leads to the change of queue-waiting-time.
4. From 2 and 3, queue-waiting-time is not just adding up the normal service time of queued requests.

3.3   Queue Length

It is simple to imagine that queue-waiting-time increases with queue length, which is also showed in Fig. 3(a). To find the accurate relationship between the two variables, we conduct four experiments corresponding to four cases as shown in Table 2. In each case, there is only one request type and the queue length increases from 0 to 40. For each queue length, we initiate all requests in a very short time. The experiment results are shown in Fig. 4.

Table 2. Experiment parameters for queue length

Case	Request type	Length
1	r_1	[0–40]
2	r_2	[0–40]
3	r_3	[0–40]
4	r_4	[0–40]

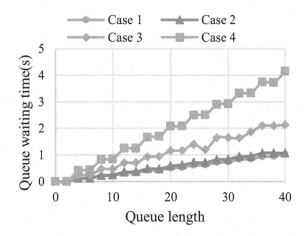

Fig. 4. Queue-waiting-time with queue length

From Fig. 4, we can see:

1. In each case, overall, queue-waiting-time increases linearly as queue length. Or more accurately, it increases a certain value at interval of four requests because the thread pool size is 4.
2. In general, the more CPU utilization demand, the sharper the slope. But the relationship is not linear which can be seen from r_1 (0%) and r_2 (30%). The slopes of them are similar but the CPU utilization demands differ greatly.

3.4   Request Order of Arrival

In this section, we study the impact of request order of arrival through numerical simulation experiments. Different orders leads to varying degrees of CPU contention. As a result, it results in different queue-waiting-time. Therefore, the impact of request order on queue-waiting-time comes from CPU contention. As we know, the impact of request type on queue-waiting-time also comes from CPU contention. Which has more influence?

Assume that there are two request types, one is CPU-bound request and the other is non-CPU-bound request. The numbers of requests corresponding to the two types are x^{cpu} and x^{ncpu}. All requests have equal normal service time 100 ms. We conduct five experiments as shown in Table 3.

Table 3. Experiment parameters for arrival order

Case	x^{cpu}: x^{ncpu}	Number of orders
1	4:12	1820
2	8:8	12870
3	12:4	1820
4	6:18	19228
5	8:24	20994

For the first three cases, we enumerate all arrival orders. When the queue length gets longer and longer, the number of arrival orders becomes very large and it is impractical to enumerate all orders. For the last two cases, we use uniform sampling method to pick sample orders which is based on *C++ Algorithm Library Function:: next_permutation*. The cumulative distribution function of request orders with queue-waiting-time is shown in Fig. 5.

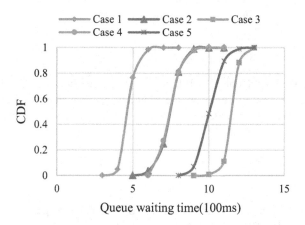

Fig. 5. CDF of request orders with queue-waiting-time

From Fig. 5, we can see that for each case, most values of queue-waiting-time are distributed in a relatively small time span compared with Fig. 4(a). Although there are some extreme orders which lead to long queue-waiting-time, the orders are very rare.

The $span^{\psi}$ of request order is no more than 0.75, while the $span^{\psi}$ of request type is about 4. Therefore, the impact of request type is far greater than the impact of request order, and we do not regard request order of arrival as a major influence factor in this paper.

4 Queue-Waiting-Time Based Load Balancing Algorithm

4.1 Online Learning Algorithm of Time-Weight

The studies of influencing factors shows that queue-waiting-time is mainly affected by request type and queue length. However, the relationship between queue-waiting-time and the two factors is difficult to precisely setup in the scenario with differentiated requests, heterogeneous cluster and dynamic environments (e.g. database size). Therefore, we model this relationship as a regression problem and then use machine learning to solve the problem. Since there is a linear correlation between queue-waiting-time and queue length as shown in Sect. 3.3, an important implication is that linear models may be appropriate for predicting queue-waiting-time. As known to all, linear regression model has outstanding advantage of low computing complexity especially for real-time applications. On the contrary, LB based on complicated load balancing algorithms itself may become a performance bottleneck for fine-grain microservices and bursty internet traffic. Therefore, we propose an online learning algorithm of time-weight OLTW (*Algorithm 1*, *based on scikit-learn library*), which is based on multivariable linear regression model as follows.

$$\psi = \sum_{i=0}^{i=N} x_i * \alpha_i = X\alpha^T \tag{4}$$

Where α_i is the coefficient of x_i. If the queue length is short, the learned coefficients have large error. In order to improve the accuracy of coefficients and considering the actual runtime environment, queue length and queue-waiting-time in train dataset are required as:

$$s.t.: \quad \sum_{i=0}^{i=N} x_i \geq \delta * \rho$$
$$\psi \leq \psi^{max}$$

Where δ is a multiple of thread pool size ρ. ψ^{max} is the max queue-waiting-time. By default, δ is 2 and ψ^{max} is 3 s. One sample contains N features and corresponding actual queue-waiting-time ψ, as $< x_1, x_2, .., x_N, \psi >$.

Algorithm 1. Online Learning algorithm of Time-Weight

```
INPUT: Recent Samples Sps,
       Initial coefficients αinit ,
       Minimum percentage (Min%) with relative error less
    than Δ%
OUTPUT:  Newest coefficients α
From sklearn.linear_model import LinearRegression as lr
begin
initialize αinit=[0]
while true
  X = [ ]
  Y = [ ]
  for i in range(0, len(Sps))
    X.append([Sps['x₁'][i],Sps['x₂'][i],…,Sps ['xₙ'][i]])
    Y.append(Sps['ψ'][i])
  endfor
  Ŷ= lr.predict(Sps)
  RE = [ ]
```

$$RE = \bigcup_{i=0}^{i=N_{Sps}} \frac{|\hat{Y}_i - Y_i|}{Y_i}$$

```
  /*Statistics percentage with relative error less than Δ%*/
  Stat=Statistics(RE, Δ%)
  if Stat < Min%
    linreg =lr(fit_intercept=False)
    linreg.fit(X, Y)
    α =linreg.coef_
  endif
endwhile
end
```

During the lifetime of an application, OLTW constantly collects the new samples and calculates the relative error between predicted values $(\hat{Y})$ and true values (Y), then statistics the percentage of relative error less than a certain threshold $\Delta\%$. Once the percentage is under a certain threshold (Min%), a retraining will be done and the newest coefficients α are sent to SQLB. The value of Min% and $\Delta\%$ are set based on the actual situation, for example in Sect. 5.1, the Min% can be set 80% and $\Delta\%$ can be set 25%. The algorithm based on thresholds greatly decreases the computational overhead and communication overhead caused by repetitive train for every newly added sample. By default, the number of Samples is 1500, and the training time is about 10 ms on machine with 2 CPU cores 2.4 GHz. Therefore, the machine learning algorithm is feasible in real production environment.

4.2   Shortest Queue-Waiting-Time Load Balancing Algorithm

The architecture of our proposed load balancer which based on OLTW and SQLB is shown in Fig. 6.

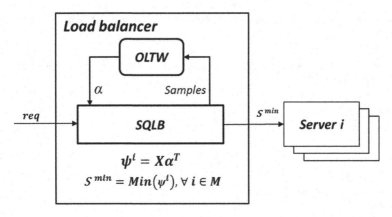

Fig. 6. Architecture of load balancer

When an incoming request arrives, firstly, SQLB calculates the queue-waiting-time of all candidate servers through Formula 4, and then selects the server with the shortest queue-waiting-time as S^{min}. Finally, load balancer dispatches the request to S^{min} (**Algorithm 2**). The server S^{min} processes the request and returns results including actual queue-waiting-time. One new sample is collected and sent to OLTW. Based on the recent samples, OLTW runs *Algorithm 1*.

Algorithm 2. Shortest Queue-waiting-time Load Balancing algorithm

---

```
INPUT: An incoming request req,
       Load state of M servers Load =<X¹, X²,…, Xᴹ>,
       Coefficients of M servers Coe=<α¹, α²,…, αᴹ >
OUTPUT: Target server Sᵐⁱⁿ
begin
initialize Tshort= inf
for (int i=0; i<M; ++i)
  ψᵢ= Load[i] * Coe[i]ᵀ
  if (ψᵢ < Tshort)
    Tshort=ψᵢ
    Sᵐⁱⁿ =i
  endif
endfor
Dispatch req to Sᵐⁱⁿ
end
```

The time complexity of Algorithm 2 is $O(N*M)$, where N is the number of request types and M is the number of servers.

5 Experimental Evaluation

To evaluate the performance of our proposed algorithm SQLB, we compare SQLB with four classical load balancing algorithms: RR, WRR, QL [8] and QSC [11] in terms of throughput, mean response time and deadline drop rate. Deadline drop refers to that the response time of a request is out of a threshold. In our experiments, the threshold is 5 s. In order to accurately evaluate the performance of our proposed load balancing algorithm and avoid the influence caused by inaccurate load state, the load balancer is based on server-side load balancing pattern [2, 8].

The microservice *fM* and LB are developed with C++ language and OLTW with Python language. Each service instance is deployed in a separate node. No database is shared among the test servers. A dedicated node acts as LB. All nodes are connected through a local fast Ethernet with 1000 Mbps bandwidth. The benchmark of request traces are generated by FGN [19] developed by Berkeley, which is widely used to generate synthesize traces corresponding to self-similar Internet traffic [20–22].

Table 4. Parameters of experimental environment

	CPU	Mem	OS	Work threads	Benchmarks
Server-1	1core 2.4 GHz	1 GB	Centos6.5	4	–
Server-2	1core 2.4 GHz	1 GB	Centos6.5	4	–
Server-3	2cores 2.4 GHz	1 GB	Centos6.5	4	–
Server-4	2cores 2.4 GHz	1 GB	Centos6.5	4	–
LB	2cores 2.4 GHz	2 GB	Centos6.5	–	–
Client	1core 2.4 GHz	1 GB	Centos6.5	–	FGN

5.1 Prediction Accuracy

In this section, we evaluate the prediction accuracy of queue-waiting-time based on OLTW for four servers as shown in Table 4, and in two cases with different CPU utilization demands as shown in Table 5.

Table 5. Parameters of two scenarios for prediction accuracy

Case	CPU utilization demand (μ)	τ (ms)	Hurst	Request rate (per second)
1	[1%, 30%, 60%, 100%]	100	0.89	140
2	[1%, 10%, 20%, 30%]	100	0.89	200

The μ of four request types in Case 1 is much larger than μ in Case 2. The μ and τ are measured in Server-1 (as reference server). The self-similar parameter Hurst of synthesize traces is 0.89 within the range [0.5, 1]. The mean request arrival rate in Case

1 and Case 2 is 140 requests per second and 200 requests per second respectively, which is over the total throughput of the four servers so that queue length and corresponding queue-waiting-time increases as time goes. Therefore different queue length and corresponding queue-waiting-time are taken into account instead of fixed ones. In one cycle, Client invokes Load Balancer continuously for 5 s and then stops to invoke until the servers become idle. At each second, both the ratio of four types and the request order of arrival are random, the interval between two adjacent requests is equal. For each server and each case, 1500 samples of train dataset and 1500 samples of test dataset are collected.

We use the train datasets to train OLTW and the train result as follows:

- In Case 1, R^2 of four servers are [0.89, 0.90, 0.95, 0.94] and the coefficients α of four servers are [[17, 29, 48, 87], [13, 31, 49, 95], [20, 26, 30, 47], [16, 29, 33, 48]].
- In Case 2, R^2 of four servers are [0.98, 0.97, 0.98, 0.98] and the coefficients α of four servers are [[22, 22, 25, 31], [23, 22, 26, 28], [23, 23, 23, 26], [24, 23, 23, 25]].

The coefficient of determination R^2 of the prediction is defined as:

$$R^2(y, \hat{y}) = 1 - \frac{\sum_{i=0}^{i=N_{Sps}} (y_i - \hat{y}_i)^2}{\sum_{i=0}^{i=N_{Sps}} (y_i - \bar{y})^2} \tag{5}$$

Where y_i is the true value, $\hat{y}_i$ is the predicted value, $\bar{y}$ is the mean of true values. The best possible score of R^2 is 1.0 and the score can be negative because the model can be arbitrarily worse.

Then we use test dataset to evaluate the prediction accuracy of queue-waiting-time for each server. We compare the prediction accuracy between OLTW and QSC [11]. QSC is an empirical model, the coefficient of i request type α_i is calculated as:

$$\alpha_i = \frac{\mu_i * \tau_i}{\sigma} \tag{6}$$

Through Formula 6, the coefficients α in QSC are:

- In Case 1, α is [1, 30, 60, 100] to Server-1 and Server-2, [0.5, 15, 30, 50] to Server-3 and Server-4.
- In Case 2, α is [1, 10, 20, 30] to Server-1 and Server-2, [0.5, 5, 10, 15] to Server-3 and Server-4.

The cumulative distribution function of test samples with relative error in two cases is shown in Fig. 7. From the figure, we can see that in Case 1, for Server-1 and Server-2, QSC has the similar prediction accuracy with OLTW, but for Server-3 and Server-4, QSC has lower prediction accuracy than OLTW. In Case 2, OLTW has much higher prediction accuracy than QSC for all servers. By comparison, OLTW is more exact than the existing empirical model QSC in predicting the queue-waiting-time. In OLTW, 80% of prediction values have relative error of less than 25% for all cases and servers. Although there are some cases which have large relative error, but the percentage is very small. Therefore, OLTW can adapt to the diversities of request types and heterogeneous servers which solves the tune problem in load balancing.

5.2   Load Balance Performance

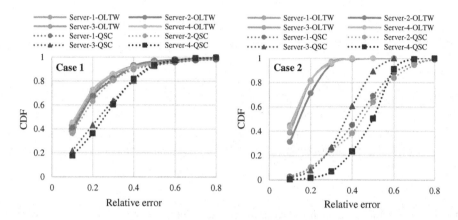

Fig. 7. CDF of test samples with relative error

For the two cases in Table 5, we increase the request rate until there is 5% deadline drop rate and the request rate is used as the throughput of the microservices cluster. At each request rate, Client invokes LB continuously for 20 s and repeats 10 times, then averages the results. The benchmarks of request traces are generated by FGN. The experiment results of the two cases are shown in Figs. 8 and 9 respectively.

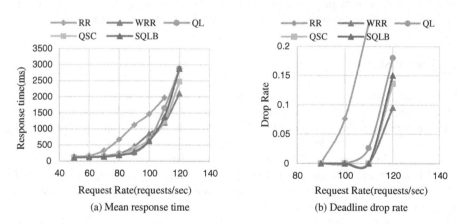

Fig. 8. Experiment results of Case 1

From Figs. 8 and 9, we can see that when the request rate is low, the mean response time is short and deadline drop rate is zero. When the request rate increases to a certain value, the mean response time increases with the request rate. When the request rate exceeds a threshold, the drop rate will increase rapidly since the server is overloaded.

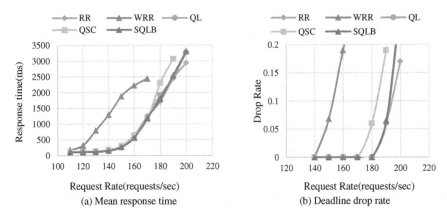

(a) Mean response time   (b) Deadline drop rate

Fig. 9. Experiment results of Case 2

RR is the worst load balancing algorithm in Case 1 but the best in Case 2. While WRR is the best in Case 1 and the worst in Case 2. Compared with QL in Case 1, the throughput of SQLB increases 4% and mean response time decreases 10% when the request rate is between 100 requests per second and throughput, and has the similar performance in Case 2. In fact, the greater diversity of requests, the worse load balancing performance of QL, this is because QL does not consider the diversity of requests. Compared with QSC in Case 2, the throughput of SQLB increases 5% and mean response time decreases 15% when the request rate is over 170 requests per second, and has the similar performance in Case 1. By comparison, SQLB has a good load balancing performance no matter in Case 1 or Case 2. This is because OLTW is adaptive and able to learn relatively accurate weights of requests types.

6   Conclusions

In this paper, queue-waiting-time is defined as load index of a server for the first time. Three factors that influence on queue-waiting-time are deeply studied and study results reveal that request type and queue length are two main factors. Then the prediction of queue-waiting-time is modeled as multivariable linear regression and an online learning algorithm of time-weight OLTW is designed, which solves the tuning problem. Based on OLTW, a shortest queue-waiting-time load balancing algorithm SQLB is proposed. Experimental results indicate that 80% prediction values of queue-waiting-time have relative error less than 25%, which is much more accurate than existing empirical model QSC, and SQLB outperforms the classical load balancing algorithms (RR, WRR, QL and QSC) in terms of throughput, mean response time and deadline drop rate.

References

1. Lewis, J., Fowler, M.: Microservices (2014). http://martinfowler.com/articles/microservices. html
2. Jenkins, J., Shipman, G.: A case study in computational caching microservices for HPC. In: IEEE Parallel and Distributed Processing Symposium Workshops, pp. 1309–1316 (2017)
3. Taibi, D., Lenarduzzi, V.: Processes, motivations, and issues for migrating to microservices architectures: an empirical investigation. IEEE Cloud Comput. 4(5), 22–32 (2017)
4. Ask Jeeves. http://www.ask.com
5. Teoma search. http://www.teoma.com
6. Zhou, J., Zhang, C.: Request-aware scheduling for busy internet services. In: IEEE International Conference on Computer Communications, pp. 1–11 (2006)
7. Gilly, K., Juiz, C.: An up-to-date survey in web load balancing. World Wide Web-Internet Web Inf. Syst. 14(2), 105–131 (2011)
8. Shen, K., Yang, T.: Cluster load balancing for fine-grain network services. In: IEEE Parallel and Distributed Processing Symposium (2002)
9. Zhang, W., Wang, H., Yu, B.: A request distribution algorithm for web server cluster. J. Netw. 6, 1760–1766 (2011)
10. Casalicchio, E., Tucci, S.: Static and dynamic scheduling algorithms for scalable web server farm. In: IEEE Parallel and Distributed Processing, pp. 369–376 (2001)
11. Zhang, L., Li, X.P.: A Content-based dynamic load-balancing algorithm for heterogeneous web server cluster. Comput. Sci. Inf. Syst. 7, 153–162 (2010)
12. Sharifian, S., Motamedi, S.A.: An approximation-based load-balancing algorithm with admission control for cluster web servers with dynamic workloads. J. Supercomput. 53, 440–463 (2010)
13. Singh, H., Kumar, S.: WSQ: web server queueing algorithm for dynamic load balancing. Wirel. Pers. Commun. 80, 229–245 (2015)
14. Acme Air sample and benchmark. https://github.com/acmeair/acmeair
15. Ueda, T., Nakaike, T., Ohara, M.: Workload characterization for microservices. In: IEEE International Symposium on Workload Characterization, pp. 1–10 (2016)
16. Ogasawara, T.: Workload characterization of server-side JavaScript. In: IEEE International Symposium on Workload Characterization, pp. 13–21 (2014)
17. Park, G., et al.: Adaptive load balancing mechanism for server cluster. In: Gavrilova, M.L., et al. (eds.) ICCSA 2006. LNCS, vol. 3983, pp. 549–557. Springer, Heidelberg (2006). https://doi.org/10.1007/11751632_60
18. Awada U.: Improving resource efficiency of container-instance clusters on clouds. In: IEEE/ACM International Symposium on Cluster, Cloud and Grid Computing, pp. 929–934 (2017)
19. Paxson, V.: Fast approximation of self-similar network traffic. ACM SIGCOMM Comput. Commun. Rev. 27, 5–18 (1997)
20. Lee, J.Y., Kim, S.: Bandwidth optimization for internet traffic in generalized processor sharing servers. IEEE Trans. Parallel Distrib. Syst. 16(4), 324–334 (2005)
21. Jin, X.: Performance analysis of priority scheduling mechanisms under heterogeneous network traffic. J. Comput. Syst. Sci. 73(8), 1207–1220 (2007)
22. Silva, R.A.C.D., Fonseca, N.L.S.D.: Topology-aware virtual machine placement in data centers. J. Grid Comput. 14, 75–90 (2016)
23. Tars, Tencent corporation (2017). https://github.com/Tencent/Tars

Author Index

Printed in the United States
By Bookmasters